BLURRING TIMESCAPES, SUBVERTING ERASURE

Blurring Timescapes, Subverting Erasure

Remembering Ghosts on the Margins of History

Edited by
Sarah Surface-Evans, A. E. Garrison,
and Kisha Supernant

First published in 2020 by
Berghahn Books
www.berghahnbooks.com

© 2020, 2024 Sarah Surface-Evans, A. E. Garrison, Kisha Supernant
First paperback edition published in 2024

All rights reserved. Except for the quotation of short passages
for the purposes of criticism and review, no part of this book
may be reproduced in any form or by any means, electronic or
mechanical, including photocopying, recording, or any information
storage and retrieval system now known or to be invented,
without written permission of the publisher.

Library of Congress Cataloging-in-Publication Data

Names: Surface-Evans, Sarah L., editor. | Garrison, A. E., editor. | Supernant, Kisha, editor.
Title: Blurring timescapes, subverting erasure : remembering ghosts on the margins of history / edited by Sarah Surface-Evans, A. E. Garrison, Kisha Supernant.
Other titles: Remembering ghosts on the margins of history
Description: First edition. | New York : Berghahn Books, [2020] | Includes bibliographical references and index.
Identifiers: LCCN 2020006126 (print) | LCCN 2020006127 (ebook) | ISBN 9781789207101 (hardback) | ISBN 9781789207118 (ebook)
Subjects: LCSH: History—Philosophy. | History—Psychological aspects. | Ghosts—Psychological aspects. | Absence (Philosophy) | Archaeology and history. | Social archaeology. | Antiquities—Psychological aspects. | Material culture—Psychological aspects. | Collective memory.
Classification: LCC D16.9 .B498 2020 (print) | LCC D16.9 (ebook) | DDC 901/.9—dc23
LC record available at https://lccn.loc.gov/2020006126

British Library Cataloguing in Publication Data

A catalogue record for this book is available from the British Library

ISBN 978-1-78920-710-1 hardback
ISBN 978-1-80539-305-4 paperback
ISBN 978-1-80539-419-8 epub
ISBN 978-1-78920-711-8 web pdf

https://doi.org/10.3167/9781789207101

Contents

List of Illustrations, Figures, and Tables vii

Acknowledgments x

Introduction 1
Sarah Surface-Evans, A. E. Garrison, and Kisha Supernant

Part I. Imagining Timescapes: Invoking Haunting, Memory, and Nostalgia

Chapter 1. Telling Ghost Stories: Communicating across Timescapes and between Worldviews 13
April M. Beisaw

Chapter 2. Material Memories: Interpreting Souvenirs and Heirlooms in the Archaeological Record 20
Erica Begun

Chapter 3. Journeys through Space and Time: Materiality, Social Memory, and Community at the City of David 33
Heather M. Van Wormer

Part II. Confronting Lingering Specters

Chapter 4. Recognizing Ghosts and Haunting in the Rural Midwest: Finding Community, Identity, and Wisdom in the Past 61
P. M. W. Lawton

Chapter 5. The Unwilling Student and the Ghost of Physical Anthropology: Public Perceptions of the Ethics of Physical Anthropology 72
Nicole M. Burt

Chapter 6. From Haunted to Haunting: Métis Ghosts in the Past
and Present 85
Kisha Supernant

Part III. Identifying Ghosts within the Capitalist Landscapes of Late Modernity

Chapter 7. Rain on the Scarecrow, Blood on the Plow: Haunting,
Trauma, and the Cruelty of the Agrarian Dream 105
Lilian Brislen

Chapter 8. Boneyard Quiet: A Ghost Story 120
A. E. Garrison

Chapter 9. Traumascapes: Progress and the Erasure of the Past 149
Sarah Surface-Evans

Chapter 10. Brickwork, Capitalism, Collective Memory, and
the Commons 171
Brigitte H. Bechtold

Epilogue. Ghosts, Haunting, and Refusals to Erasure 185
Kisha Supernant, April M. Beisaw, A. E. Garrison, and Sarah Surface-Evans

Index 196

Illustrations, Figures, and Tables

Illustrations

1.1. Screen capture of silent film "1940 Hudson Valley Dig," showing Mary Butler Lewis driving to her 1940 Hudson Valley archaeology survey site from the Blodgett building at Vassar College, where the author now conducts similar work. Source: https://archive.org/details/upenn-f16-0444_1940_Hudson_Valley_Dig.   16

1.2. A small portion of Vassar College's expansive Main Building by full moonlight. The windows of the author's third-floor apartment are visible at the far right, above the lamppost. The college president's office is just below, on the second floor. Photo by the author.   17

2.1. Marine shell (possibly *Pleuroploca* sp.) from Burial 34. Photo by the author.   27

2.2. Amethyst pendant from Burial 36 at Structure 19. Photo by the author.   27

2.3. Polished blackware jar from Structure 19. Photo by the author.   28

2.4. Patzcuaro-style figurines found at Structure 19. Photo by the author.   28

3.1. Garden marker. Photo by the author.   35

3.2. Shiloh gardens and Mary's mausoleum. Photo by the author.   35

3.3. Jerusalem and Bethlehem, with Benjamin Purnell (in white hat) front and center. Courtesy of Communal Societies Collection, Hamilton College, Clinton, NY.   43

3.4. Shiloh at the House of David. Photo by the author.   44

3.5. Mary's auditorium. Photo by the author.   46

3.6. New Shiloh headquarters, Mary's City of David. Photo by the author. 47

3.7. Laundry and garage. Photo by the author. 48

3.8. Two different brick materials. Photo by the author. 48

3.9. Aerial view of Mary's City of David, 1936. Courtesy of Communal Societies Collection, Hamilton College. 49

3.10. Advertisement for Jewish resorters. Courtesy of Communal Societies Collection, Hamilton College. 51

3.11. Mary's Vegetarian Restaurant. Photo by the author. 52

5.1. Activity table located in the main gallery area at the Cleveland Museum of Natural History. Note that it is a plastic teaching skull. Photo by the author. 77

6.1. Author's great-great-grandparents, Marie Flora Gauthier and Alexis Supernant. Photograph provided by Cliff Supernault. 96

9.1a to 9.1c. Aspects of gentrification (construction, demolition, and rebranding) I pass by regularly while walking and running in my neighborhood. Photos by the author. 151

9.2a to 9.2d. Photos of an old building, taken while on a walk with my son; and the demolition of the same building. Photos by the author. 155

9.3a and 9.3b. The Scott Garden and Jenison House. Photos by the author. 159

9.4a and 9.4b. The substation and walls during construction. Note the "three stacks" motif in Illustration 9.4b, with the actual stacks in the background. The blank panels on either side of the "three stacks" sculpture are meant for artist-commissioned murals. Photos by the author. 163

10.1. Factory on East Carson Street, South Pittsburgh, 8 April 2018. Photo by the author. 175

10.2. Terraced (row) houses on Havelock Street in Kettering, England, 25 November 2018. Photo by the author. 177

10.3. Restored passage in St. Pancras International, London, April 2018. Photo by the author. 179

10.4. The last of a set of row houses on S 5th and Cabot Way. South Pittsburgh, April 2018. Photo by the author. 180

10.5. Bricks becoming pebbles and sand on the south shore of the Firth of Forth, Scotland, June 2018. Photo by the author. 182

Figures

2.1. Map of Mesoamerica showing locations of key regions discussed, including the Patzcuaro Basin and Teotihuacan. Map by the author (Begun 2013). 23

3.1. Map of Mary's City of David. Map by the author. 50

5.1. Flowchart illustrating the relationship between the starting category of the visitor and the resulting type of conversation. Figure by the author. 79

6.1. Map showing Métis homeland and known Métis wintering sites. Map by the author. 89

6.2. Métis archaeological sites in Canada. Map by the author. 92

6.3. Artifact count from Cabin 3 at Buffalo Lake Métis wintering site, showing a high number of personal objects, 99 percent of which are beads. Figure by the author. 94

9.1. Map of neighborhoods near Scott Garden. Map by the author. 160

Table

5.1. Explanation of the categories of museum adult learners. Table by the author. 78

Acknowledgments

The authors wish to acknowledge all those ghosts and specters that have made themselves felt and seen.

Introduction

SARAH SURFACE-EVANS, A. E. GARRISON,
and KISHA SUPERNANT

Do you believe in ghosts?

What if we told you that you don't have to believe in ghosts to feel the impact of their haunting? That strange tingling down your spine that you feel when you pass the run-down ruins of a farm or factory is your body communicating to you. Haunting is a communication of something that is difficult to articulate. Haunting is an unspoken question that settles into our thinking and guides a seeking out of answers that might never come. Ghosts are the manifestation of something missing. Something indescribable. Something unseen, lingering in the shadows of everyday experience.

When ghosts present themselves, they are messengers of complicated stories that are often difficult to understand or to contemplate. Ghosts confront us with "truths" we may not wish to hear, which may be why we fear ghosts. The popularity of "ruin porn," ghost tours, ghost-hunting television shows, and references to ghosts in popular music and film speaks to our uneasy fascination with specters. Do we run from ghosts or do we listen to their stories? We invite you to join us as we travel through timescapes and visit ghosts, not as gawkers seeking a thrill, but approaching the spectral with the curiosity to learn what they have to teach us.

Social scientists, historians, and literary critics are increasingly turning to the concept of "haunting" as a way of acknowledging and attempting to describe what cannot be known but is felt and experienced nonetheless (Beisaw 2016; Bell 1997; Blanco 2012; González-Tennant 2016, 2018; Gordon 1997; Hill 2013; Hudson 2017; Miles 2015; Starzmann and Roby 2016; Surface-Evans and Jones, forthcoming). A growing body of theory is emerging to focus inquiry on dimensions beyond what is recognized as traditionally empirical, such as the entangled and interrelated concepts of memory, materiality, nostalgia, trauma, and haunting. However, we recognize that these are loosely woven concepts, whose connections require further stitching to create a picture of haunting. The authors in this volume demonstrate that specters do have empirical grounding and can be examined as institutions and social systems. The material remains of the past can become crossroads of memory to be activated in the present. Yet each author engages with memory or nostalgia evoked by materiality of social institutions in separate, but interrelated ways. In order for ghosts to flow and "haunt" they need to be free to move and be defined by each author and each reader. This is because the ghostly apparitions of capitalism and colonialism make themselves felt in different ways. By telling their stories we invite you step into the past.

The research presented in this volume draws on archaeological, historical, sociological, and ethnographic data. It is grounded in science and evidence. We identify the materiality of memory within objects, people, and landscapes. We tell ghost stories that invite hauntings by the specters of the past in the present (Bechtold, Chapter 10; Van Wormer, Chapter 3). We are haunted in remembering what we have not seen but dreamed or imagined (Garrison, Chapter 8). The practice of remembering and looking for ghosts seeks to undo the dehumanizing elements of social structures and, at times, our own disciplines (Burt, Chapter 5; Supernant, Chapter 6). Why do we share this research as ghost stories? Ghosts transmit knowledge in surprising and unusual ways. They are a way to return to a narrative and literary tradition that is not part of modernity and scientific writing. They are a way of reaching across the material into depths that connect us to one another through time and space.

By embracing the ghostly or spectral we can compress time and experience a fourth dimension. We can time travel in our minds and with our emotions. Such imaginings are meaningful ways for us to engage with the people of the past in the present and future. This is what we mean by *blurring timescapes*. This volume is an attempt to go beyond the casual experience of place and time and to allow ourselves to become, albeit temporarily, possessed by the past that is imprinted on places or people, in bricks or stories, through souvenirs or songs. The authors invite us to move beyond our normal sensory experience or "affect" and connect to people (real or fictional) through empathetic imagining.

Affect is how we experience feeling and emotion. We suggest that haunting is a type of affect that transcends temporality. The difficulty comes in describing these feelings and identifying their source(s) (Gordon 1997). This volume is an experiment in searching for and describing specters, exposing those hidden and unseen pasts and presents that haunt. We manifest ghosts in the telling and identifying of specters, and that requires an approach that is different from typical scientific writing. While scientists who look to the past to understand present social conditions are often "haunted," they seldom describe the affect of such realizations in academic writing (Beisaw, Chapter 1). Archaeology, in particular, is vulnerable to feelings of haunting, as our goal is to make sense of material culture from another time. We are not encouraged to present our work in ways that would ask the audience to explore, with us, something that is difficult to explain (Burt, Chapter 5), even if that invitation could open a window through time in a powerful way.

This collection of research critically evaluates perceptions and interpretations of the past and their impacts on the present. The act of remembering is subversion. This is what we mean by *subverting erasure*. The authors in this volume ask, what happens when the memories of a place, people, and events are systematically erased, forgotten, and covered up? And how are the stories we tell shaped by nostalgia or ghosts we imagine within the practice of social science? The authors explore hidden narratives and examine the social mechanisms operating on and organizing what is remembered and what is lost to time (Bechtold, Chapter 10; Surface-Evans, Chapter 9). Others consider the material residues of remembering, how objects and their meaning transcend time and sometimes space (Begun, Chapter 2; Lawton, Chapter 4; Van Wormer, Chapter 3).

The authors in this volume demonstrate the value of conceiving of ghosts, not just as metaphors, but for making the past more concrete (Bechtold, Chapter 10; Surface-Evans, Chapter 9). We seek to *remember ghosts*, because they are often where the stories of everyday people are found, relegated to *the margins of history*. Confronting ghosts also allows us to exorcise the negative specters of colonialism, racism, gentrification, and capitalism (Burt, Chapter 5; Garrison, Chapter 8; Lawton, Chapter 4; Supernant, Chapter 6; Surface-Evans, Chapter 9). In other words, the telling of ghost stories can prevent the erasure of the very things that create ghosts. Many of the researchers in this volume take an activist stance: as we uncover the sources of ghosts, we are able to offer solutions to problems in the present (Brislen, Chapter 7; Lawton, Chapter 4; Surface-Evans, Chapter 9). The sharing of ghost stories accesses the power of imagination and compassion.

This volume also is an experiment in vulnerability, as much as it is an empirically driven affect study. Each story shared in this volume is connected to its author in deeply personal ways. Science removes the scientist, in most cases, from the results of their work. This volume calls on the authors to speak their hauntings through their research, requiring their presence as ghosts in the tellings themselves (Garrison, Chapter 8; Supernant, Chapter 6; Surface-Evans, Chapter 9). From this perspective, haunting is a type of experience and theoretical framing that brings us closer to understanding and empathizing with people, past and present. Telling these ghostly stories also helps us problematize the atemporality of our disciplines, in that stories about haunting are nonlinear, unlike typical scientific narratives. The ability to empathize with our fellow human beings is increasingly important in a world marked by fear and violence (Johnson 1997), because it helps to open the doors of understanding and mutual respect. Empathy also helps us visualize the patterns in history and, in some circumstances, the patterns of exploitation present within social institutions. In these ways, ghost stories help us acknowledge the forgotten from our pasts, recognize the paths others have walked, and show us ways toward a future where those silenced by power might have more space to speak their own truths.

The volume is organized into three overlapping themes: imagining timescapes, confronting lingering specters, and identifying ghosts within the capitalist landscapes of late modernity. Engaging across time, space, and discipline, the authors in these sections explore haunting from a broad perspective, bringing new understandings of haunting into the social sciences to conceptualize how the past haunts the present and the future.

Imagining Timescapes: Invoking Haunting, Memory, and Nostalgia

How easily time seems to slip away when we're in it. How quickly it seems we forget what we are supposed to remember. Or, we can just as easily remember what never was—conjuring the past from a photo in the right light and company. People experience *meaning*, some of it shared and some of it unfamiliar to them, but nonetheless we assign meaning to past events and the objects tied to those events. People sort through piles of knickknacks at a flea market or leave in their closets, basements, and attics the objects inherited from prior generations. We experience time, from day to day, in many directions, and our experiences with time are subject to a variety of different social realities. Through our equally varied cultures, we experience the past alongside and *in* our presents, existing as stories and material objects from times not our own. After all, when the stories fall silent finally, all that remains are the objects and places that mattered enough that the keepsakes remain. Memories are imperfect, and our remembrances of the past may be clouded by the seduction of nostalgia. These are tricky rememberings—hazy memories filled in with what might or not be true—filled in by these same beguiling imaginings that would change our visions. The meaning of events and objects may change from person to person and over time, building in the stories of times, places, and the ghosts that would bring it all together.

The chapters in this section animate the strands of time and space that stretch between human communities, allowing the reader to see the blending together of layers that form the connections we share. We share these connections through objects of meaning that house our memories: pictures, letters, even kitchen appliances. We share these connections in the objects we keep—from a journey, an adventure, an extraordinary experience that might never happen again. Our attachment to the objects and items associated with those moments bring eternal life to memories and people.

In Chapter 1, the reader will meander across the Vassar College campus in the mysterious midnight of upstate New York, with April M. Beisaw spooking at the corners where history tells us, *Someone lingers here*. Vassar only serves as the center of the conjuring, however; as its affects and magic spread out in many directions, Beisaw delights in the spaces between what we see and what we feel on the backs of our necks. At the same time, the crossing over between these ambiguous dimensional cusps creates a bind that holds our stories of others—and therefore, stories of us—together.

Erica Begun asks us to open our visions in other ways in her chapter, "Material Memories: Interpreting Souvenirs and Heirlooms in the Archaeological Record" (Chapter 2). The sometimes intentional, sometimes accidental sharing of material objects spins gossamer strands between the Teotihuacan and Michoacán people. Begun parallels her own social and cultural experiences with family heirlooms as a strand woven into the narrative of a human experience of attachment to objects that matter, however they matter, to those of us making their meaning.

In Chapter 3, Heather M. Van Wormer asks us to linger slightly longer in the doorway, imagining what revelry, heartbreak, and threads of passionate devotion create in the emptiness that deceives. She explores the City of David, a once thriving community in southeast Michigan, home to believers whose lives would take them in unexpected directions. And yet, even as the lives of those she narrates diverge, they remain "at home" in this haunted space, their places at the table kept warm for their return. It is in this chapter that the closeness of family is revealed as a haunting, that the ways in which we *believe* our truths to manifest create dimensions for our forever and the eternities of those we love. The strands of Van Wormer's narrative hold together the lasting connections, unseen, regardless of any one person's faith or devotion, between those that walk the earth of material reality, and those that remain in the shadows—but remain, nonetheless.

Confronting Lingering Specters

We are haunted by our own disciplinary past—its misdeeds and colonialist foundations. We cannot hope to expose the specters of wider social systems without confronting our own skeletons in the closet. The chapters in Part II of this volume focus on the ghosts of the disciplines of archaeology and biological anthropology, including the erasure of the past in Saginaw Valley, Michigan (Lawton, Chapter 4), the lingering specters of race in museum education (Burt, Chapter 5), and how erasures of personal and professional histories can have profound impacts on understandings of Indigenous identity (Supernant, Chapter 6). In each case, erasure is resisted through haunting, where the ghosts refuse to be forgotten and insert themselves, sometimes forcefully, into the present.

P. M. W. Lawton, in Chapter 4, invites the reader to consider haunted ruralscapes, where erasure of deep Indigenous histories is accomplished through agricultural practice and settler colonialism. The demands of farming require removal of sacred places, such as Chisin or "Big Rock" near Chesaning, where a large limestone boulder was destroyed by early settlers for its material value. Tying into themes of Part III, Lawton explores the role that an ethic of consumption plays in the Saginaw Valley today, where rural farmers, feeling deeply threatened by the ghosts of the past and the uncertainty of the future, resist the actions of a large corporation to seize part of their lands for development.

Museums are deeply haunted places, a premise on which Nicole M. Burt founds her discussion of public education in biological anthropology at the Cleveland Museum of Natural History. Although her own training taught her about racist and sexist biases pervading early physical anthropology, the publics served by the museum are not haunted in the same way as practitioners. Museums curate and display specimens often acquired through questionable ethical practice, but museums that ignore or gloss over past ethical wrongdoings diminish their ability to haunt the visitors as productive teaching tools. Providing examples of her own interactions with various public audiences in Cleveland, Burt calls on museum practitioners to develop strong pedagogical tools to engage the public and expand their worldview, so they too can be haunted.

The final chapter in this section is a tale of personal haunting and professional practice. Beginning with a ghost story, Kisha Supernant takes the reader on a journey through her development as an archaeologist, weaving together a personal narrative of discovering her own ancestors and relatives and her move from being haunted by her own past with one of actively haunting the present and future. Using a case study of the Métis Nation in Canada, a postcontact Indigenous community of which she is a part, Supernant demonstrates how the nation-state of Canada sought to erase the Métis from the present. This attempted erasure led to misrepresentations of the Métis as merely mixed Indigenous and non-Indigenous. Supernant uses a Métis framework to explore the Métis archaeological record, allowing a Métis past to haunt the present and the future of Canada.

Identifying Ghosts within the Capitalist Landscapes of Late Modernity

The last four chapters in this volume show us how the past, present, and future are knitted together through experiences of loss, trauma, and injustice brought about by capitalism. While all the chapters in this volume "blur timescapes," those in Part III demonstrate the damage caused by ignoring traumas of the past. The voices of ghosts speak to us through those who remain—whether they choose to acknowledge the ghostly presence or not. Many traumas are a result of the social structures embedded in capitalistic enterprise. The "bones" (Garrison, Chapter 8) and bricks (Bechtold, Chapter 10) of capitalism can be found exposed in shallow graves across both urban and rural spaces (Brislen, Chapter 7).

In Chapter 7, Lilian Brislen helps us feel the harmful consequences of running from ghosts: in particular, the past trauma caused by the US farm crisis of the 1980s. She describes the historical contexts of the events leading to the crisis and how the aftereffects leave specters across rural America. Through the analysis of popular music during and after the crisis, she shows how forgetting endangers farmers' identities and future success as it perpetuates a harmful "capitalist fantasy" that is impossible to fulfill. She suggests that healing is to be found not in attempting to escape ghosts but in finding peace in living with them—and, in the process, better understanding ourselves.

A. E. Garrison conjures the ghosts of the recent, industrial past of Lansing, Michigan, in Chapter 8. Her visitation to the realm of memory, what was or may have been, is informed by documents, photos, and imagination. She envisions a past filled with the emotions and movement of everyday people and helps us visualize the web of connections linking past to present. She shows us how the whims of institutions controlled by the powerful and moneyed class continue to mold and affect society today. She points out the variability in human experience: how racism and classism determine who was included, who is remembered, and what is "preserved." The slow deterioration of place is a form of trauma that is barely perceptible on a conscious level.

Sarah Surface-Evans is haunted by the ways gentrification has transformed her community. As an archaeologist who studies material culture, she cannot help but notice how the erasure of the material touchstones of community memory and identity through gentrification is a form of trauma. In Chapter 9, she argues that traumascapes of structural violence are created whenever memories are contested and subverted by the powerful. Justified in their actions to create "progress" and remove "blight," city governments are complicit in the creation of urban traumascapes. Trauma lingers in places and passes through generations, causing disorientation of memory. Surface-Evans discusses how archaeologists have the tools to help communities affected by gentrification and calls for archaeological activism to heal the wounds of traumascapes.

Brigitte H. Bechtold manifests ghosts through the medium of brickwork in Chapter 10. Sharing her personal experiences with brickwork throughout her life and in many working-class communities in Europe, the United Kingdom, and the United States, she shows us the connections of past and present lives built into our cityscapes. She helps us explore different experiences of timescapes, too, distinguishing between chronological time, social time, and capitalist time. Bechtold also considers what is lost when capitalist time takes precedence and brickwork is valued by its profitability rather than by its ability to store the narratives that are part of the intellectual commons of communities. Modern forms of community social action, such as "buildering" and "yarn bombing," have the potential to create a space for resistance to the erosion of community memory and to subvert the power of capitalist time.

An Invitation

As you read through the chapters in this volume, we invite you to be haunted, to allow yourself to notice the prickle that raises hairs at the back of your neck. Haunting is a powerful way to move through time-space, compressing human experience through the affect of specters. Haunting invites remembrance of things, places, peoples, and times that would otherwise be forgotten. Let us remember together, to bring the past into the present and into new imagined futures.

Take my hand and follow me into the dark unknown.

Dr. Sarah Surface-Evans is Associate Professor of Anthropology at Central Michigan University. Her community-based archaeological research investigates cultural landscapes in the Great Lakes region of the United States. Her recent publication "A Landscape of Assimilation and Resistance: The Mount Pleasant Indian Industrial Boarding School" in the *International Journal of Historical Archaeology* examines the gendered and powered components of institutional design at Federal Indian Boarding Schools. This ongoing research was recognized for a Michigan Governor's Award for Historic Preservation in 2016. She has a forthcoming publication that utilizes "haunting" as a way conceptualize the trauma of colonial landscapes.

Dr. A. E. Garrison is Assistant Professor of Sociology at Central Michigan University. She earned her doctorate in Rural Sociology from the University of Missouri in 2011. Her work focuses on the development of graphic sociological methodology for scholarship and pedagogy. Her graphic work includes "Ghosts of Infertility: Haunted by Realities of Reproductive Death" (2016). Garrison's research interests also include social consequences resulting from urban planning policies, impacting urban infrastructure in Rust Belt cities. Her work in this subject area includes "Boneyards of the *Sortatropolis*: Exploring a City of Industrial Secrets – Lansing, Michigan (Part 1)" (2017).

Dr. Kisha Supernant is Métis and Associate Professor in the Department of Anthropology and Director of the Institute of Prairie and Indigenous Archaeology at the University of Alberta. She is the Director of the Exploring Métis Identity Through Archaeology (EMITA) Project and has published widely in national and international journals, including *PNAS, Journal of Archaeological Science, Journal of Anthropological Archaeology*, and the *Canadian Journal of Archaeology* and is co-editing a forthcoming book entitled *Archaeologies of the Heart*. An award-winning researcher, teacher, and writer, she is actively involved in research on cultural identities, landscapes, collaborative Indigenous archaeology, Métis archaeology, and heart-centered archaeological practice.

References

Beisaw, April. 2016. "Ghost Hunting as Archaeology: Archaeology as Ghost Hunting." In *Lost City, Found Pyramid: Understanding Alternative Archaeologies and Pseudoscientific Practices*, ed. Jeb J. Card and David S. Anderson, 185–198. Tuscaloosa: University of Alabama Press.
Bell, Michael Mayerfeld. 1997. "The Ghosts of Place." *Theory and Society* 26(6): 813–836.
Blanco, Maria del Pilar. 2012. *Ghost-Watching American Modernity: Haunting, Landscape, and the Hemispheric Imagination*. New York: Fordham University Press.
González-Tennant, Edward. 2016. "Hate Sits in Places: Folk Knowledge and the Power of Place in Rosewood, Florida." In *Excavating Memory: Material Culture Approaches to Sites of Remembering and Forgetting*, ed. Maria T. Starzmann and John R. Roby, 218–241. Gainesville: University Press of Florida.
———. 2018. *The Rosewood Massacre: An Archaeology and History of Intersectional Violence*. Gainesville: University Press of Florida.
Gordon, Avery F. 1997. *Ghostly Matters: Haunting and the Sociological Imagination*. Minneapolis: University of Minnesota Press.
Hill, Lisa. 2013. "Archaeologies and Geographies of the Post-Industrial Past: Landscape Memory, and the Spectral." *Cultural Geographies* 20(3): 379–396.
Hudson, Martyn. 2017. *Ghosts, Landscapes, and Social Memory*. New York: Routledge.
Miles, Tiya. 2015. *Tales from the Haunted South: Dark Tourism and Memories of Slavery from the Civil War Era*. Chapel Hill: University of North Carolina Press.
Johnson, Barbara Rose, ed. 1997. *Life and Death Matters: Human Rights and the Environment at the End of the Millennium*. Walnut Creek, CA: AltaMira Press.
Starzmann, Maria Theresia, and John H. Roby, eds. 2016. *Excavating Memory: Sites of Remembering and Forgetting*. Gainesville: University Press of Florida.
Surface-Evans, Sarah, and Sarah J. Jones. Forthcoming. "Discourses of the Haunted: An Intersubjective Approach to Archaeology at the Mount Pleasant Indian Industrial Boarding School." In special issue, *Archaeological Papers of the American Anthropological Association*, ed. Tiffany Cain and Teresa Raczek.

PART I

Imagining Timescapes
Invoking Haunting, Memory, and Nostalgia

CHAPTER 1

Telling Ghost Stories
Communicating across Timescapes and between Worldviews

APRIL M. BEISAW

Introduction

Academic writing is often linear. First, we establish a problem to be investigated. Then we select methods for assessing evidence and explain the data compiled. We attempt to connect the results to a broader picture. Finally, readers are left with one or more takeaway messages: this place is important, or these objects reveal a new pattern. Such a predictable writing format rarely moves the reader, but it allows similarly trained experts to skim content and extract the facts they are looking for. Once an article is read and relevant notes are taken, the reader need not return to the original and probably has little desire to.

Ghost stories, in contrast, linger in the mind of a reader or listener because a well-told ghost story is delightful thing to experience. They are often short and to the point but peppered with foggy details that convey ambiance and relatability. Dates are often relative (after the war, before women had the right to vote) and names seem familiar, to create a sense that this could have happened to you or someone you know. Ghost stories do not contain unnecessary details, which would only serve to jostle the listener into the cold cruel world of facts and figures. There is nothing that must be recalled, other than the feeling of wonder and the takeaway message: Don't forget what has happened here. Don't go where you don't belong. Every life comes to an end.

There are certainly times and places for academic communications, whether written or oral, but there are also times and places for the playful space that can be found in ghost stories. While some archaeologists spend a good deal of time debunking such tales, those efforts can devalue the connections to time, place, and ancestors that ghost stories so effortlessly convey. The listeners and tellers of a ghost tale do not necessarily need a lecture on science fact. Science can do a lot, but it cannot explain connections that seem to transcend time. Science is not the only way of knowing.

Other archaeologists have begun to explore this space. For example, Shannon Lee Dawdy's (2016) recent work on New Orleans includes many examples of how ghost stories attach to that city's material culture. There, "old houses and objects are mediums for the spirits of the dead" (8) that coauthor the past with the living (50–51). Dawdy identifies rules around what ghost stories are told and who tells them, with locals considering the tales told by tour guides as "lies and fabrications" compared to the "colorful enough stories" woven by locals (69). The cultural anthropologist Michele Hanks (2015) finds similar concern over truth in her ethnography of ghost tourism. The "real" ghost stories are not lies, but knowledge is required to be able to discern stories manufactured as pure fiction from those that are relaying emotions about what really happened here. Both Hanks (2015: 141) and Dawdy (2016: 73) find that locals who know the true history of a place can tell its ghost stories better than any spiritual medium and any for-hire storyteller.

I consider myself both a scientist and a teller of ghost stories. Everywhere I go I find haunted places, and this is not a cause for concern. My academic career has spanned more than two decades. The things I learned in my early career as a chemist, my transitionary career as an environmental scientist, and my long-term career as an archaeologist have provided me with a breadth of knowledge such that the landscapes I move through speak to me. I see cycles of life and death everywhere: in invasive species that came from elsewhere but fight to make this new place their home, in cemeteries that contain monuments to those who refuse to be forgotten, in decaying buildings that linger long past their usefulness. I have come know the patterns of humanity: where people tend to live, how they experience life there, common ways of dying, and means of memorializing lost friends and relatives. Sometimes a house, a gravestone, a broken toy, or an old tree is all that is left of past peoples or places. When you know the science and humanity of life and death, it is easy to feel the ghosts of place, as defined by Michael Mayerfield Bell (1997).

The ghosts of place do not need paranormal powers to manifest or convey messages for the living. Haunted places are simply locations where the living can slip from the present into a real, imagined, or idealized past. The boundaries between now and then are thinnest at ruins, sacred sites, sites of exceptional beauty, and places whose history can be felt by those with sufficient knowledge or empathy. To connect to the story of a place is to experience its ghosts. If you want to see what I mean, come with me for a virtual ghost tour of the haunted landscape where I now work, Vassar College. After we return from that journey, I will leave you to experience the rest of the chapters of this book on your own. Then, in the epilogue, I'll present you with my ghost tour of this book. To create both tours, I distilled vast amounts of information into short stories that encourage us to linger on the landscape. As you read each, consider how knowledge and empathy are all that are needed to communicate across time and between worldviews.

The Ghosts of My Work

When I arrived at Vassar College, in Poughkeepsie, New York, its 150th anniversary celebration had just ended. The college created numerous web pages that summarized seemingly small bits of history with too many names and dates that meant little to me. Overwhelmed by information that I struggled to connect with, I turned my attention toward learning the past of the anthropology department. At the heart of my investigation was a personal need to understand the maze of a building that housed my office and lab as well as an academic need to learn the origins of artifacts stored in cigar and handkerchief boxes in a particularly odd wooden cabinet.

From those web pages and through conversations with some of my colleagues, the building started to make sense. Built to house the short-lived discipline of euthenics (not eugenics), Blodgett Hall contains a series of half-floors. Each half-floor was intended for a different aspect of this study of human well-being, such as education, home economics, and contagious diseases. What was once a hyperorganized structure is now a chaotic maze. More than a century of renovations has moved walls around in a way that is reminiscent of the Winchester Mystery House. The exterior of my office door pronounces this space as Blodgett 318. Yet the interior of that same door marks it as Blodgett 233. A yellowed paper with Chinese writing on it adorns a handsome old bookcase in the office. I have been told the note explains the organization of books once housed within it. The owner of those manuscripts died long ago but those who remember him have asked me to leave the note in place.

Investigating the origins of the artifacts curated in Blodgett alongside me, I have learned much about a museum that was once housed in the basement. Some of the numbered artifacts that I have found must have come from it. I have also learned about those anthropologists who walked the halls before me; Ruth Benedict, the cultural anthropologist, and Mary Butler Lewis, the archaeologist, were both students here. Mary was also employed by Vassar, for a short time. On the internet, I found a silent movie showing her and some Vassar students doing archaeology in the Hudson Valley. It shows her excavating in the field and loading equipment into a car (Illustration 1.1) parked behind what is now my lab. The video was all I needed to start seeing Mary in Blodgett. Approximately sixty years separates us in time but Blodgett and archaeology unite us in space and activity. Knowing about these ghosts grounded me in the heritage of my new home.

Illustration 1.1. Screen capture of silent film "1940 Hudson Valley Dig," showing Mary Butler Lewis driving to her 1940 Hudson Valley archaeology survey site from the Blodgett building at Vassar College, where the author now conducts similar work. Source: https://archive.org/details/upenn-f16-0444_1940_Hudson_Valley_Dig.

The demands of being on the tenure track pulled me away from Vassar's past as I worked at getting the publications, teaching evaluations, and service record that would ensure my own future there. Once tenure seemed secured, meaning I was no longer on a series of short-term contracts, I felt my attention being pulled back to the Vassar landscape and the stories it held. This pull was not purely academic. I was now living in Main Building, a building constructed in 1863 and listed on the National Register of Historic Places (see Illustration 1.2). The entire college was once housed in Main's five stories. As in Blodgett, anachronistic features are everywhere in Main. The placement of certain doors and windows seems nonsensical. Ghost stories are tied to many of these strange spaces and to the building as a whole. Main is haunted by the college's founder, Matthew Vassar, who died in this building while reading his retirement speech. I was now living in what was once his apartment and swearing that I would retire well before my own death. Please remind me of that promise once I hit retirement age.

While living in Main, I compiled all the ghost stories of the building that I could find. The college's online archives include student diaries and issues of the school paper. I searched for terms like "ghost," "spirit," and "dead." Often these led to phrases like "she didn't have a ghost of a chance" or "I'm just not in the spirit," but between those results I discovered ghosts. The building came

Illustration 1.2. A small portion of Vassar College's expansive Main Building by full moonlight. The windows of the author's third-floor apartment are visible at the far right, above the lamppost. The college president's office is just below, on the second floor. Photo by the author.

alive for me and established another historical connection that I just had to honor. Several accounts documented an 1885 visit to Vassar by Mark Twain. Among other activities, Twain told ghost stories to students gathered in one of Main's parlors. I had already started doing the same thing, but now I could add Twain's story to my repertoire.

Main Building is Vassar's largest dorm. It houses more than three hundred students and the families of two faculty members. Fortunately, the other faculty member living here also has a love for ghost stories. We advertised a "Ghosts of Main" storytelling event around Halloween, and students packed into the multipurpose room. There, I told them about Matthew Vassar but also about Gertrude Bronson, Vassar class of 1895. Gertrude died in Cleveland, Ohio, the year after graduation. Her story claims that because this is where she was happiest in life, Gertrude returned to spend her afterlife in Main. She makes her presence felt by moving chairs, opening and closing doors, or watching students walking to and from class from her third-floor window. Her name is supposedly carved into that window's sill. Main has way too many windows to mount an organized search, and more than a few layers of paint have been laid down since Gertrude's death, but that does not stop students from checking their own windowsills for her name as soon as they learn about Gertrude.

Vassar, like most US colleges, has several suicide-related ghost stories. Folklorist Elizabeth Tucker (2005) has shown how these stories provide colleges with a safe way to talk about the stress that comes with living away from home and preparing for a future career. One of Main's suicide stories is also useful for explaining why this college does not have class valedictorians. It goes like this. A pair of close friends and roommates were in competition to be named valedictorian. One day they had a fight and the girl currently in second place shoved her competitor out of their dorm room window. Unable to believe what she had done, the murderous student hanged herself. Now, ghostly scratching noises can be heard as the would-be valedictorian keeps trying to climb back into her room.

Vassar's Main Building is both huge and old. Drafty windows, antique heating systems, and all-too-friendly rodents generate a wealth of noises and cold spots, not to mention the occasional unexpected door closure. Ghost stories help transform these realities into a shared backdrop of lives lived. Upon hearing Main's ghost stories, students tend to go looking for physical evidence of the tales told. Their once familiar place is now simultaneously more mysterious and more meaningful. Students always ask if I know who lived in their dorm room before them and if anyone has reported a ghost sighting in it. I do my best to answer questions and incorporate new reports into later ghost story events, but I am often overwhelmed with information. My default response is that if Vassar students who died elsewhere return to haunt their Main dorm rooms, Jackie Kennedy Onassis may be hanging out in Room 312.

Once the Pandora's box of ghost stories is open, it is difficult to close. After approximately 150 hours of archival research, I began to offer walking ghost tours of the Vassar College campus. The hour-long walking tour includes stories of past students, staff, presidents, trustees, and donors. Because we are all part of how this place functions, we have all made it into Vassar's unofficial history—its ghost stories. For the walking tour's debut, over seventy-five students came out to stroll the campus in the dark, and many remarked on how they had never seen the chapel's stained-glass windows aglow at night or noticed that the lightning rod of the Skinner Hall of Music is a series of musical notes. As we walked from one stop to the next, students told each other their own ghost stories. It seems that everyone is a skeptic in daylight but more willing to consider certain possibilities in the dark.

In ghost stories, peoples, places, and their interrelationships are more important than dates and names. What happened first may have been predestined and what happened later may give the earlier occurrence more gravitas. What happened to me might happen to you. Even if we don't know each other, we can be connected by a ghost and its story. We all want to live out eternity where we were happiest; we have all stood at a window and watched others pass by below us; we have all gotten so wrapped up in competition that we have lost a friend and regretted it later.

To Be Continued . . .

Ghost tours disrupt established hierarchies and emphasize liminality (Hanks 2015: 82). Because ghosts are in a transitional state, encountering them brings the audience to a place that they do not usually experience, one that is in between here and there—a threshold. The same can be done with the narrative tool of "to be continued." This chapter ends somewhat prematurely to bring you to a liminal threshold and allow you to experience suspense. The chapters that follow are written in an academic mode, even though space is made for a blurring of time. Then, in the epilogue, you will find my ghost tour of those same chapters. As with Vassar's tour, I attempt to distill vast amounts of information into short stories that encourage us to linger with emotions felt and lessons learned. By reading my tour after the chapters that inspired it, you will see how ghost stories need not lie or mislead. The truer the tale, the more likely the ghosts are to remain with you.

Dr. April M. Beisaw is an Associate Professor of Anthropology at Vassar College, Poughkeepsie, NY. There she teaches courses on Native North America, repatriation, forensic anthropology, and historical archaeology. Her most recent book is *Identifying and Interpreting Animal Bones: A Manual*, published by Texas A&M University Press. Her next book will be on the New York City water system and the towns that have been sacrificed to create and maintain city reservoirs. She is also an associate editor for the journal *Historical Archaeology*.

References

Bell, Michael Mayerfeld. 1997. "The Ghosts of Place." *Theory and Society* 26(6): 813–836.
Dawdy, Shannon Lee. 2016. *Patina: A Profane Archaeology*. Chicago: University of Chicago Press.
Hanks, Michele. 2015. *Haunted Heritage: The Cultural Politics of Ghost Tourism, Populism, and the Past*. Walnut Creek, CA: Left Coast Press.
Tucker, Elizabeth. 2005. "Ghosts in Mirrors: Reflections of the Self." *Journal of American Folklore* 118(468): 186–203.

CHAPTER 2

Material Memories

Interpreting Souvenirs and Heirlooms in the Archaeological Record

ERICA BEGUN

As archaeologists, we love to study burials. Through mortuary analysis we can seek to tell the stories of the people whose remains we study in addition to learning much about those who buried them. Every culture has differing degrees of comfort with allowing the remains of the dead to linger in the spheres of the living. Some cultures bury their dead in cemeteries, others choose to cremate their dead; some keep their dead close, others push them far away. Because of their own cultural views, many people might find the idea of burying a loved one within or under their house a bit ghoulish, as if by keeping the dead close we might be inviting them to linger in unexpected ways or somehow taint our living space with death's presence. However, for many Mesoamerican cultures, especially those of central and western Mexico, this was a common practice with altars and buried cache offerings often associated with the burial locations. By burying the dead within the household, the living could protect the graves and keep their dead close, thus inviting them to continue to be a presence in the world of the living. Through this, we see the important role that ancestors may have played in the household rituals present during this time.

We often think of hauntings as an inherently negative experience. Ghosts are born from trauma, grief, and unexpected loss, which serve to intimately connect the memory of the deceased to the trauma of death. Peaceful deaths at the end of long lives rarely result in hauntings within "Westernized" views of ghosts. As a reflection of the trauma enmeshed with ghosts and hauntings, the actions of the ghosts themselves are usually disruptive, if not hostile and destructive, as they continue to cause damage to the living through their presence and actions. These are the ghosts and hauntings that garner public awareness and make for exciting Hollywood horror stories. However, there is a softer side to ghosts as well—one that is often overlooked or unexpressed but plays no less significant a role in many cultures. There is a fine line between memory and ghosts, and when these are combined without the trauma of death, you can see the emergence of spirits as active figures in the lives of the living in the form of ancestral spirits. These are "ghosts" that can be safely welcomed as the relationships and connections between family and friends are maintained past the limits of life. Kisha Supernant (see Chapter 6) discusses the ghostly feeling of connection between the past and present that is common not just in archaeological experience but in human experience in general. While there are many ways to see such a haunting, one way in which this ghostly presence of the dead can be seen is in the significance of heirlooms and, by extension, souvenirs.

When my grandfather died, my mother claimed his Cuisinart. She brought it from Michigan to where we lived in Wisconsin. She kept that Cuisinart until I was in college (about a dozen years), before it finally broke down and she was forced to replace it. The brand of the food processor did not matter, nor did the fancy features she could have gotten with a newer model. She did not want a new one and would not have gotten one had the ancient Cuisinart not fallen apart on her. What mattered was that it had been owned by her father, and by using it, she was bringing a piece of his life (and his love of cooking) into her own home so that the tools he had used to nurture his family would now help nurture her own. The importance of the Cuisinart was that it served as a focal point for her memories of her father. Through the act of bringing the Cuisinart into her home, my mother was inviting the ghost of her father to linger as an active presence in our lives through the use of a material object that held significance for both of them.

My mother's story is not unique. But it is one that is often hard to see archaeologically. We are limited in scope to what we find in the archaeological record. Objects, soil colors, and bones are all full of information that we, as archaeologists, are trained to understand. However, much about the human experience is not so easily quantified. It is much harder to give voice to some ghosts of the past, bringing to life the memories and stories of those long gone. Archaeologists rely heavily on the concept of context—the spatial, temporal, and relational information about material remains gained from excavations—in order to interpret the archaeological record. We draw meaning from the material culture of the past based on these relationships. When we find artifacts outside of the expected range of contexts—for example, a thirty-year-old Cuisinart alongside otherwise state-of-the-art kitchen tools—we seek to understand the chain of events that led to this disruption in the typical patterns of use and behavior. In many cases, no reason for such shifts in behavior is apparent, and we can do little more than assume there was a reason, even if we do not know what it may have been. These objects and behaviors are often chalked up to "ritual" as a catch-all for behaviors we cannot fully understand but that clearly had meaning to the culture we are studying.

This chapter explores the intersection between memory and material culture in a community in ancient Mexico. I argue that what had initially seemed like evidence of a West Mexican ethnic enclave at the urban center of Teotihuacan may be evidence of a much deeper story about the lives of people long gone. Archaeological evidence of a direct connection between Teotihuacan and north-central Michoacán has been scarce. That is not to say there were not complex interactions between the regions—we know that these connections existed—but many unanswered questions remain. Several publications discuss the potential connections between Teotihuacan and Michoacán, most centering around the human remains (White et al. 2004a, 2004b), burial styles (Gómez 1998, 2002; Gómez and Gazzola 2007), and burial assemblage ceramics (Gómez 1998, 2002; Gómez and Gazzola 2007) found in one small compound (called N1W5, Structure 19) in the western outskirts of the city. It was this exciting research that brought me to work at Teotihuacan, as I sought to tease out a deeper understanding of the ties between these two neighboring regions. However, my research at the Michoacán-affiliated compound of N1W5:19 did not serve to strengthen these connections as I had hoped it would. Instead of a vibrant community from north-central Michoacán, working to maintain their ethnic identity, I found that much of the ceramic and almost all of the lithic materials were of local origin. There was no production of Michoacán-esque goods within the compound—a stark contrast to their neighbors in the rest of the Oaxacan barrio who were continuing to produce Oaxacan-style goods with local, Teotihuacan-sourced materials. The Michoacán materials seemed contained, even isolated, within small parts of the N1W5:19 compound. Despite this, tantalizing pieces of evidence, most clearly in the form of ceramics, suggested that a connection to Michoacán did exist.

As a result of this research, I suggest that the presence of Michoacán pottery at Teotihuacan does not reflect a direct, long-term cultural affiliation between the N1W5:19 compound and the greater cultural entity of Classic period Michoacán. Rather, the short-term nature of the occupation and the presentation of the materials suggest something both less grand and arguably more complex in the form of memory objects. It seems that these pieces of material culture, which likely originate in the Lake Cuitzeo and/or Lake Patzcuaro regions of north-central Michoacán (Figure 2.1), serve not just as markers of ethnic presence but also as possible evidence of heirlooms and souvenirs in the lives of a small group of Teotihuacan residents with a Michoacán affinity. If this is true, archaeologists might apply the notion of heirlooming to explain many of these objects that seem out of spatial-temporal context and thus can begin to tell a deeper, richer, and fuller story of those who have come before us. Like my mother, these people sought to maintain a connection through objects of memory, choosing to collect, keep, and value over time the material remains of their

Figure 2.1. Map of Mesoamerica showing locations of key regions discussed, including the Patzcuaro Basin and Teotihuacan.
Map by the author (Begun 2013).

memories and, thus, their lives. In particular, I look at two social and behavioral phenomena for explanations: souvenirs and heirlooming.

Souvenirs as Memory of Time and Place

Souvenirs carry with them the memory of a place or event. According to Statista.com ("Global Tourism Industry" 2018), modern global tourism is a multitrillion-dollar industry. This includes many facets of travel and tourism, meaning that a significant portion of the money from tourism is spent on souvenirs. It is foolish to think that such behaviors are limited to modern cultures. Indeed, Hume (2014) and Popkin (2018) suggest that the earliest well-documented evidence for collecting such objects dates to the Roman period but that the practice is far older. Graburn (2000) adds that not all souvenirs mark travel events; they can also reflect memories of historic events (e.g., Bradley 2000) that individuals wish to remember or connect with personally.

A growing body of anthropological literature deals with the material culture of tourism, specifically souvenirs (e.g., Gordon 1986; Hitchcock and Teague 2000; Morgan and Pritchard 2005). These studies on the importance of souvenir collecting and self-identity formation can inform our understanding of the material culture of the past. Ownership of a souvenir marks a person as one who has been somewhere and has returned changed from that journey. Souvenirs reflect the desire to carry that past experience into the present and future, using the object as a tool of remembrance (Popkin 2018). As Van Wormer (Chapter 3) touches on, the souvenir itself serves as a tangible connection to the memories of the travel event and the experiences had there. Its significance may be to either the culture or place where it originated, but it is separate from "normal" life. People have a "need to bring things home with them" because travel is otherwise ephemeral and liminal, a fleeting yet sacred and extraordinary experience (Gordon 1986: 136). Travel is often a period of liminality, and the souvenir serves to mark both the liminal experience of travel and the changed status of the traveler upon return. Souvenirs "prove" that something important happened, something worthy of remembrance. Thus, the souvenir serves as a portable but physical link between a visitor and the place and/or people they visited, allowing one to recall a time and place that may be distant from one's home.

Heirlooming

In much the same way that souvenirs invoke the memory of a place, heirlooms reflect the memory of past people and relationships. By definition, heirlooms are material objects that are passed generationally between members of a kin group and hold a certain significance within that familiar group. This process of keeping objects within a social context after the passing of an earlier owner, sometimes called "temporal curation" (Thomas 1976: 128), highlights the significance of an object that is found outside of normal temporal contexts. An heirloom possesses an innate duality regarding the use of an artifact in that it may be used for the original function of the object or as a memory marker (Thomas 1976) of significant events in the lives of the original owners. When an heirloom experiences generational ownership, it "exemplif[ies] a kind of lateral cycling, which occurs when an object is transferred from one user to another without a change (or at least minimal changes) in the object or its use" (Lillios 1999: 239). In this way, the life of the material culture extends far beyond that of the original owner, bringing with it a sense of memory of previous owners and their lives. As objects are passed down through the generations, so too are the stories that accompany them. The object itself is imbued with memory and serves as a connection to lives once lived. Thus, the object is filled with the specter of the past individual, which can also be curated and cherished along with the physical object.

Heirlooms act as the voice of the ghosts of the past for those who inherit these important objects. The result of the connections between person and object, and of the changing relationship between the living, the dead, and the material culture left behind, is that objects of memory hold a special role in the material record. The significance of these objects can lead to reuse, recycling, repair, or repurposing as future generations seek to keep the memory of the dead alive through the object to which the person is connected. What this means for archaeology is that there can be a lag between when an object was produced and when it finally enters the archaeological record—meaning that the object is found out of its usual contexts in time and/or space, confusing otherwise straightforward interpretations of a site. This can be further complicated if nonrelated individuals find a connection to an object and seek to curate materials for other, personal reasons in the form of collections (Walker Tubb, 2006).

Teotihuacan Background

Teotihuacan represents a major multiethnic urban center in the central highlands of Mexico (Figure 2.1). The city was occupied between AD 100 and 750, during the Classic period of Mesoamerican prehistory. During this time, Teotihuacan's influence spread far across Mesoamerica. Oddly, there is little evidence of direct conquest or political control outside of the Basin of Mexico. Instead, the power of Teotihuacan seems to have been closely tied to economic control over valuable resources, such as the famous green-gold Pachuca obsidian source in nearby Hidalgo. As a result of the city's control over this obsidian source, many smaller, less urbanized parts of Mesoamerica sought ways to connect themselves to the power and economic system of Teotihuacan through long-distance trade networks.

Much of the recent work at Teotihuacan has focused on gaining a better understanding of the earliest occupation at the site (e.g., Sergio Gómez's Tunnel Project). Interspersed throughout the work on understanding the complex nature of the city itself are many projects looking at the perceived "foreign" elements found throughout the city. The best known and researched of these areas are the Maya and Oaxacan barrios, which represent trade and residential/ethnic enclaves, respectively. Contained within the Oaxacan barrio is a small apartment compound labeled N1W5:19. Archaeologist Sergio Gómez has identified this compound as having a connection to a West Mexican/Michoacán presence within the city of Teotihuacan.

Evidence for a Michoacán Presence at N1W5:19

Previous work at the N1W5:19 compound revealed a number of artifacts that established connections between Michoacán and Teotihuacan (Gómez 1998, 2002; Gómez and Gazzola 2007). Gómez (1998, 2002) reported on a number of the findings from his 1991 excavations; however, most were focused on the burial contexts. The burials suggested that a handful of the interments at the compound showed cultural affiliation with a nonlocal (and non-Zapotec) cultural presence in the form of Michoacán-style grave goods that had been placed into the burials of certain individuals. Just as we use clothing, language, food, and many other aspects of culture to identify our own affiliations, so too do our styles of burial tell a cultural story. In addition to the unusual grave goods, Gómez discovered two tombs at the compound that appear to have been constructed in a style similar to the shaft tomb tradition of Early Classic West Mexico (Cowgill 1997; Gómez 1998). As is the case in many Classic period cultures of central and western Mesoamerica, the occupants of N1W5:19 chose to bury their dead in the courtyards and under the dirt floors of their compound (Begun 2013; Gómez 1998, 2002; Gómez and Gazzola 2007).

Based on the tomb construction and the presence of a few ceramic vessels and figurines, along with a single West Mexican (Ucareo)–sourced prismatic blade, Gómez (1998, 2002; Gómez and Gazzola 2007) asserted that a connection was to be drawn between the occupants of the compound and Michoacán. Indeed, it is within these burials that we see some of the strongest connections between the occupants of the compound and West Mexico. Christine White et al. (2004a, 2004b) presented isotopic analysis of the human remains that both strengthened and complicated this association. These data suggests that the individuals in these Michoacán-style graves were originally Teotihuacan natives who had spent a large amount of time in the north-central region of Michoacán before returning to Teotihuacan, where they ultimately died and were buried in a peripheral apartment complex closely tied to the Oaxacan barrio. It remains possible that rather than actively associating themselves with Michoacán, the population of N1W5:19 maintained a minimal material cultural tie to Michoacán. Whether this was unintentional (owing to issues of distance and transport difficulty) or intentional (a conscious effort toward assimilation into local customs and traditions) remains unclear. While the existing material record does not support a long-lasting ethnic enclave of Michoacán people within the Oaxacan barrio, it remains possible that the people of the N1W5:19 compound may have exhibited and displayed their ethnic ties to Michoacán in more ephemeral ways, such as through language, food, or clothing styles, which have not left a lasting presence in the archaeological record. In this way, their presence in the city itself represents a tantalizingly ephemeral specter of culture.

Their positioning in a low-rank compound that was peripheral both to the foreign enclave of the Oaxacans and to the city itself suggests a high degree of marginalization. In other words, despite their connections to Teotihuacan, they were seen as inherently foreign and settled within one of the foreigner enclaves at the periphery of the city. While they may not have been overtly foreign, the N1W5:19 compound reflects a group with significant ties to both Teotihuacan and the north-central region of Michoacán, which were overt enough to marginalize the community within the city's broader population.

While there is lithic, shell (Illustration 2.1), and lapidary (Illustration 2.2) evidence supporting a connection to West Mexico (Begun 2013), much of the material evidence supporting a Michoacán affinity or presence at the compound comes from the ceramic assemblages. The vast majority (over 98 percent) of the ceramic materials excavated and analyzed from the compound reflect the local ceramic assemblage of Teotihuacan (see Begun 2013). The remaining materials were clearly identified through visual and chemical analyses as having nonlocal origins (Begun 2013). Materials from Michoacán were exceedingly rare, even among the foreign ceramics. A total of 65 sherds out of a total of 40,949 from the household, and 4 pieces (all whole vessels) out of 2,571 total sherds and vessels from the burials, could be visually identified as having Michoacán origins. Of the 65 Michoacán-associated sherds, the majority were either a thin, highly polished blackware (Illustration 2.3) or a polished redware that bore a resemblance to known ceramics types from north-central Michoacán (see Begun 2013; Carot 2001; Pollard 2007). These ceramics were mostly broken pot sherds, a small number of which had been carved and painted (al secco style); small jars; and a handful of figurines of styles that do not occur locally at Teotihuacan. These figurines very closely resemble those of the Patzcuaro style found in the north-central parts of Michoacán (Begun 2008) (Illustration 2.4).

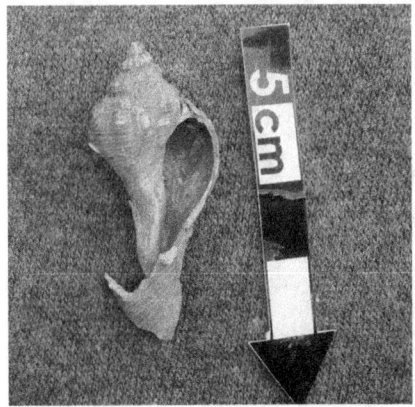

Illustration 2.1. Marine shell (possibly *Pleuroploca* sp.) from Burial 34.
Photo by the author.

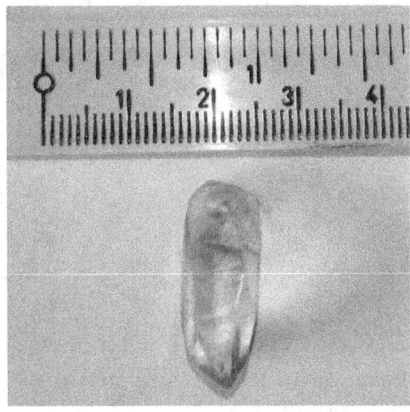

Illustration 2.2. Amethyst pendant from Burial 36 at Structure 19.
Photo by the author.

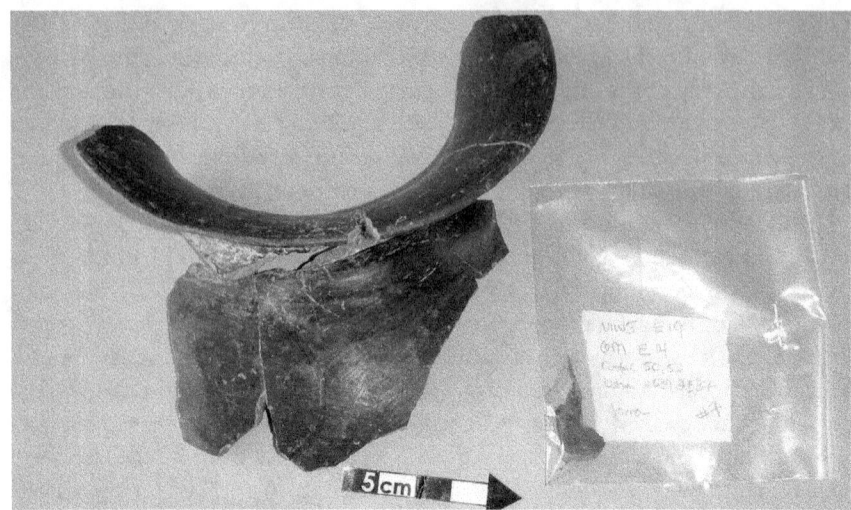

Illustration 2.3. Polished blackware jar from Structure 19.
Photo by the author.

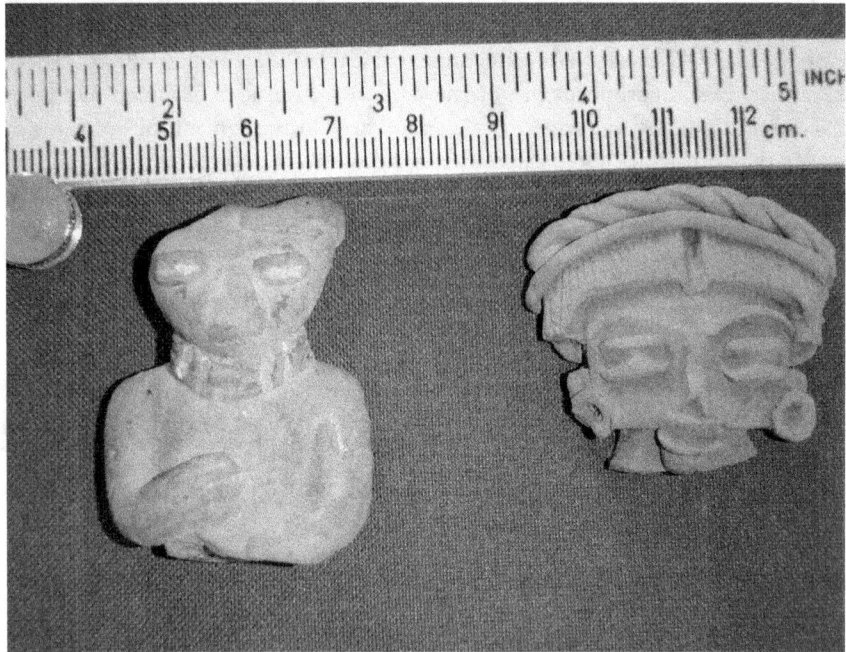

Illustration 2.4. Patzcuaro-style figurines found at Structure 19.
Photo by the author.

Instrumental Neutron Activation Analysis (INAA) confirmed that the highly polished, thin, fine-paste blackware was indeed not of local origins but failed to pinpoint its actual place of origin (Neff 2011). Other, similar materials have been found within the Lake Cuitzeo region of Michoacán, suggesting this as a possible source for the blackware. Two samples of a polished redware were identified as likely coming from the Lake Patzcuaro region (Neff 2011). This strongly suggests that at least some of the nonlocal materials found at the N1W5:19 compound originated in the north-central part of Michoacán.

Objects of Memory at N1W5:19

The Michoacán-associated materials were discovered in two distinct contexts: whole pots that were found in burials and broken sherds found in household midden contexts. It seems plausible that important vessels and figurines linking the occupants of N1W5:19 back to Michoacán were treated as both souvenirs and heirloom objects because of their rarity (see Lillios 1999), or at least that they serve as evidence of "temporal curation" behaviors (Thomas 1976: 128). While there is little evidence that the people of N1W5:19 were engaging in the use of Michoacán materials themselves for ritual worship, the presence of such materials in many of the burials from the earlier occupation periods of the compound is significant, as is the lack of Michoacán-associated materials in the later period burials. The initial use of the objects as grave goods demonstrates the closer connection between those individuals and Michoacán. This pattern changes rapidly, likely following the deaths of those who had traveled to distant lands and brought back objects of significance. Within the span of a generation, the value of the objects moved away from their significance as marking interactions or personal affiliations with the west to a more ephemeral social identity as material markers of memory and objects of remembrance. In this way, they moved from the realm of souvenir into that of heirloom. The connection to the previous owner overshadowed the significance of an object's geographical origin as it became a placeholder for the memory of the dead. These objects, no longer suitable for burial, were curated within the household to serve as anchor points for memory.

Thus, it is possible that they were passed down from one generation to the next, displayed, or used as markers of ties to a distant place or deceased family. As souvenirs, they could have had symbolic significance connecting the owners of the objects to the region they, or their ancestors, had visited. It is not unusual for people to collect and keep objects that symbolize a piece of that place, sometimes in a very literal sense, like soil, rocks, ceramics, or plants (Van Wormer, Chapter 3). As heirlooms, their presence in the compound may indicate an attempt by the occupants to maintain their connections—whether of ethnic origin, cultural affiliation, or travel—through the keeping of objects of memory (Lillios 1999). The fact that these vessels disappear from the archaeological record around the time that the compound becomes more fully occupied by people with an Oaxacan cultural affiliation cannot be ignored. Nor can the fact that after about fifty to a hundred years these objects appear solely as shattered refuse in household fill and midden context.

There seems to be no evidence that the people of N1W5:19 attempted to repair such vessels when broken, although attempts at repair were made on other costly vessels. While it may be that repairs were not possible (as was the case with my grandfather's Cuisinart), it is even more likely that as the populace of the compound became more removed from their Michoacán connections and/or origins, the value of the pottery as a point of ethnic identity or as a marker of the memory of a distant location lessened over time. As a result, when a vessel or object broke (or was intentionally broken) it was discarded rather than repaired because keeping it was no longer so closely connected to the memory of the dead. In their breakage, the vessels could no longer contain what they were meant to hold in either a physical or metaphysical sense. Similarly, the figurines, which can very directly represent corporeality, may have lost their supernatural significance when broken. If the breakage of these objects was intentional, it reflects a conscious desire to distance oneself from the materiality of memory represented by heirlooms. Through the breaking of the objects, the connection to the specter of the deceased may too have been severed. Once the connections were severed, the objects lost their significance and thus could be disposed of without fear or worry of offending a supernatural presence.

Conclusion

The past is a story of lives that have been lived. In its own way, archaeology is a discipline surrounded and informed by ghosts. Just as it is often said that ghosts are tied to objects of importance to their lives, so too are the stories of the past tied to the things left behind. While over time the meaning of these objects—both souvenirs and heirlooms—can change, they remain an intriguing window into how people blend memory and materiality. Archaeologists are adept at teasing out the threads of complex human behavior from the material record. However, some behaviors are easier to see archaeologically than others. Due to the ephemerality of memory, it is highly likely that such complex meanings are easily lost in our interpretations of the archaeological record. Often, items that may have been curated by families over generations end up being labeled as "ritual objects" due to their odd temporal contexts. Others, for which the meaning may have shifted over time, appear forgotten and discarded in ancient trash deposits, thereby losing their social meaning and significance. By seeking alternative ways of understanding the complexity of human behaviors that result in objects being found out of temporal context, archaeologists may be better able to understand the ways in which ancient people sought to express and preserve their own memories of the past.

Dr. Erica Begun holds a doctorate in Anthropology from the University of Iowa, specializing in the archaeology of prehistoric Mesoamerica. She has a passion for ceramics in general, and figurines in particular. In addition, her research often focuses on the intersection between ceramics and ethnic identity among the Pre-Tarascan populations of North-Central Michoacán, Mexico.

References

Begun, Erica. 2008. "The Many Faces of Figurines: Figurines as Markers of Ethnicity in Michoacan." *Ancient Mesoamerica* 19(2): 311–318.
———. 2013. "Detecting Ethnicity at Teotihuacan through Archaeology: The West Mexican Presence at Structure N1W5:19." Ph.D. dissertation. Iowa City: University of Iowa.
Bradley, Katherine. 2000. "Women's Suffrage Souvenirs." In Hitchcock and Teague, eds., *Souvenirs*, 79–90.
Carot, Patricia. 2001. *Le site de Loma Alta, Lac de Zacapu, Michoacán. Mexique*. Paris Monographs in American Archaeology. BAR International Series. Oxford: Archaeopress.
Cowgill, George. 1997. "State and Society at Teotihuacan, Mexico." *Annual Review of Anthropology* 26: 129–161.
"Global Tourism Industry: Statistics and Facts." 2018. Statista, 21 August. Retrieved 5 April 2018 from https://www.statista.com/topics/962/global-tourism/.
Gómez, Sergio. 1998. "Nuevos datos sobre la relación de Teotihuacan y el Occidente de México." *Antropología e Historia del Occidente de México: XXIV Mesa Redonda de la Sociedad Mexicana de Antropología*, 1461–1493. Mexico City: Sociedada Mexicana de Antropología, Universidad Nacional Autónoma de Mexico.
———. 2002. "Presencia del Occidente de México en Teotihuacán: Aproximaciones a la política exterior del estado Teotihuacano." In *Ideología y política a través de materiales, imágenes y símbolos*, ed. María Elena Ruiz Gallut, 563–625. Mexico City: Universidad Nacional Autónoma de México.
Gómez, Sergio, and Julie Gazzola. 2007. "Análisis de las Relaciones Entre Teotihuacan y el Occidente de Mexico." In *Dinámicas Culturales entre el Occidente, el Centro-Norte y la Cuenca de México, del Preclásico al Epiclasico*, ed. Brigitte Faugère-Kalfon, 113–135. Mexico City: Centro de Estudios Mexicanos y Centroamericanos, El Colegio de Michoacán.
Gordon, Barbara. 1986. "The Souvenir: Messenger of the Extraordinary." *Journal of Popular Culture* 20(3): 135–146.
Graburn, Michael. 2000. "Foreword." In Hitchcock and Teague, eds., *Souvenirs*, xii–xvii.

Hitchcock, Michael, and Ken Teague, eds. 2000. *Souvenirs: The Material Culture of Tourism.* London: University of North London.

Lillios, Katina T. 1999. "Objects of Memory: The Ethnography and Archaeology of Heirlooms." *Journal of Archaeological Method and Theory* 6(3): 235–262.

Morgan, Nigel, and Annette Pritchard. 2005. "On Souvenirs and Metonymy: Narratives of Memory, Metaphor, and Materiality." *Tourist Studies* 5(1): 29–53.

Neff, Hector. 2011. "INAA Result Report." Prepared for Erica Begun. University of Missouri.

Pollard, Helen. 2007. "Manual Visual de la Cerámica Prehispánica: Cuenca de Patzcuaro, Michoacán." Unpublished presentation. East Lansing: Michigan State University.

Popkin, Mary. 2018. "Urban Images in Glass from the Late Roman Empire: The Souvenir Flasks of Puteoli and Baiae." *American Journal of Archaeology* 122(3): 427–462.

Thomas, David Hurst. 1976. "A Diegueno Shaman's Wand: An Object Lesson Illustrating the 'Heirloom Hypothesis.'" *Journal of California Anthropology* 3(1): 128–132.

Walker Tubb, Kathryn. 2006. "Artifacts and Emotion." In *Archaeology, Heritage, and the Antiquities Trade*, ed. Neil Brodie, Morag M. Kersel, Christina Luke, and Kathryn Walker Tubb. Gainesville: University Press of Florida.

White, Christine, Michael Spence, Fred Longstaffe, and Kimberly Law. 2004a. "Demography and Ethnic Continuity in the Tlailotlacan Enclave of Teotihuacan: The Evidence from Stable Oxygen Isotopes." *Journal of Anthropological Archaeology* 23(4): 385–403.

White, Christine, Rebecca Storey, Fred Longstaffe, and Michael Spence. 2004b. "Immigration, Assimilation, and Status in the Ancient City of Teotihuacan: Stable Isotope Evidence from Tlajinga 33." *Latin American Antiquity* 15(2): 176–198.

CHAPTER 3

Journeys through Space and Time

Materiality, Social Memory, and Community at the City of David

HEATHER M. VAN WORMER

It is a cool, crisp sunny fall day—one of my favorite kinds of days in southwest Michigan. It is somewhere in my second or third year doing research at the City of David, a religious colony, and I am still getting my bearings in both the large site and its complex history. My main informant, Ron, and I are walking to the carpenter's shop to get tools we need for a project in the museum. As we walk, I ask about a tree that we are passing. I do not recognize the species. He tells me what kind it is and which family had brought it with them from Australia. Ron then tells me that when the family came, the daughter, Chicki, was only about five years old; he asks me if I know how she got her nickname. I do not, so he tells me a story about how her brothers were several years older than she was and did not really want their little sister hanging around them and their friends. They tried numerous strategies to lose her but never succeeded. Hence, they started calling her Chicki, like a young chicken that has impressed itself on a person and will not stop following at their heels. Ron chuckles and tells me that Chicki is still like that, so many years later. As we near the carpenter's shop, Ron asks if I want a room for the night so I don't have to drive back to Grand Rapids in the dark. I respond that that would be lovely, if he has a room to spare. He tells me that I can sleep in Cowboy's room on the second floor of the Shiloh headquarters building, just at the top of the stairs—he says this is an appropriate room for me to stay in, as both Cowboy and I are from the far western United States originally. I ask if he is sure Cowboy won't mind, and Ron assures me that Cowboy is away from the colony at the moment and won't mind at all.

A year or so later, I remember this seemingly mundane conversation with a start—while working in the archive I learn that Cowboy has not been there for many decades and Chicki was a child in the 1940s. Ron graduated from art school in San Francisco the late 1970s and returned to the colony where he had visited his grandparents as a child and where he has been a member ever since. Ron could not possibly have known Cowboy or been there to know Chicki as a child. I wonder why he used the present tense when telling me about them and how he came by these memories. For the first eight or so years I worked at the colony, in numerous conversations across all kinds of contexts, I encountered members speaking of past colonists using the present tense. And it took several years of study to even recognize the significance of this or to connect it to processes of social memory.

In 2000, I started doing research at the City of David, which is located in Benton Harbor, Michigan. It took a long time for me to figure out who, and how many people, lived at the colony. This is partly because not all community members wanted to interact with a nonbeliever from the outside, and thus some would leave the area when I arrived at a building or event. Part of this difficulty was due to the fact that one of my first "assigned" tasks was to catalog the nearly two hundred linear feet of archival material at the colony—publications, letters, photographs, etc.—representing nearly one hundred years and more than a thousand residents. It took me a lot of time to keep numerous names (often family members), places, and eras straight, not to mention how trying to understand a theological tradition that prides itself on being intelligible only to the "chosen" believers creates its own series of challenges.

During those early years, in conversations with different colony members, I noticed that present members remember previous members in interesting ways. Often, when at the colony, walking by a particular building, remarking on a plant in the garden, or discussing a current situation, they remember individuals no longer living or events that happened long ago. These are not just memorized and standardized stories, nor the same set of tired anecdotes. It is as if the past member is still there, or as if the person relating the story witnessed the event. Sometimes these stories are triggered by very clear markers to individuals, such as plants or other contributions they made to the colony (Illustrations 3.1 and 3.2). Other times these remembrances come from unmarked material objects, buildings, or landscape features, as if they are vessels for these memories and past members.

In the initial years of research, I found this to be somewhat confusing—I wondered about how many people lived there whom I never saw. By 2008 I was formally documenting buildings and landscapes in order to write the nomination that made Mary's City of David a historic district on the National Register of Historic Places. And by that time I was also more familiar with the archival materials; I was able to recognize these names and understand that many of the people in these stories are gone—in some cases, gone long ago. Once I was able to place those names in appropriate time periods in the history of the colony, it became apparent that often the speaker could not have personally known the colonists in these memories. But, in some ways, the people in the stories are still

Illustration 3.1. Garden marker.
Photo by the author.

Illustration 3.2. Shiloh gardens and Mary's mausoleum.
Photo by the author.

present at the colony. I do not mean that present-day members see or talk to ghosts, or that extra places are set at the dinner table for those who are no longer living. What I mean is that past members are remembered in sometimes very personal ways—and in this "remembering," the past interweaves with the present and influences current definitions of identity and community. These past members are not seen as ghosts haunting the present. Instead, community members who die in the faith will be with the surviving members again, in the Millennium, and remembering them in the present is a form of community maintenance. And this remembering has deep connections to material culture.

Our daily lives are filled with objects and arrangements of material things, and these objects communicate, situate, and condition human interaction and shape the ways in which we experience and interpret the world. As Anthony Giddens and others have argued, "social life . . . is always spatially dependent." In this way, material culture can be seen as "a situated practice through which groups construct identity, remember, and control knowledge" (Giddens 1984: 25). Material culture reflects and reinforces our behavior and beliefs, and it is a powerful tool for conditioning worldviews.

The architects of intentional communities understand this and use material culture to reinforce their mutual knowledge in overt ways. They deliberately attempt to restructure fundamental social relations such as class, family, and gender—and these are reflected and reinforced in their carefully prescribed material world. Material culture is used to set themselves apart from the outside world (through clothing, uses of technology, and industrial endeavors), to reflect ideology and social structure (through landscape designs, subsistence practices, settlement patterning, architectural forms), and to reinforce ideology and social relations within the group. Material culture both reflects and reinforces social ideals, and community members are keenly aware of the symbolic meanings represented in artifacts. These communities choose to literally live within those symbol systems, both socially and physically. In order for these ideologies to become worldviews their symbols and structures must become routinized, with a more mundane, unmarked existence—to make them "everyday" and taken for granted (Bourdieu [1977] 1993: 164–71).

In this chapter I discuss the connections between these social or collective memories and colony identity. I argue that these memories are an outgrowth of past social relations in the colony, embedded in the specific religious beliefs and contextualized in present-day definitions of community. I explore the timescapes created by the shared memories in the intentional community of the City of David. After a discussion of intentional communities in the context of the United States, and in the context of culture change, I briefly outline the history of the City of David, and then I discuss how collective memory is connected to the material realm. This is a story of how the intangible theological ideals of a community became tangible through their association with parts of the community landscape and materiality. I argue that these rememberings, while not "ghosts" or "hauntings" in the stereotypical ways we normally think of them, are nonetheless a form of positive "haunting" and a means for this community to form meaningful connections between their past, present, and future.

Communitarian Movements and Intentional Communities

The communitarian impulse has had a constant presence in North America from the very first European settlers. Nineteenth-century American society saw the founding of literally hundreds of communitarian groups (Mandelker 1984; Oved 1988; Pitzer 1997). These communities were founded on planned ideologies and were often aimed at reforming society. Bounded by common beliefs, these communities arose as an attempt to live within the ideals outlined in those beliefs, and were often religious in nature (examples include the Shakers, the Mormons, and the Oneida Perfectionists). Other communities were committed to changing the fundamental structure of society but did not emphasize a particular religious belief (for example, the Fourierists, Harmony, and New Harmony), while still others emphasized mainly economic ideals and reforms (examples include Communia in Iowa, the Kaweah colony in California, Llano Del Rio outside of Los Angeles, and Newllano in Louisiana).

The term "intentional community" is relatively recent in the literature and is used very purposefully. The communities that are considered "communal" or "communitarian" are an incredibly diverse set of social groups and are often evolving. Attempts to categorize this diverse set have resulted in several different characterizations (secular and nonsecular; collective, cooperative, and communal, etc.), but none that aid in the understanding of these communities in a broader anthropological perspective. Communal living has numerous forms: in some groups, members share all possessions in common; in others, members retain ownership of personal items and only share economic interests and community-wide endeavors. Further, the degree of "communalness" changes over time in many groups as they adapt to various internal and external pressures.

For these reasons, most communal studies scholars have adopted the term "intentional community." As Timothy Miller notes,

> it makes sense to define communitarianism not so much in terms of form as in terms of impulse, of motivation. When people chose to live together and share at least some of their resources for the common good or for the betterment of the world, something communal has happened. Once the prime impulse has proceeded to be embodied in a particular outward form, we are talking details, not essence. (1998: xix)

In this way an attempt can be made to understand the ideological and social processes that form the basis of communitarianism, instead of just the material reflection that they make. Miller goes on to suggest a set of criteria necessary to define an intentional community:

1. "a sense of common purpose and of separation from the dominant society";
2. "some form and level of self-denial, of voluntary suppression of individual choice for the good of the group";
3. "geographic closeness and a clear spatial focus";
4. members with regular, personal interaction at a level deeper than is found in the larger society;
5. economic sharing in some form;
6. actually attempting to live their communal design in a real existence; and
7. a size of more than five individuals, "some of whom must be unrelated by biology or exclusive intimate relationship." (xx–xxii)

Scholarly literature about intentional communities focuses on reconstructing the history of specific groups and charting how they change over time. In part, this focus is a temporal phenomenon, and by the early 1980s scholars were examining intentional communities in increasingly analytical ways. While large numbers of more recent works still operate within this case history approach, many also investigate wider topics and ask broader questions that cannot be addressed by examining just one community. These topics include the importance and wider implications of communal studies; reasons why (and when) intentional communities are founded, and why they fail; aspects of seclusionism and interactions with the outside world; and relationships within an intentional community and their impact on maintaining social structure.

The most impactful contributions from studies of intentional communities arguably come from the connections between social reform and large-scale rapid social change in the larger society. As Donald Pitzer notes, "approximately 600 communal societies are known to have existed in English colonial America and the United States before 1965" (1984: 219–20). In addition, he states that during "the communal explosion since 1965, which can only be described as a new order of communitarian phenomenon, 100,000 communal groups have been formed in this country" (220) and argues for their importance in multiple dialogues in the social sciences. Susan Love Brown (2002) discusses the significance of intentional communities in their relationships to states. She argues that "all communities in the world today exist within the context of larger societies" and that these communities "constitute viable units for the study of state societies" as a "powerful means of integrating the individual and society" while "providing a focus for the study of change" (153). She goes on to assert that one type of community, the intentional community, is "a product of state societies" and that "intentional communities as revitalization movements constitute an important form of cultural critique" (153). Through the process of creating their social structure and community, intentional community members are (directly or indirectly) enumerating what they find wrong with the larger society. Susan Matarese and Paul Salmon demonstrate that intentional communities are places where problematic behavior patterns found in the larger society are more easily minimized and that "communal societies may also be viewed as therapeutic environments where individuals experiencing a sense of religious or social crisis could find either temporary or permanent relief from the harsh realities of the outside world" (1995: 25; see also Oved 1983). In a similar vein, Peter Forster and William Metcalf argue that communal groups are, in addition to being laboratories of social experimentation and change, also "the outcome of society's attempts to marginalise its change agents" (2000: 1) and fulfill the function of "removing or isolating 'disruptive' people from the rest of mainstream society" (3).

Others have pointed to the documented episodes of increased numbers of "foundings" of intentional communities and the connections to larger societal and cultural change. Michael Barkun (1984) documents four waves of intense communal activity: the early nineteenth-century religious revival inspired by William Miller; the rise of popularism in the very end of the nineteenth century, with many more secular groups and definitive links between models of human salvation and economic success; a third wave connected to unprecedented levels of federal government involvement in restructuring the economy and social life; and, not surprisingly, during the 1960s, closely linked to rapid changes in society, technologically, politically, economically, and socially. Barkun also argues that these waves of intense communal activity are linked to and caused by the expansion and contraction of the economy (43). Berry (1992) expands this argument, asserting that these communitarian foundings were caused by patterns in economic crises, specifically correlated with declines in prices, asset values, and wealth. While most communitarian researchers agree that economics played an important role in this pattern, they argue that looking for explanations in purely economic arenas misses the mark (Albanese 1999; Butler and Numbers 1993; Chamberlain 1980; Doan 1987; Hayden 1976; Kanter 1972; Kark 1995; Kraushaar 1980; Mandelker 1984; Oved 1988; Pitzer 1997). Instead, they point to intense periods of social change as a causal factor in the founding of communitarian groups.

Nonetheless, the fact that the foundings of these communities tend to cycle with periods of intense social change (e.g., the Industrial Revolution) has remained a central interest in many theoretical discussions. This is largely because, if true, the idealized social structure put in place by intentional communities and their subsequent change over time reflect perceptions of and reactions to larger social phenomena. The degree of their isolation from the wider society, however, does not remove intentional communities from the larger society, and while they reject some cultural ideals, they invariably incorporate others.

The House of David is no exception. While it rejected mass consumerism, increasing social anonymity, and vices like alcohol, the House of David opened an amusement park and sent jazz bands throughout the country. Clearly, the relationship with the outside world and its ideologies is a complex one; there is no wholesale acceptance or rejection of social trends and ideologies within these communities. Further, this blending of selected aspects of the external world with the daily functioning inside the community was (and still is) an essential balancing act that kept individual members from experiencing too much of a schism with their previous life and beliefs.

History of the City of David

The Christian Israelites differ from many other millennial groups in a couple of respects. Following a line of seven prophets called the messengers, starting in 1792 with Joanna Southcott (Adkin 1990: 8–11; Fogarty 1981: 1–27; Miller 1998: 80), they believe that the divine has both male and female components (Taylor 1992: 20). The Christian Israelites believe that the first coming of Christ was embodied in the form of Jesus. They believe that Jesus and Christ are two separate entities, as can be seen in the following passage written a few years after the House of David was founded in Benton Harbor:

> Many good theologians have never noticed the difference between Jesus and Christ. Remember, Jesus had a beginning of days, and Christ was the High Priest after the order of Melchizedek, having neither beginning of days nor end of life. Jesus was never called Christ til Christ, the High Priest rested upon Him at the River Jordan and showed the full power of God, and then He was called Jesus Christ, because Christ took possession of Jesus. Jesus spiritually means a pure cleansed body. Jesus was the sacrifice—a lamb without blemish—and Christ (God) was the sacrificer. Sometimes Jesus spake to the people, and sometimes Christ, the Spirit of God spake. Christ said: Before Abraham was, I am. He was the "I am" that appeared to Moses in the bush; and Jesus said: I and My Father are one. Christ withdrew from Jesus on the cross; and Jesus said: My God, My God, why hast Thou forsaken Me? Jesus could not have died if Christ had not withdrawn as it were for a moment to make the sacrifice; for Jesus had to give up His mortal life (the blood) for the Immortal. The Spirit then entered into His body and raised Him up; who then said: I am He that was dead and am alive, and behold I am alive forevermore. (Purnell [1906]: 12; spelling as in original)

In this way, the Christian Israelites see Christ as the spirit that worked through Jesus, and they believe this will happen again.

The purpose of the first coming (in the male form of Jesus) was for soul salvation, they believe, and it was a free gift of grace. The purpose of the second coming (with Christ appearing this time in female form) is for the Ingathering, or the assembling of the twelve scattered tribes of Israel. In addition, they believe not only that believers' souls are immortal but that their bodies will be as well (Ephesians 5:23). This immortality is achieved in four stages, as outlined by Benjamin Purnell. The first stage is "the condition of man since Adam's fall." Once the various works of the divinely inspired messengers are accepted and the individual joins the Ingathering, the second level is achieved. At the third level the individual experiences an "intensification of the spirit through the acceptance of the branch (the spiritual grafting to the vine of God) and being sustained by the spirit." During life at the third level, the individual's blood is cleansed and purified, thereby preparing the individual for the fourth or personal Millennium (Adkin 1990: 33).

The colony and colony experience are considered to be transitionary in nature. Members have left one existence (the outside world), but they have not yet arrived at their destination (the Millennium). For this reason, the colony and colony life are seen as a place of transition—not in the former world, but not yet in the next world. Benjamin Purnell characterized it in the following way:

> There must of a necessity be a preparation for Israel; and as Israel are called out of the world and yet cannot enter into the new world until prepared, and therefore there must be a place prepared between the two worlds for separation, and preparation, and a proving and a crucifixion, and a battling, and a struggle, as two nations in the womb of providence, and to be separated. (1915–25: 3:69)

This passage aptly describes expectations of the colony. The colony at Benton Harbor was not supposed to be utopian or perfect in any way—perfection is in the Millennium, which has not yet arrived. For this reason, unlike other contemporary intentional communities, members of the colony do not emphasize perfecting their surroundings, or creating heaven on earth. Instead, the colony is a place of trial and preparation for believers. One community member said of this passage,

> It has been a favorite of mine as it describes the true nature of the community ... which was never set as a utopia, but much rather a place of trial, preparation and faced with injustices that are hopefully used by the divine wisdom to shake loose from us anything that is not of necessity. I remember Melvin Tucker [colony member] once told me that during the time of the separation that Mary [Purnell] told him he had come to the place where you could give up ... "be ready to give up everything but your faith." That is pretty much the sum total ... when nothing is in contention for your attention and daily practice of your faith ... coming to see everything through the eye of faith. My findings thus far on this path is ... Mary was right. (R. James Taylor, personal communication, 29 October 2003)

The transitionary nature of colony life and gender complimentarity are important aspects of the ideology at the colony. They shape not only members' faith but also the organization of their social and material world, including landscape, architecture, and daily life, challenging the views and values of the outside world. The colony, then, is a place of trial and preparation for believers, and the value of living one's faith—which is emphasized repeatedly in colony activities and personal accounts—becomes the essence of daily life for colony members.

While Christian Israelite history goes back hundreds of years, the Benton Harbor colony started with the seventh messenger, Benjamin and Mary Purnell (Adkin 1990: 14–15). The Purnells and several followers established the community in 1903 and began preparing a settlement for the primary purpose of Ingathering. The settlement became known as the House of David. Members of the colony undergo a physical and spiritual purification in preparation for the Millennium, which includes not cutting one's hair (Leviticus 19:27, 20:26–28, 21:5), not consuming alcohol (Numbers 6:3), living communally (Acts 2:3), practicing vegetarianism (Genesis 1:29; Leviticus 19:26), remaining celibate (1 Corinthians 7), and living one's faith. All of these are temporary practices to prepare the individual for the Millennium and immortality. They also believe that the "dead" (nonbelievers) should deal with the dead, and this extended to funerals and burials—members did not participate in preparing their recently deceased loved ones for burial, nor did they attend funerals or wear black clothing.

During its first four years in Benton Harbor, the colony grew steadily. Israelites from as far away as Australia, where Benjamin and Mary visited and established an outpost in 1904, were "called home" to Benton Harbor (Fogarty 1981: 55), with many more patiently waiting for the completion of buildings to house them. The monthly *Shiloh Messenger of Wisdom* included the following notice from 1907 until well into the 1920s:

> Important Notice: Owing to the desire of many to come to the House of David faster than we are able to build and prepare places for them, we wish it understood by all such, that in order to save us and themselves much unnecessary trouble, they should correspond with us before making arrangements to come. It is absolutely necessary that each and every case be given due consideration and the applicant await the call to come home, as there must be order in the Lord's house.

Early buildings were designed with dining facilities in the basement and business offices on the ground floor, while the upper floors housed colony members (Adkin 1990: 18–19). Many of these buildings are full of details that symbolize the Ingathering. As can be seen in the photo postcard (Illustration 3.3), the buildings Jerusalem and Bethlehem were connected by a triple archway, which was marked "The House of David 1906" and symbolized the joining of the Fifth and Sixth Churches to form the Seventh Church of Israel (18). Other architectural details communicate Israelite beliefs, such as the trumpets

Illustration 3.3. Jerusalem and Bethlehem, with Benjamin Purnell (in white hat) front and center.
Courtesy of Communal Societies Collection, Hamilton College.

carved into each panel of each stair step in Bethlehem, symbolizing the call for the Ingathering, and the wooden three-link chain above the entrance to Jerusalem, signifying faith, hope, and charity (19). This trend continued in the House of David's future construction, and the buildings became more ornate (Illustration 3.4).

Several other industries were developed to further the expansion of the colony: a block factory for building materials, an electricity plant, greenhouses, a wagon and carriage shop, and a water system. Construction of a new auditorium for religious meetings was underway, and at least fourteen missionary teams were circulating the country (Adkin 1990: 20). Community businesses continued to expand, including several farms, a blacksmith shop, a planing mill, a bakery, an ice cream parlor, and a zoo with exotic animals brought by newly arriving members (Miller 1998: 81–82). By 1907, 387 people lived at the House of David (Adkin 1990: 23), and at its peak in the 1920s, nearly 1,000 people lived in the colony.

The House of David attracted (and encouraged) large numbers of curious people from the outside world to come and observe its members. However, because the zoo and the ice cream parlor were located directly behind colony housing, visitors often entered the residences in order to observe the colonists

Illustration 3.4. Shiloh at the House of David.
Photo by the author.

(Adkin 1990: 23). In order both to solve the privacy problem and capitalize on the community's notoriety, Benjamin built an amusement park south of the main colony buildings (24). The local newspaper described the first summer of the park as follows:

> Citizens of Benton Harbor and Berrien county would scarcely believe, had they visited the place less than a year ago, that it was possible to make such a vast improvement. An improvement that without cost affords a place of amusement and recreation for ten thousand people. Strange as it may seem, nevertheless it is so and the park speaks for itself. Lighted by hundreds of electric lights, furnished with a large amphitheatre, with rustic benches, bridges and driveways and a large lagoon in the centre and twelve different kinds of mineral water flowing from as many fountains, the park during the past month has been visited by thousands of resorters and Benton Harbor people. (*News Palladium*, 20 July 1908)

Entertainment in the park included an arcade, the zoo, the aviary, an ice cream parlor, and House of David bands. The first passenger miniature train was in operation by the end of 1908, and in 1920 eight of these trains ran in the Eden Springs Amusement Park (several recently restored and now running through the park again, thanks to the nonprofit Friends of Eden Springs). The auditorium and swimming pool were completed by 1910, and a greenhouse adjacent to the zoo was finished the following year. Other attractions included a bowling alley and numerous souvenir shops (Adkin 1990: 350).

By 1915 the colony had made a lucrative business of another pastime: baseball. A 3,500-seat baseball stadium was constructed south of the amusement park. The House of David probably became best known for its baseball teams. The home team played a regular schedule, and at the traveling team played between 180 and 225 games a year. This barnstorming teams traveled to every state in the United States as well as to Canada, Mexico, and most cities in Europe, bringing the bearded players international fame (Adkin 1990: 25; Hawkins and Bertolino 2000). In addition to the baseball teams, the colony sent several musical ensembles around the country; the Syncopep Serenaders, one of the House of David jazz bands, became quite well known (Taylor 1996: 44).

As happens with many intentional communities, the House of David's financial success caused an increase in materialism, and colony relationships suffered. By the 1920s the colony was embroiled in several legal battles (Adkin 1990: 99–115) and it suffered an onslaught of public scorn and tabloid-like national newspaper coverage. Rumors of Benjamin's alleged sexual misconduct turned into a civil trial, and ex-members banded together (complaining also of Benjamin's fancy dress, food, and excessive wealth, particularly in contrast to other colony members) in the hopes of cashing in if the state succeeded in taking control of colony resources (89–93). These former members were awarded some money to replace the funds they had initially brought to the colony and to cover estimated wages while members; however, they were not nearly as successful as they had hoped, and Benjamin was found guilty on only one count: perjury. Benjamin died shortly after this ruling, and factions within the House of David began warring openly over control of the colony and its resources.

At this time, the colony had approximately four hundred members, who were split evenly into two factions. One faction followed Benjamin's wife, Mary, whom they believed to be "Shiloh Twain," or the female half of the seventh messenger (Adkin 1990: 187). The other faction followed Judge Thomas Dewhirst, a longtime pillar of the community. When the members chose sides, marriages and families split down the middle, never to re-establish contact. In early 1930 the two factions reached a settlement, and since the Christian Israelites were the largest landowners in all of southwestern Michigan at this time, there was much to divide. The property awarded to the Dewhirst faction included all of the real estate on the north side of Britain Avenue, the amusement park, the European Hotel, several farms, the beer gardens, High Island and the lumbering operation, and the properties in Australia (352–54). Mary's faction received several farms, the unfinished House of David Hotel, sixty thousand dollars in cash, and other properties (210–11, 354–55). Mary renamed her settlement City of David and on 1 April she and her 217 followers, loaded up with all of their personal possessions and some household goods, moved two blocks east.

With only one building to serve as a residence, temporary tents were set up and construction began immediately (Adkin 1990: 212). The emphasis at the new colony was very different than at the old colony. As early as the 1910s,

Mary had warned House of David members of the dangers of materialism. She had remarked on several occasions that business priorities should not outweigh religious ones (Frost 2014). Thus, from the start, Mary concentrated on getting back to the basics of the Israelite faith. As one colony member explained it to me, Dewhirst was a businessman, and Mary was a preacher. And one of the first buildings the City of David completed was the auditorium, where she preached (Illustration 3.5).

At the time of the split, a redefinition occurred, particularly for the City of David. If one were to attempt to understand this redefinition solely through historical sources, however, the impact of the split on the members of the City of David would be seriously underestimated. Little changed structurally in the shift from the House of David to the City of David in 1930. The bureaucratic offices remained the same, with a board of trustees, a secretary, and other organizational positions operating in much the same way and with many of the same tasks and responsibilities as at the House of David. Mary's publications, as one might expect, continued to match remarkably closely with Benjamin's and with those of the previous six messengers. In many ways, Mary took the members back to the central tenets of their theology that she felt had been ignored with the increasing materialism and demonstrations of wealth at the old colony.

Illustration 3.5. Mary's auditorium.
Photo by the author.

The new colony's architecture provides examples of this. Unlike the architecture at the old colony, the City of David built efficient and functional buildings with very little in the way of embellishments (Illustrations 3.6 and 3.7). This is not because they did not have the skills or craftsmen at the colony; on the contrary, the members of the City of David were (and are) an extraordinarily talented group, and many of the old colony's architects and carpenters followed Mary. The buildings at the City of David were meant to be used, not to emphasize the wealth or success of the colony. These buildings emphasize the practical and transitionary nature of the colony in their design and construction materials. For example, the first floor of the garage building was constructed out of newly made colony bricks on two sides, while the other two sides were constructed out of surplus concrete blocks (Illustration 3.8). This pattern repeats in numerous buildings.

The members of the City of David spent much of their time at the locations for the various colony industries. Many worked on the numerous farms, and the colony produced fruits of various kinds, grains, dairy, eggs, maple syrup, sorghum, beans, potatoes, oats, tomatoes, and other crops. Meals were eaten communally, although not in one central location. Instead, colony members ate where they worked with their fellow colonists. They attended weekly prayer meetings, with much music and reading of religious texts. Individual members were strongly encouraged to expand their interests and talents, and many members were recognized for their exceptional vocational, musical, and sports abil-

Illustration 3.6. New Shiloh headquarters, Mary's City of David.
Photo by the author.

Illustration 3.7. Laundry and garage.
Photo by the author.

Illustration 3.8. Two different brick materials.
Photo by the author.

ities. Individual talent and aptitude was not regarded in the same way at the House of David. Even today, at the City of David, individuals and their skills are highly prized and celebrated. If someone excels at some task or is particularly good at something, they are kept in that job and will supervise that work. Many individuals ran aspects of City of David affairs for decades because they had shown skill at it. Examples include Bob Vierlitz, who managed the Rocky Farm for more than thirty years, and Frank Rosetta's management of the greenhouses for decades, and Mary Kolesar, who ran the printing office for more than fifty years. Colony members at the City of David were assigned tasks based on their skills and preferences, and individuals who excelled at particular duties were encouraged. This recognizing of exceptional individuals and talents is, in my opinion, directly related to the Christian Israelite theology based on the seven messengers—a tradition that recognizes and prizes exceptional individuals.

By 1936 the City of David had accomplished a tremendous amount (Illustration 3.9 and Figure 3.1). The colony now had many buildings, and the farms were producing particularly well. Several businesses were also in full swing, including the hotel, cafe, and bakery. The City of David started a resort business, but this one was different from the old colony's amusement park in several respects. While both colonies established firm lines between believers/insiders and nonbelievers/outsiders, the way these delineations worked in everyday practice differed significantly in two ways. First, at Mary's City of David, the resort cabins were located at the center of the colony and the two groups were often in contact (Figure 3.1; all buildings labeled "4"). This was quite a change from the old colony, where strict rules prohibited contact between the House of David members and their clientele at the amusement park. Second, the resort catered to a primarily Jewish clientele from Chicago (Illustration 3.10).

Illustration 3.9. Aerial view of Mary's City of David, 1936.
Courtesy of Communal Societies Collection, Hamilton College.

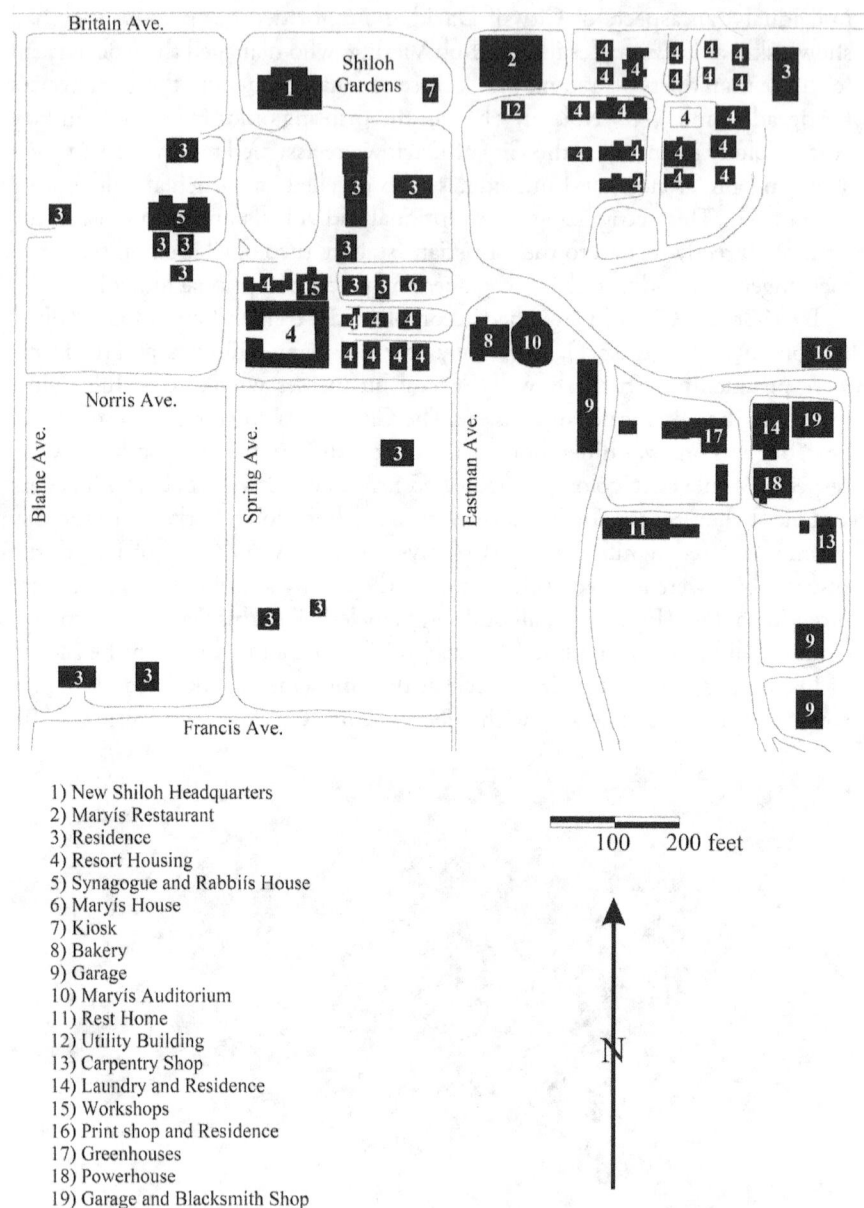

1) New Shiloh Headquarters
2) Mary's Restaurant
3) Residence
4) Resort Housing
5) Synagogue and Rabbi's House
6) Mary's House
7) Kiosk
8) Bakery
9) Garage
10) Mary's Auditorium
11) Rest Home
12) Utility Building
13) Carpentry Shop
14) Laundry and Residence
15) Workshops
16) Print shop and Residence
17) Greenhouses
18) Powerhouse
19) Garage and Blacksmith Shop

Figure 3.1. Map of Mary's City of David.
Map by the author.

Illustration 3.10. Advertisement for Jewish resorters.
Courtesy of Communal Societies Collection, Hamilton College.

Because the colony offered vegetarian meals, both downtown and in the newly opened Mary's Restaurant (Illustration 3.11), resorters could easily keep kosher during their summer vacations. The relationship between the City of David and the Jewish resorters became a strong one, and in 1938 Mary built a Jewish hospital and a synagogue, to which a rabbi's house was added in 1942 (Taylor 1996: 116). Although the hospital closed within a year, the synagogue was in operation until 1976 (Adkin 1990: 258, 281), and even today, former resorters come back to the colony for reunions and visits.

These business endeavors represent a stark contrast to those that the old colony continued to develop. The House of David owned businesses that catered to the public, but these were not always businesses that they would have patronized themselves (for example, the brewery and beer garden in the amusement park). The City of David, instead of merely providing services that would produce capital, took something from their religious life and invited the outside world in to share it with them. These differences continue to the present day, although there is now some communication between the two colonies. This complex history and its many personalities form the central part of the social and communal memory for the colony. And the buildings and landscapes are tangible manifestations of these memories and community members.

Illustration 3.11. Mary's Vegetarian Restaurant.
Photo by the author.

Social and Collective Memory

While puzzling about how memory functions in the present-day City of David, I started to explore definitions and discussions of collective and social memory. The term "collective memory" originated with a student of Durkheim's named Maurice Halbwachs (Crane 1997: 1376; Coser 1992). Halbwachs used the concept of collective memory as a means of explaining how "the past" is remembered in different social environments, such as families, religious groups, and social classes. He argued that humans, from a very early age, never exist in a solitary world. We are always members of various groups, immersed in these identities, and this provides a framework for individual remembrances (1992: 126). He argued that memories are not stored in our minds; instead, the ability to remember is contingent upon external stimuli (such as talking with a friend or visiting a specific place) and is also fragmentary (Douglas 1980: 5).

For this reason, Halbwachs argued that one had to understand the social context in order to understand a person's or a group's memory of the past. To remember means to be tied to collective frameworks of social reference points that allow memories to be coordinated in time and space (Vromen 1993: 511; Whitehead 2009: 128–29). Not only are memories acquired through society, Halbwachs argued, but they are recalled, recognized, and located socially (1992: 38). And memory orders experience and ensures the continuity of collectivities (Olick and Robbins 1998: 109). To remember, one needs others; to remember is to understand a relation (Vromen 1993: 511). Thus, memorable events in the lives of groups to which the individual belongs serve as a coherent system of reference points for recall. In this way, memory is a process, not a thing—or, as one scholar put it, "collective memory is both a mirror and a lamp—a model of and a model for society" (Olick and Robbins 1998: 124). And the past is formed in consciousness through what Halbwachs termed "the mnemonic agencies" of social relationships, of objects, of landscapes invested with social meanings (Halbwachs [1950] 1980: 106–7; Olick and Robbins 1998: 111; Whitehead 2009: 131). It is represented in objects and places that "store" meanings in a concentrated manner—meanings that are shared by a group of people who take them for granted.

Memory at the City of David

At the City of David, one can see these social or collective memory processes in action, particularly in the ways that past members and events are a part of daily life. In this instance, I argue that they are also an outgrowth of the colony's religious beliefs and practices in a way that Halbwach's framework does not address. Memories of past colony members do not exist solely in the realm of the past. Timescapes break down and, in some ways, present colony members are part of a community that exists outside of the boundaries of linear time. Social memory creates a space where past colony members are present in daily life for current colony members, but the inclusion of absent members in daily life is not a new practice; it was common in eras past. Important and central members were often away from the colony for long periods of time, as numerous preachers spread the word, bands spread the music, and baseball teams spread the game. While not physically present, these members kept in close touch with "home" through letters and were still actively participating in colony decisions and social life. For example, in a letter to Francis Thorpe, the secretary of the colony for many years and manager of the baseball team, Mary wrote,

> Well Francis, we sure are busy here at Home canning beans, tomatoes, apples, and peaches—dear Mrs. Morrell is donating her peaches again to us—she has just phoned for us to send a truck for some more which makes the third lot—God is so good to us. We have our early dutch picked and expect to pick the wealthy's in a week or two. Bob has another beautiful patch of tomatoes, our melons are just ripe—we have some very nice roasting ears and I hope you will be Home to enjoy some of them. Francis I paid off the note at the Bank so do not worry over that anymore . . .
> We have the window cards all ready to print but we cannot find JessLee's cut—have you got it with you or can you tell us where to find it—did you have one or two of JessLee's—Gideon says you borrowed his. So be of good cheer and write as often as you can. (22 August 1932)

Such interactions give us an important glimpse of not only the travelers' experiences but also the definitions of "home" for colony members. They also reinforce the high value placed on individual talents and skills, both for believers and for the prophets they follow.

The origins, travels, and work of individual members are marked and remembered, often in the landscape of the colony itself. For example, many different flowers, shrubs, and trees are marked with signs, naming the species of plant, the geographic origin, and the associated colony member (Illustration 3.1). Others are not visibly marked, but their history and significance are commonly known—and often casually mentioned in conversation—by colony members. This functions to keep the past alive in the present. But this practice is more than just remembering; it has deeper roots in their faith. As one community member put it, "History and the faith go together—they cannot be separated."

The religious tenets of the Christian Israelites reinforce the importance of maintaining connections to past members. They believe that those who die in the full faith, without the promise of the Millennium fulfilled, will be counted among the worthy. While they will not receive "terrestrial salvation" (a temple of flesh and bone), they will receive "celestial salvation" and become spiritual advisors and ministering angels to the elect. In this way, the processes of social memory at the City of David diverge from the ones that Halbwachs and others describe. Not only do the past and the present converge, but the future is part of this timescape as well. Given the sacrifices necessary for colony life, memories of past colony members provide current colony members with the comfort that they, too, will be remembered. Remembering creates inclusion and a sense of belonging to something larger. The act of remembering the past reinforces identity and belief in the present. Remembering individuals and events in the past is also remembering the promise of the future, of the Millennium. The practices of prophesying the future and remembering the past are intertwined. Historical accounts shared by members of the City of David are living histories that build community and provide affinity. Remembering bridges the faith in the past, present, and future. Social memory at the City of David teaches us that timescapes are complicated—that the past, present, and future coexist within our beliefs and are demonstrated in the places that humans create.

Dr. Heather M. Van Wormer is an associate professor and the chair of the Anthropology Department at Grand Valley State University in western Michigan. As a past president of the Communal Studies Association and the current editor of *Communal Societies*, her research focuses on material culture and ideology in past and present intentional communities, as well as their place in broader social movements. She has done historical and ethnographic research for nearly twenty years at Mary's City of David, as well as several years of fieldwork at the Wilderland community on the Coromandel Peninsula in New Zealand.

References

Adkin, Clare, Jr. 1990. *Brother Benjamin: A History of the Israelite House of David*. Berrien Springs, MI: Andrews University Press.
Albanese, Catherine L. 1999. *America: Religions and Religion*. Belmont, CA: Wadsworth
Bourdieu, Pierre. (1977) 1993. *Outline of a Theory of Practice*. New York: Cambridge University Press.
Butler, Jonathan M., and Ronald L. Numbers. 1993. "Introduction." In *The Disappointed: Millerism and Millenarianism in the Nineteenth Century*, ed. by Ronald L. Numbers and Jonathan M. Butler, xv–xxiv. Knoxville: University of Tennessee Press.
Barkun, Michael. 1984. "Communal Societies as Cyclical Phenomena." *Communal Societies* 4: 35–48.
Berry, Brian J. L. 1992. *America's Utopian Experiments: Communal Havens from Long-Wave Crises*. Hanover, NH: University Press of New England.

Brown, Susan Love. 2002. "Community as Cultural Critique." *Intentional Community: An Anthropological Perspective*, ed. Susan Love Brown, 153–179. Albany: State University of New York Press.

Chamberlain, John V. 1980. "The Spiritual Impetus to Community." In *Utopias: The American Experience*, ed. G. B. Moment and O. F. Kraushaar, 126–139. Metuchen, NJ: Scarecrow.

Coser, Lewis A., ed. 1992. "Introduction." In *Maurice Halbwachs on Collective Memory*, 1–34. Chicago: University of Chicago Press.

Crane, Susan A. 1997. "Writing the Individual Back into Collective Memory." *American Historical Review* 102 (5): 1372–1385.

Doan, Ruth Alden. 1987. *The Miller Heresy, Millennialism, and American Culture*. Philadelphia: Temple University Press.

Douglas, Mary. 1980. "Introduction: Maurice Halbwachs (1877–1945)." In Halbwachs, *The Collective Memory*, 1–21.

Fogarty, Robert. 1981. *The Righteous Remnant: The House of David*. Kent, OH: Kent State University Press.

Forster, Peter Michael, and William James Metcalf. 2000. "Communal Groups: Social Laboratories or Places of Exile?" in *Communal Societies* 20: 1–12.

Frost, Julieanna. 2014. *The Worthy Virgins: Mary Purnell and Her City of David*. Clinton, NY: Richard W. Couper Press.

Giddens, Anthony. 1984. *The Constitution of Society*. Berkeley: University of California Press.

Halbwachs, Maurice. (1950) 1980. *The Collective Memory*. New York: Harper and Row.

———. 1992. *On Collective Memory*, trans. and ed. Lewis A. Coser. Chicago: University of Chicago Press.

Hawkins, Joel, and Terry Bertolino. 2000. *Images of America: The House of David Baseball Team*. Chicago: Arcadia.

Hayden, Dolores. 1976. *Seven American Utopias: The Architecture of Communitarian Socialism, 1790–1975*. Cambridge, MA: MIT Press.

House of David, 1907. "Notice," *Shiloh Messenger of Wisdom*, p. 8. Benton Harbor, MI.

Kanter, Rosabeth Moss. 1972. *Commitment and Community: Communes and Utopias in Sociological Perspective*. Cambridge, MA: Harvard University Press.

Kark, Ruth. 1995. "Post Civil War American Communes: A Millenarian Utopian Commune Linking Chicago and Nas, Sweden, to Jerusalem." *Communal Societies* 15: 75–114.

Kraushaar, Otto F. 1980. "America: Symbol of a Fresh Start." In *Utopias: The American Experience*, ed. G. B. Moment and O. F. Kraushaar, 11-29. Metuchen, NJ: Scarecrow.

Mandelker, Ira L. 1984. *Religion, Society, and Utopia in Nineteenth-Century America*. Amherst: University of Massachusetts Press.

Matarese, Susan, and Paul Salmon. 1995. "Assessing Psychopathology in Communal Societies." *Communal Societies* 15: 25–54.

Miller, Timothy. 1998. *The Quest for Utopia in Twentieth-Century America*, vol. 1, 1900–1960. Syracuse, NY: Syracuse University Press.

Olick, Jeffrey K., and Joyce Robbins. 1998. "Social Memory Studies: From 'Collective Memory' to the Historical Sociology of Mnemonic Practices." *Annual Review of Sociology* 24: 105–140.

Oved, Yaacov. 1983. "Communes and the Outside World: Seclusion and Involvement." *Communal Societies* 3: 83–92.

Oved, Yaacov. 1988. *Two Hundred Years of American Communes*. New Brunswick, NJ: Transaction Books.

Pitzer, Donald E. 1984. "Collectivism, Community and Commitment: America's Religious Communal Utopias from the Shakers to Jonestown." In *Utopias*, ed. P. Alexander and R. Gill, 119–135. London: Duckworth.

———. 1997. "Introduction." In *America's Communal Utopias*, ed. Donald E. Pitzer, 3–13. Chapel Hill: University of North Carolina Press.

Purnell, Benjamin. n.d. [1906]. *The Little Book*. Benton Harbor, MI: House of David. Reprinted by Mary Purnell as *The Preachers' Book: The Last Message of Life to Israel, Who Are Scattered Abroad*, Benton Harbor, MI: City of David.

Purnell, Benjamin. 1915–25. *Ball of Fire*, 6 vols (vols. 1–3 *The Rolling Ball of Fire*; vols. 4–6 *The Flaming Ball of Fire*). Benton Harbor, MI: House of David.

Taylor, R. James. 1992. *200 Years: Joanna Southcott, 1792 through the City of David, 1992: A History of the Seven Churches of Israel of the Latter Day*. Benton Harbor, MI: City of David.

Taylor, R. James. 1996. *Mary's City of David: A Pictorial History of the Israelite House of David as Reorganized by Mary Purnell*. Benton Harbor, MI: Mary's City of David.

Vromen, Suzanne. 1993. "Maurice Halbwachs on Collective Memory." *American Journal of Sociology* 99(2): 510–512.

Whitehead, Anne. 2009. *Memory*. New York: Routledge.

PART II

Confronting Lingering Specters

CHAPTER 4

Recognizing Ghosts and Haunting in the Rural Midwest
Finding Community, Identity, and Wisdom in the Past

P. M. W. LAWTON

When ghosts appear, it usually signifies that something is wrong (Gordon 1997). In the uneasy aftermath of American colonization, it should surprise no one that ghosts are everywhere within the American landscape (Miles 2015). Occasionally ghosts can lead us to recognize the hard truth of our colonial pasts. Perhaps they can even lead us to being better neighbors and more community-minded individuals. Learning to see ghosts can often come from understanding and recognizing tragic histories (see Brislen, Chapter 7; Supernant, Chapter 6; Surface-Evans, Chapter 9). The scientific approach of archaeology can help uncover such stories. Archaeology is a form of storytelling that asks us to imagine a place in another time and to think about the lives of the people living in that time and place. It may be said that archaeologists manifest ghosts when they interpret an archaeological site. It is not simply the recovery of pot sherds or projectile points that is important but the stories that they tell us about the past.

Garrison (Chapter 8) and Surface-Evans (Chapter 9) explore the haunting of urban landscapes and the specter of capitalist progress involved in the Rust Belt city of Lansing, Michigan. This chapter asks readers to journey north and east (a day's travel by foot, an hour by car) to another concept: that of ruralscapes haunted by colonialism (see also Brislen, Chapter 7; Supernant, Chapter 6). Chesaning, a small farming community in the heart of Michigan's Saginaw Valley, has many of its own ghosts. Algonquin for "place of the Big Rock," Chesaning is a name that commemorates something that is no longer there. Chisin (the Big Rock) was destroyed by settlers, and according to local historians Mark and Irma Ireland (1966), the leaders of the community decided to disguise this fact by attaching the name to another rock. Fortunately, Indigenous sources Totush (Mills 1918) and Eli Thomas (Vogel 1986) continued to attest that the Big Rock of modern Chesaning was not and had never been Chisin. For those who know Chisin's story it can feel as if something is missing. "Sometimes the things we miss are the very things that haunt us the most" (Mahnke 2018), much like echoes of memory.

Memories and the Politics of Power

Remembering is a critical part of human experience, though one that is often tricky. Memory is an artifact of human experience, and different perspectives recall the same events differently. In *Remembering the Modoc War: Redemptive Violence and the Making of American Innocence*, Boyd Cothran (2014) discusses memory as a political vehicle for false innocence. Time and time again, those perpetuating violence toward Native Americans during westward expansion of American colonialism would wash their proverbial hands clean with stories promoting their innocence riddled with excuses for their brutal conduct. For a century, perpetrators of the Wounded Knee and Sand Creek massacres were commemorated for their "bravery" (Kelman 2013).

Accompanying the physical violence perpetrated in each case was the violence of subversion and erasure of Native American voices. The narrative was reversed to make white settlers innocent and the true victims the aggressors. Yet, the ghosts refused to be silent. The Sand Creek Massacre has been the subject of recent archaeological investigations, the results of which have been used to re-interpret the tragic event (Kelman 2013). The results of these investigations have corroborated the Indigenous narrative that the victims had been peacefully gathered before the massacre. Other sites have received a similar re-examination in the quest to better understand the past.

In some instances, descendant communities and researchers have successfully collaborated to reclaim the "truth." Unfortunately, this has not been the result for other truths (see Supernant, Chapter 6), such as the history of Chisin on the Shiawassee River. When we fail to remember the truth, ghosts become most active. They are reminding us of hidden and contested stories. Remembering is essential to allow ghosts to rest. Remembering can defend us from the repetition of past mistakes. Remembering may also bring communities together in a unique and powerful manner (see Surface-Evans, Chapter 9). Whether we remember with an artifact, a place, or a text, the endeavor can be valuable. Archaeological materials often provide haunting reminders of a time long past when the land was the home of another people with a different way of life.

Saukenauk

To understand the ghosts of a place, you must first know its history. The story of the Saginaw Valley in present-day Michigan began long before Henry Nouvel's documented journey into the region in 1675 (Kelton 2010). Significant archaeological sites attest that the valley was home to Native Americans for thousands of years. "Saginaw" is derived from the name Saukenauk, Algonquin for "place of the Sauks" (Butterfield 1918). The Saginaw Valley was allegedly the home of the Sauk and Fox until the area became contested land in the Beaver Wars (1630–1701).

Early on in the Beaver Wars, between 1630 and 1660, the Fire Nation was driven from their homes in southeastern Michigan by Neutral and Ottawa attackers (Cleland 1992). The Fire Nation were noted to include several Algonquin-speaking agricultural groups who outnumbered the Neutral, Huron, and Iroquois combined (Cleland 1992). The Fire Nation may have included the Fox, Mascounten, Miami, Potawatomi, and Sauk. Due to the war, an exodus had occurred by 1660; as a result, the area is supposed to have been largely abandoned for the remainder of the seventeenth century.

This was the first making of ghosts in the Saginaw Valley. By the 1680s it was the Chippewa who had begun to call the valley home. The Chippewa and their allies referred to the valley as the haunted hunting ground. Oral histories recorded in the late nineteenth century recount the conquest of the Saginaw Valley and of ghosts left behind by their victims (Butterfield 1918). Historians suggest that these "ghost sightings" may have been actual flesh and blood refugees who remained in their war-torn homeland or even Iroquois hunting parties. Reports from early pioneers and antiquarians suggest that mass graves may be located along the tributaries of the valley, and local lore posits that they are the result of the series of battles that drove the Fire Nation to the west side of Lake Michigan. While Mackinac and Detroit experienced fur trade and colonization directly, the Chippewa and Ottawa living in the interior of Lower Michigan experienced less European interference and therefore have little to no historical documentation. The documentation that is available, however, paints a dark tale, and one that would not end there.

The 1819 Treaty of Saginaw established several reservations throughout the valley. The treaty permitted those living on the reserves to continue to hunt, fish, and collect in those adjacent lands not yet sold by the federal government to settlers. For nearly two decades some of the Chippewa and Ottawa of the valley would be legally permitted to remain in their homes. Unfortunately, the years leading up to and following the 1819 Treaty of Saginaw were not easy on the Chippewa and Ottawa living in southern Michigan. Extensive fires (1790–1805) ravaged much of the low-lying vegetation important to deer populations. The cold, wet summers of 1816, 1824, and 1830 ruined the crops, rice stands, and fishing upon which they relied (Prince 1997). During the 1830s, disease troubled Native American communities in the valley, killing their people and often driving others away as they attempted to survive epidemics (Lee 1837; Schoolcraft 1837).

By 1837 with the signing of the Treaty of Detroit, the Saginaw treaty reservations were sold to the United States as well. Although the new treaty stipulated that the Native Americans leave Michigan, many took their annuities and purchased land nearby. A few others did not leave their reservation villages at all, managing to purchase lots on the former Saginaw reservations. Unfortunately, the lands upon which they once hunted and the rivers in which they fished were being replaced by cornfields, log ponds, and mills. The lands became barren from overlogging and the consequent erosion, and the landscape was changed in ways that must have been startling.

One reservation, called the Big Rock, on the Shiawassee River, comprised ten thousand acres and was the second-largest in the Treaty of Saginaw. Chisin (the Big Rock) was located along a documented Chippewa trail that had once connected the Shiawassee rapids to the Detroit-Saginaw trail to the east. On some clear nights, ghosts of travelers from times long past might be seen taking a rest at the lonely rock, perhaps leaving some message or token on the boulder before continuing on their way to Chisin for the annual corn festival.

Though initially less impacted than larger coastal Native American communities, Chisin was eventually settled by Americans from western New York in 1842. The American settlers who came here named the village "Chesaning" after Chisin. According to annuity and allotment records, those who lived at the Big Rock reservation selected lands in northwestern Isabella County and near the north part of Saginaw Bay in Bay County (Wyckoff 2016). Not long after the Chippewa left, the landscape was changed dramatically at Chisin. Within a decade, mills had been built on the banks of the river and the pioneer town of Chesaning had begun. This stark transformation of the landscape is the second creation of ghosts, as places and spaces once important to the Chippewa and others who came before them were destroyed.

Today, only stories of the natural wonder that was Chisin remain. In 1836, state geologist Douglas Houghton visited the reservation during a survey down the Shiawassee valley. Houghton's observations impart several interesting pieces of information. For instance, "At the Indian Village (in the bed of the stream) saw boulder of lime rock weighing several tons," he writes. Houghton also explains how the reservation was a gateway to the "wild" north, noting that they had met the latitude of the evergreens. Here pines and hemlock began to throw out darkening canopies. He was awakened that night by a wolf's long howl. Houghton's rapture from the surrounding nature did not, however, prevent him from noting the value of the limestone in the river, foreshadowing its eventual destruction by mining. Oral histories of the stone still exist around the area even though its physical remnants were carted away long ago. The stone in the river was taken by settlers who wished to utilize it for lime while also removing it as an obstruction to travel and damming (likely between about 1840 and 1846). Today, the area where the stone once sat is a small community park, though no commemoration to the natural wonder or the people who named it is to be found. Chesaning clings to mementos of its identity by transforming a commonplace boulder into "the Big Rock." This boulder lies in the yard of Big Rock Elementary School, but this narrative forgets that the actual Chisin was destroyed, the river was altered for mills, and the trees felled for lumber (Ireland and Ireland 1966). We can see how even more ghosts emerge from this shifting of the historical narrative—effectively erasing the damaging toll on the landscape taken by American settlers. As a result of this perpetuating false story, many of the sacred and important places of Michigan's First Nations exist in plain sight but go unrecognized by current inhabitants. Indigenous place-names remain throughout the United States, a reminder of the toll of settler colonialism. These places are displaced from their origins and stories, memories subverted, because of what was forgotten.

False Mementos of Identity

Across the United States are landscapes replete with buried histories of Native Americans. Even in those corners that never became great cities, nor saw the horrors of war, there are memories of profound sadness. The aggressive removal of Native Americans from their ancestral lands, the deadly toll of disease, and destructive federal policies all had lasting impacts on Indigenous communities (Cleland 1992). I propose that the trauma (Surface-Evans, Chapter 9) of colonialism was made all the more painful by the subsequent changes to the land itself. The Great Lakes landscape would be forever changed by American settlers' new land-management styles and perceptions of their environment. Where valuable deer-hunting grounds once existed now stood large corn fields. Favorite fishing spots were disrupted by dams. Many Native Americans believe spirits can live in inanimate objects, like trees, lakes, mountains, and stones (Baierlein 1996; Bender 2011). Glacial erratics, often lonely stones on an otherwise unremarkable landscape, are commonly described as "manitou stones," *manitou* being the Anishinaabemowin word for "spirit." According to myths retold by some Anishinabeg, the manitou lived inside of large stones and rock overhangs (Cleland 1992). Such features can sometimes still be found on the present-day landscape. These visible landmarks and their surrounding landscapes confer identity and histories onto the members of local groups and form "a network of meaningful connections for communication and identity" (Van Dyke et al. 2016: 205).

Almost immediately from its inception, the US government began to enact a policy of removal against the First Nations of North America. Though some individuals were able to stay and purchase allotments in a part of their former homeland, most Native Americans were forced to move. The trauma of leaving their home, the place where their ancestors lived and died for generations, was compounded by the erasure of the lands on which they depended (Supernant, Chapter 6). As settlers arrived in greater numbers they drained the wetlands for farming, dammed the rivers for energy, and clear-cut the woodland for timber. These sacred landscapes became marred and were unrecognizable in the aftermath.

The haunted traces of removal are felt in large and small communities alike. Traumascapes are permitted to persist without a common knowledge of their source and can remain present throughout time (McAtackney and Ryzewski 2017; Surface-Evans, Chapter 9). Attempting to bury them by altering the narrative does not put the ghosts of the land and dispossessed to rest. Despite the associated discomfort, it is always better to confront the difficult parts of colonial history (see Burt, Chapter 5). In a world where authorities are sometimes culpable of willful erasure, there must remain those dedicated to remembering, because forgetting has consequences.

"Surplus Land" and Contemporary Reckonings with the Past

Today, parts of rural America, including the fertile Saginaw Valley of Michigan, are experiencing dramatic changes. Whether it is the pressure to increase housing capacity for growing communities or to provide land for an alleged progressive economic venture, these changes are often carried out without the consent of the people. When these projects are proposed, they are touted as having greater "value" than the current occupants' use of the land. When capitalist values dominate, local governments will be persuaded to vote in favor of eminent domain to facilitate the project. Eminent domain, and its sacrifice of private property rights, is often seen as a necessary evil. For those on the receiving end, though, it is a traumatic experience. This seemingly "un-American" confiscation of land has clear links to federal American Indian policy.

The settlement of the United States largely depended upon the theft of Native homelands. Under the Dawes Act, the US government mandated that tribes dissolve their reservations into private land lots. There was an important clause in the allotment act language, one that would come back to haunt the descendants of the American colonists two hundred years later: the surplus-land clause permitted white settlers to purchase former tribal lands not immediately redistributed to Native American families (Leeds 2013). The US government believed not only that the Native Americans did not need the lands but also, it was further implied, that they would not use these lands as well as another might. Supreme Court Justice John Marshall infamously said, "To leave them [Native Americans] in possession of their country was to leave the country a wilderness" (Johnson v. M'Intosh - 21 U.S. (8 Wheat.) 543 (1823)). Such a view ignored Indigenous property law systems and agricultural endeavors. Despite having been accomplished farmers and land managers for centuries, Indigenous people were labeled "savage" by the racist and ethnocentric policy of the US federal government. The treaties that the United States imposed upon Native Americans were often called "bad paper" by those deceived and dispossessed by them. This bad paper now haunts some of the descendants of the people who engineered the whole affair.

The same reasoning once used to dispossess Indigenous people of their land is now being used to seize land from middle-class rural families in Wisconsin. A large corporation has made a deal with the state of Wisconsin to build facilities and supply jobs near the city of Mount Pleasant. Seizure of property by Foxconn Technology Group is a controversial demonstration of the damaging power of eminent domain. Foxconn has promised to use the land in Mount Pleasant, Wisconsin, to provide jobs at a television factory. In response, the town board has agreed to label the family homes and farms that are setting in the way as "blight," allowing Foxconn to take control of the land for their facilities. Blight can be assigned to any property that is not being "used effectively," is "predominantly open," has a "diversity of ownership," or "substantially impairs or arrests the *sound growth* of the community" (Beachy 2018). Redistribution of this kind usually dispossesses the powerless to advantage the powerful (see also Surface-Evans, Chapter 9). Places like Mount Pleasant and the Saginaw Valley are particularly vulnerable because many people live in communities that fit the loose definitions provided by the law (predominantly open, diverse ownership) and, with the growth of municipalities nearby, their continued ownership could be seen as preventing "sound growth" for the community. Ultimately, if property owners are not providing the "best use" of a lot, the law affords seizure for building televisions. The ghosts of America's racist policies return to haunt white American landowners today.

I first encountered eminent domain while working as an archaeological contractor on a natural gas pipeline project in the Midwest. Our crews were run off properties with shotguns, dive-bombed by crop dusters, and sprayed with Roundup because we were seen as agents of the land grab. Many of the landowners had been previously unaware that eminent domain could be used to allow a pipeline to cross their property. Sometimes entire communities were against the pipeline, but as long as a certain percentage of the land was owned by those who opted in for the project, those against it had no say in the matter.

Archaeology and preservation become relevant because development projects supported by eminent domain have a high potential to disturb or destroy archaeological sites of pre-colonial and early colonial history. For example, the Foxconn facility is planning to use Lake Michigan water during its day-to-day operations. Nearshore locations such as this have a very high chance of intersecting previously undocumented archaeological sites. Opportunities to preserve or learn from any existing sites will disappear as lands move into private corporate ownership. US laws governing historic preservation exclude private land from requirements that historic significance be assessed before destruction. Therefore, eminent domain has the potential to destroy ancient and colonial-era sites alongside the historic homes and farmsteads being unceremoniously dismantled. All of this history is simultaneously erased. Ironically, the ignorance of colonial-era events dispossessing Native American communities subverts the history of the United States, repeatedly favoring the wealthy and powerful. Archaeology has the potential to bring these stories back into American consciousness.

Conclusion

Researchers are beginning to explore how archaeology can contribute to recognizing traumascapes (McAtackney and Ryzewski 2017; Surface-Evans, Chapter 9). By including community participation in the fieldwork, research, and public policy spheres of an archaeological recovery project, more diverse viewpoints can be considered. Memories often involve events shared with other people, and everyone's memory is unique to their own experience. Sharing the experience of building something together, whether it is a preservation program or a community center, can establish feelings of belonging among collaborators (Turner 2005). Engagement improves the lives of community members, creates common ground for discussion, and promotes alliances among people of differing backgrounds (Little 2007). Addressing the impacts of the past and the erasures of history can restore a sense of community while we learn from the lives of our ancestors. The only concession that the past requires is a truthful representation. Ghosts must be recognized. The past does not want things, and ghosts are not so concerned with reparations of the physical variety. They simply wish for the truth of what happened to be recognized (Moore 2006).

Public outreach in archaeology is nothing new, though more archaeologists are gradually realizing how important engagement is. If we cannot find a way to reach our communities, funding for archaeological research will wither and laws protecting archaeological heritage may even be repealed. More immediately, sites are being destroyed every day by sand mining, construction, and other forms of private development. No laws exist to protect archaeological sites on private land. Only when landowners themselves know and care about the importance of what lies beneath the surface will research, preservation, and commemoration occur.

Returning to the ghosts of the Saginaw Valley and Chisin, archaeology has the potential to reconnect the present community with an accurate representation of the colonial American history of the region. To increase visibility of the local history, heritage monuments that do not gloss over colonial events could be placed around communities. In the case of Chesaning, a sign should commemorate each of Chisin's locations: one at the park where the river rock once lived and another for the glacial erratic by the elementary school, to highlight why the memory of the river rock was erased. Such an undertaking should proceed as collaboration between the local community and the descendants of removed Native American groups. Presentations on the history of the region would also be an excellent tool for public engagement. If community interest is sufficient, public archaeology initiatives could result. Although historic documents regarding the Chisin village are short and unspecific, a series of early maps may one day direct community archaeology initiatives to rediscover it (Bureau of American Ethnology 1897; Farmer 1836; Risdon 1825). Since all of the locations depicted align spatially with plowed farm fields outside of town, archaeological deposits may continue to be intact inside and below the plow zone. Pedestrian survey, one of the oldest archaeological methods, remains popular because it does not disturb vegetation or the soil and is easy to conduct with volunteers of all experience levels. By also utilizing modern technological approaches to facilitate stewardship, such a project could develop a new respect for archaeological science in rural publics as well as an understanding for how preservation efforts restore the voices of the less powerful.

Chisin is in many ways a microcosm, one of many small communities across the country that maintain the potential for recognizing and engaging the past. The buried heritage of the rural United States has the potential to teach us about important moments in a community's story. Changing the present often begins with sharing those silenced parts of history, those pasts that have been avoided or dismissed (West 1999). Communities who encounter their colonial past learn from it in order to inform their future. Eminent domain has become a tool to be abused by powerful and influential developers. However, by recognizing unpleasant chapters of colonial American history, one can learn the nature and origins of those powers that continue to abuse the disadvantaged.

P. M. W. Lawton has served as an archaeological consultant throughout the Eastern United States for several years. From 2014 to 2016 he studied Cultural Resource Management (CRM) at Central Michigan University. He is interested in educating the public about archaeology, integrating new field methods, and working with descendant communities.

References

Baierlein, E. R. 1996. *In the Wilderness with the Red Indians: German Missionary to the Michigan Indians, 1847–1853*, trans. Anita Boldt. Detroit: Wayne State University Press.

Beachy, Sara K. 2018. "Foxconn and Eminent Domain: Using Blighted Property Designations to Redevelop Land." *Inside Track*, July 18. State Bar of Wisconsin. Retrieved 16 October 2019 from https://www.wisbar.org/NewsPublications/InsideTrack/Pages/article.aspx?Volume=10&Issue=12&ArticleID=26461.

Bender, Herman. 2011. "The Spirit of Manitou across North America." In *Archaeology Experiences Spirituality?*, ed. Dragos Gheorghiu. Newcastle upon Tyne, UK: Cambridge Scholars.

Bureau of American Ethnology. 1897. *Michigan from Saginaw Bay to Lake Erie*. Bureau of American Ethnology 18th Annual Report (1896–97). Baltimore: A. Hoen and Co. Lith.

Butterfield, George Ernest. 1918. "Native Life—Legendary History of the Sauk Indians." In *Bay County: Past and Present*, ed. George E. Butterfield, 29–31. Bay City, MI: C. & J. Gregory.

Cleland, Charles E. 1992. *Rites of Conquest: The History and Culture of Michigan's Native Americans*. Ann Arbor: University of Michigan Press.

Cothran, Boyd. 2014. *Remembering the Modoc War: Redemptive Violence and the Making of American Innocence*. Chapel Hill: University of North Carolina Press.

Farmer, John. 1836. *An Improved Edition of the Map of the Surveyed Part of the Territory of Michigan*. Map. New York: J. H. Colton and Co.

Gordon, Avery F. 1997. *Ghostly Matters: Haunting and the Sociological Imagination*. Minneapolis: University of Minnesota Press.

Houghton, Douglass. *Douglass Houghton Papers: 1829–1845. Field Notes*. Retrieved 21 September 2017 from https://babel.hathitrust.org/cgi/pt?id=mdp.39015094724641.

Ireland, Mark Lorin, and Irma Thompson Ireland. 1966. *Place of the Big Rock: Chesaning, Michigan, 1842–1950*. Chesaning, MI: Chesaning Public Library.

Johnson v. M'Intosh - 21 U.S. (8 Wheat.) 543 (1823).

Kelman, Ari. 2013. *A Misplaced Massacre: Struggling over the Memory of Sand Creek*. Cambridge, MA: Harvard University Press.

Kelton, Dwight H. 2010. *Annals of Fort Mackinac*. Charleston, SC: Nabu Press.

Kitichinouk, May May. Letter to Henry Schoolcraft, Owasso, Michigan. 9 June 1838. Located at: Ziibiwing Center of Anishinabe Culture and Lifeways Archives.

Lee, William L. Letter to Henry Schoolcraft, Detroit. 25 October 1837. Located at: Ziibiwing Center of Anishinabe Culture and Lifeways Archives.

———. "Speech by Nawm-che-mee." Letter to Henry Schoolcraft, Detroit. 26 June 1839. Located at: Ziibiwing Center of Anishinabe Culture and Lifeways Archives.

Leeds, Stacy L. 2013. "By Eminent Domain or Some Other Name: A Tribal Perspective on Taking Land." *Tulsa Law Review* 41(1): 51–77.

Little, Barbara J. 2007. "Archaeology and Civic Engagement." In *Archaeology as a Tool of Civic Engagement*, ed. Barbara J. Little and Paul A. Shackel, 1–22. Lanham, MD: AltaMira Press.

Mahnke, Aaron. 2018. "Devil in the Details." Episode 102, *Lore* (podcast), 26 November.

McAtackney, Laura, and Krysta Ryzewski. 2017. *Contemporary Archaeology and the City: Creativity, Ruination, and Political Action*. Oxford: Oxford University Press.

Miles, Tiya. 2015. *Tales from the Haunted South: Dark Tourism and Memories of Slavery from the Civil War Era*. Chapel Hill: University of North Carolina Press.

Mills, James Cooke. 1918. *History of Saginaw County, Michigan; Historical, Commercial, Biographical*. Saginaw, MI: Seemann & Peters.

Moore, Lawrence E. 2006. "CRM: Beyond Its Peak." *SAA Archaeological Record* 6(1): 30–33.

Prince, Hugh C. 1997. *Wetlands of the American Midwest: A Historical Geography of Changing Attitudes*. Chicago: University of Chicago Press.

Risdon, O. 1825. *Map of the Surveyed Part of the Territory of Michigan*. Map. Albany, NY: Rawdown, Clark, and Co. Retrieved 22 October 2017 from https://quod.lib.umich.edu/c/clark1ic/x-000081782/39015091187123.

Schoolcraft, Henry. Letter to C. A. Smith, Michilimackinac. 9 October 1837. Located at: Ziibiwing Center of Anishinabe Culture and Lifeways Archives.

Turner, Frederick. 2005. "Civic Ritual and Political Healing." *American Arts Quarterly* 22(1): 8–13.

Van Dyke, Ruth M., R. Kyle Bocinsky, Tucker Robinson, and Thomas C. Windes. 2016. "Great Houses, Shrines, and High Places: A GIS Viewshed Analysis of the Chacoan World." *American Antiquity* 81(2): 205–230.

Vogel, Virgil J. 1986. *Indian Names in Michigan*. Ann Arbor: University of Michigan.

West, Patricia. 1999. *Domesticating History: The Political Origins of America's House Museums*. Washington, DC: Smithsonian Books.

Wyckoff, Larry. 2016. "The Chippewas of Saginaw, Swan Creek, and Black River of Michigan and the Allotment of Their Lands under the Treaties of August 2, 1855 and October 18, 1864." Retrieved 8 September 2018 from https://www.academia.edu/28208175/The_Chippewas_of_Saginaw_Swan_Creek_and_Black_River_of_Michigan_and_the_Allotment_of_their_Lands_under_the_Treaties_of_August_2_1855_and_October_18_1864.

CHAPTER 5

The Unwilling Student and the Ghost of Physical Anthropology
Public Perceptions of the Ethics of Physical Anthropology

NICOLE M. BURT

How to Recognize a Haunting

I fell in love with natural history because my parents took me to every museum, historical house, roadside attraction, and science center that could be reached by car in northern Wisconsin. I was awestruck by the amazing science I saw and the discoveries of the scientists. Even more than the science I loved the act of remembering that happened in these places. I embraced the connection with other families throughout time and space, all of whom left a bit of themselves behind to haunt. This love led me to Beloit College and my initial formal training in biological anthropology and museum studies. During my formal education, I became aware that everything I learned had to first pass through the mind of another human. The development of scientific knowledge leaves the ghost of that person's beliefs and biases on their research. A haunting in this context fits Avery Gordon's definition: "one way in which abusive systems of power make themselves known and their impacts felt in everyday life, especially when they are supposedly over and done with" (2011: 2). In this way, a field of study, hypotheses, research, or even science itself can be haunted by the beliefs and biases of its creator and the system within which it was created. Just as Sarah Surface-Evans (Chapter 9) discusses the haunting of place and the trauma of moving through these transformed spaces, practitioners have to re-engage and re-experience past scientific practice even when inhabiting the new modern ethics of science. It is important to examine uncomfortable truths that may allow bias to continue unchecked in research and practice.

I am not the only anthropologist who has wondered how to separate science facts and the scientists who originally interpreted them. Aleš Hrdlička (1869–1943), a biological anthropologist who helped define the field, wrote about the need for and the possible impossibility of fully separating scientific research from the people and societies that create it. As Michael Blakey (1987) points out, Hrdlička's own work was not free of racial, classist, and sexist bias. Biological anthropology has been working on confronting these issues via practice, pedagogy, and professional standards (DeWitte 2015; Ellison 2018; Turner, Wagner, and Cabana 2018). Ethics are a huge part of formal biological anthropology teaching, but my work as a curator puts me in constant contact with public audiences who do not have this ethical background. I found that the more I tried to discuss topics such as forensics, health disparities in Cleveland, and my own research on modern diet, the more troubling I found some of the interactions. Rather than walk away, I wanted to engage. I began to wonder, why is there such a disconnect between the ethics of my field and what people perceive them to be? I realized that practitioners are not the only ones being haunted; these ghosts are also part of the public perception of and interaction with biological anthropology and museums. Public disconnect from the ethics of science, and the difficulties in teaching a haunting history to laypeople, is the focus of this chapter.

History and Ethics in Biological Anthropology

When I was first learning evolutionary theory, we read both *On the Origin of Species* and *The Descent of Man* by Charles Darwin. What became apparent to me was that my peers and even my professor seemed willing to give Darwin a pass and not comment on the problematic passages of the latter book in particular. My copy is heavily highlighted with notes featuring sad faces and exclamation points as I realized that even Darwin could let you down. Jonathan Marks succinctly states the difference between the two books: "he [Darwin] consciously omitted humans from his earlier book, and thus omitted as well the quaint Victorian cultural prejudices he would later impose upon them" (2017: 13). The clear implication in Darwin's *Descent of Man* is that non-Europeans are less evolved than Europeans and biologically more similar to the great apes. Clearly, this is completely false and a misrepresentation of human evolution. It is easy to reject such statements as a scientist. Yet, my disappointment is repeated every Darwin Day where the conversation rarely touches on the differences between Victorian and modern scientific ethics and practice. The only experience much of the public will have with evolutionary theory is discussing Darwin and his major works. The lack of criticism or ethical interpretation of Darwin's history clearly affects people's understanding, or lack of understanding, of evolution and anthropology. Science educators often assume that the public knows science is no longer done in the Victorian model, but this does not seem to be true. Over time, memories may fade, with only an outline of the whole remaining in peoples' minds. Often what persists in memory is a specter of a past idea rather than the embodiment of new practice. Bruce MacFadden et al. (2007) found that only 30 percent of their sample of natural history museum visitors could explain natural selection, and many respondents gave teleological explanations to explain questions about microevolution. Scientists have moved on, but the public imagination is still focused on the memory of an older understanding. In this way, old ideas rejected by science can continue to haunt and undermine modern interpretations and ethics (particularly when the field presents or celebrates history without context).

Biological anthropology has a long history of both research on and engagement with ethics.[1] The history of anthropology is complicated to teach because much of it is horrifying, embarrassing, and completely opposite to current ethical standards. Politicians, the public, and sometimes the scientists themselves have misused or misinterpreted evolutionary theory and biological anthropology practices to objectify, oppress, and otherwise harm. These are the ghosts that often manifest in a modern context, particularly in cases where anthropologists are engaging with descendant communities. Introductory textbooks are forced to deal with the complicated history of the field, which some do better than others—just like individual professors. These brief introductions might be all a student knows of research ethics before they continue on to graduate school or join the workforce. Most of the work on creating a unified ethical framework for the field is done in the literature and by the continued efforts of the American Association of Physical Anthropology (AAPA) to formalize the field's research ethics (Turner et al. 2018). Ethics are alive and changing. They require engagement and reflection. Evaluating past practice, however, can be unpleasant because of both the awkwardness of critiquing peers and the trauma of having to engage with unethical work deeply enough to critique it (Brislen, Chapter 7; Surface-Evans, Chapter 9; Supernant, Chapter 6). By reimagining a biological anthropology that fully engages with ethics, I am asking practitioners to confront traumascapes and ghosts that linger and hide beside scientific discoveries.

As a field, can we ask laypeople to engage with science ethics when they are not exposed to the depth of scholarship and history that surrounds biological anthropology ethics? When discussing methods with the public, do we have a responsibility to discuss the ethics of how living or skeletal communities come to be studied for science? When doing modern health disparity research, do researchers discuss whether the research is taking advantage of an at-risk population or is addressing an inequality? The public is already confronting ethics because it is the underpinning all human interactions. However, these interactions occur without the benefit of engagement in the conversation by practitioners. I propose that just as anthropologists are honest with their students about these realities, so too must they be honest with community partners and the general public. To have a working set of ethical guidelines, everyone needs to be aware of the standards, not only practitioners. As a curator, this is something I grapple with often as I need to present to the public: families, schoolchildren, retirees, people on vacation, people on dates, and people visiting town with nothing else to do. Occasionally these are formal lectures, but more often than not, I have five minutes with a person while standing under a dinosaur.

Museum Teaching—What Is the Difference?

Museums are unique institutions with a long and complicated history of their own. Here I am particularly concerned with the adult learning done in museums. Museums are a ghostly landscape, haunted by past scientists and their specimens. Not all people are equally attuned to ghosts or as susceptible to ghost stories. Often museum ghosts are more visible to practitioners than to patrons. Practitioners are trained to view both the object and its context, while the patron is given a curated experience. It is the context or meaning of the object that haunts. As museum practitioners we try to control the gallery environment to make it enjoyable. We shape the visitors' experience to lead them to our scientific message. Andromache Gazi writes, "In interpreting objects and themes, exhibitions create new worlds which are usually perceived by visitors as 'true' and 'authentic' because of the museum's status and cultural authority" (2014: 2). In creating authentic experiences many forget or are unaware of the invisible cultural framework that supports those facts and can haunt an exhibit or program. Museums are powerful stewards of knowledge. The authority of the museum gives its truth precedence over other ways of knowing the past. Ideally, gallery designs would be inclusive and equally enticing to all. However, research has shown that the museum experience itself can be disorienting and Othering, just as it can be transformative (Archer et al. 2016; Marandino 2016; Tinning 2018). A diverse public requires a diverse lens that may be difficult for the institution to provide. In relationships of unequal power, referencing differences can essentialize difference (Eckert 2016; Fabian 2006; Schiller 2016). Museums are cultural institutions that strive to maintain a diverse lens for projecting knowledge. As Kisha Supernant (Chapter 6) writes, anthropologists need to engage with communities in meaningful ways that respect and preserve the views of these communities and do not contribute to their erasure. By ignoring a haunting, we, as practitioners, may not understand why a community is not engaging with our work (Lawton, Chapter 4). Modern museums have a role to play in decolonization beyond the repatriation of remains and rewriting of labels that explain specimens.

The role of museums is in flux owing to the modern ethical framework that causes us to rethink collection and exhibit policies for human remains and other culturally sensitive objects (Di Domenico 2015; Tonner 2016). The new ethical and cultural landscapes surrounding museums are often viewed as threats to the essence of the museum identity, but what new identity should the museum inhabit? The museum is not only a repository for biodiversity but also a place of cultural memory for both the ghosts we welcome and those that frighten us. MariaLaura Di Domenico (2015) suggests that the new museum identity must work as either an ethical mediator or educational entertainment. I would expand on this conversation to move from gallery experiences and collections to adult learning in museums, to say museum educators are an extension of gallery space and continue to shape the visitor experience and knowledge constructed there. Thoughtful museum design of both galleries and programs can be a place of empowerment focused on critical thinking and the evaluation of dominant cultural stories (Grenier 2010; Heimlich and Horr 2010; Sandlin, Wright, and Clark 2011; Tinning 2018). As practitioners, we know that we are constructing a story for the public, but this is a two-way process. The other active agents in this space are the museum visitors who come with their own expectations, agendas, and ghosts. While museums are places for ghosts, the ghosts summoned will be personal—each formed from the intersection of the place mixed with personal experience. As practitioners we need to be aware of how history lives differently within each visitor. When we try to keep less desirable topics hidden, we risk looking uninformed or, worse yet, as quietly accepting that the ends (scientific knowledge) justify the means (exploitation of communities).

The informal learning done in museum galleries is fundamentally different from the formal teacher/student relationship. Informal adult education must be initiated by the visitor and will build on the learners' interests to suit their goals for the interaction over those of the institutions (Heimlich and Horr 2010; Rogoff et al. 2016; Sandlin et al. 2011). To teach in a museum, you need to entice the unwilling student to learn or they move on to the next area. Museums can be part but not all of the educational process, as they generally lack the ability to follow up (Tran 2007). There is no single public pedagogy of adult learning, but there is a strong group of theorists focused on a functional pedagogy that is open to the unknowable and comfortable with ambiguity in the creation of meaning (Grenier 2010; Sandlin et al. 2011; Tran 2007). A tall order for most scientists, but to engage on tough issues such as ethics, practitioners must leave space for the complexity of the visitor, the objects, the science, and ourselves.

Case Study: Think and Drink with the Extinct

As a curator at a natural history museum, I give many public talks on research, evolution, and a variety of other topics. The informal teaching in museums involves people of all ages (preschool to adults). My focus here is on adult audiences who move into a student position as part of our interactions. They come to the experience with their own history or ghosts that relate to their own history and relationship to science. The ghosts will be obvious to the student but distant or insubstantial to the teacher. The strength and types of ghosts accompanying a learner will affect their willingness to be a student and their interest in what I as a museum professional wants to teach them. By identifying myself as a scientist, I may embody a particularly unpleasant ghost of scientific misconduct. By acknowledging the ghosts, I can separate them from modern physical anthropology and myself. This case study is an informal reflection focusing on one kind of gallery presentation, *Think and Drink with the Extinct*. I outline my process in providing this adult learning program before discussing how this experience can be translated into pedagogy.

Think and Drink with the Extinct is an adult program held from 5:00 p.m. to 9:00 p.m. once a month at the Cleveland Museum of Natural History, featuring a bar, music, and snacks (Illustration 5.1). Each event in the series has a

Illustration 5.1. Activity table located in the main gallery area at the Cleveland Museum of Natural History. Note that it is a plastic teaching skull.
Photo by the author.

topic, and experts lead activity tables so visitors can interact with "real" science. Visitors are allowed to move through the gallery space and approach the tables and the experts they wish to talk with. These experts may be museum personnel or invited guests from other institutions. Generally, more than a thousand people attend the forensic/biological anthropology–themed events. The environment is loud and busy, with visitors sometimes having to wait in line to talk to one of the experts or even view the activities.

For the past four years, I have focused my section of these events on the biological profile with a focus on the science of understanding bodies and the methods involved. I cover age, biological sex, height, and pathology. In the initial design of my programs, I intentionally excluded ancestry as another part of the biological profile, in order to avoid talking about the complexity and history of the race concept at an event where I did not have the time to discuss nuance. Details about race as a biocultural construct or the history of ancestry in the biological profile all seemed too big to focus on. I teach entire classes on this at the museum (Clementz et al. 2017) and was not sure how to engage the topic in an ethical way in the time frame of the event. However, despite my intention to avoid the subject, ancestry and ethics emerged in the conversations at these early events anyway.

Before each event, I write a lesson plan and get my activities ready. Following each event, I assess the success of both the lesson plan (Did I convey the facts or learning objectives of the night efficiently?) and the activity (Did people touch what they were supposed to touch?). Due to the density of interaction, this reflection is done after the event and is not supported by specific statistics or numbers of visitors. Further, I have not done any evaluation of content effect via a pre- and post-activity survey. To analyze the events in such detail would change the dynamic and the informality of the process. In reflecting on my practice, I fit the hundreds of interactions into three categories: "I totally agree with you," "Non-engagement," and "That is just your opinion" (Table 5.1).

Table 5.1. Explanation of the categories of museum adult learners. Table by the author.

Category	Explanation
I totally agree with you	An engaged learner who comes to the interaction with some level of knowledge of the material due to personal interest. Even if knowledge is limited this learner is ready to learn.
Non-engagement	A potential learner who does not approach the activity table or who does not engage at the table.
That is just your opinion	A learner who engages with the educator but rejects what they are saying directly.

I will use these interaction categories to discuss how the starting category of the visitor dictates the nature of the conversation we can have as an instructor/student pair. I have categorized visitors by willingness to participate in the learning activity, which is further complicated by their personal level of familiarity with the subject and/or with the ghosts of the field. For example, some visitors may identify as part of a group historically marginalized or abused by unethical practices of the scientific community and this will play a role in the interaction. As an educator, there is no way to predict the category of the interaction before it happens. Instead, you have to be prepared to go where each interaction leads. Each interaction is an isolated event and you need to restart at zero with each individual.

At the start of each interaction, I outline the topic and highlight the key points of the activity table. First is aging methods: children are growing, and adults are deteriorating. Next is biological sex: focusing on key features of the pelvis and the minimal sexual dimorphism within human populations. I move on to stature estimation from bones followed by the importance of looking at pathology and seeing if there is a pattern of violence or disease.

Anatomy of an Interaction

An interaction with a visitor can be very messy, jumping between topics and following a conversational flow rather than a traditional lecture format in which the instructor talks and questions follow. To describe verbal experiences as a written transcript, I separate out the interactions and present them in a linear arrangement as a conversation flowchart (Figure 5.1). The narrative below describes the paths of possible interactions.

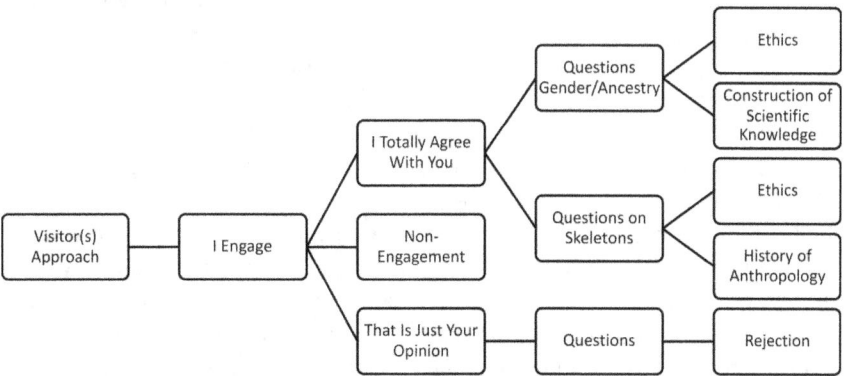

Figure 5.1. Flowchart illustrating the relationship between the starting category of the visitor and the resulting type of conversation.
Figure by the author.

The first interaction category is "I totally agree with you." This group usually has heard the phrase "biological sex" and may start a conversation about sex and gender. They usually point to a skeleton and ask whether it is male or female, to which I respond that it is probably female (or whatever I have determined). This typically triggers a conversation about human size variation or how averages work and the problem with norms. Often this is followed by a question about how science is a process and what it can or cannot do. Visitors may ask, "If there is population variation, why aren't you assigning race like they do on *Law and Order?*" This triggers a discussion about how race is a biocultural construct that does not correspond to human population variation, and this in turn feeds into a conversation on racially driven policies and structural racism that contributes to health disparities in the United States and around the world.

Clearly, the conversation moves quickly to important ethical issues being dealt with in the fields of anthropology and medicine. The conversation has flowed from the initial discussion of research to a discussion of structural racism. I want to stress that the dynamic is very different from a lecture. While I am an expert, this is an active conversation of the topic that intersects with current events and history. The atmosphere of the museum gallery further shapes the conversation and calls to mind the history of science. Again, these conversations are short, between five and twenty minutes, and I have almost no chance of following up. I may suggest a book or a blog to get them pointed in the right direction, or the conversation may continue along a new line of questions: "Where do the bodies come from?" Or, "Who takes part in anthropological studies?" This triggers a conversation about biological supply companies, body donation options, and the history of where anatomical specimens come from. A conversation about informed consent and how scientific research is conducted in living populations will accompany this. Again, the conversation can get into some big issues facing museums and their collections. When starting with an engaged participant I find that the conversations are productive. When the conversation encounters the ghost of colonialism or a traumascape, as defined in this volume (Garrison, Chapter 8; Lawton, Chapter 4; Surface-Evans, Chapter 9), we can discuss and process it together. The conversations are productive for both the student and the instructor.

To some, it may seem risky to discuss with the lay public the problematic nature of historical approaches to anatomical collections and community work that was done *on* communities rather than *with* communities. In my experience, being upfront about this history is important and is valued by the museum visitor and community members. Of course, sometimes they put you in the position of chastising them for wanting unethical practices or minimizing the importance of consent. This highlights the conflict inherent in museum education: if the conversation is perceived as boring or the visitor does not want their worldview challenged, they can simply walk away and not engage. The "Non-engagement" conversation can happen at any time. Some individuals will simply not approach you, but some will come up and then, rather than responding to your questions, walk away. I think "Non-engagement" is the smallest category, but this may be a biased assessment, because when engaged with a participant I cannot also focus on individuals who are not approaching.

The final conversation type is "That is just your opinion" (see Figure 5.1). The conversation is the same on my part but with a big difference in response. This is someone who actively engages you but then directly rejects what you are saying. I have had interactions where people specifically say they do not believe what I am saying or that the data is incorrect. Or sometimes they bring in counterarguments based on news reports or other sources of knowledge. For example, I often talk about vaccinations and the scientific misconduct that led to the popular idea that they cause autism (Harris 2010). To a layperson discounting retracted studies may appear as cherry picking of the data, when in fact I am rejecting falsified data. The rejection of scientific findings or frameworks is not unique to the museum setting or my presentations. But it is this interaction that I think is crucial for creating a pedagogy that can transform an unwilling student into an active participant and consumer of scientific information. As scientists, we often assume that the public is ready to hear and act on our findings and suggestions, but the majority of people have no experience in translating data into behavior. It is unfair to ask the public to behave as a scientist would without providing training on how to do the interpretation.

Building a Pedagogy

Most scientists in the current era engage with the public on some level, either in person or via social media. I am certain that all scientists and educators have been told that the data and science we discuss are just our opinions by people who disagree. Of course, in the context of what I am discussing with them, I have already established that I am rejecting the conclusions of past scientists—so they, in turn, are choosing to reject me. This is a crucial interaction and the thing that makes me dedicated to informal science education. I want people to think critically about science and its conclusions; however, I do not want them to reject scientific findings without engagement. I want a public that can think critically, and I want to create a learning environment where participants can develop the skills to do this. A quote from Marks on the subject of science and beliefs is particularly illustrative of this goal: "So, the issue should not be, how do we make everybody believe what they are told in the name of science? But rather, how do we make wise distinctions within the corpus of science to gauge what we should and should not make everybody believe?" (Marks 2012: 102).

The informal education experience, as discussed in this chapter, is an opportunity to discuss the scientific process along with research and findings. Through conversation and activities, scientists can help the public deal with the masses of information they confront every day. A public informal learning pedagogy of discourse and reconceptualization, as proposed by Basil Bernstein (1999) and Martha Marandino (2016), has the potential to move isolated museum programs to functioning pedagogy that actively challenges the accepted history, ghosts of the field, and trauma associated with the science being taught. Museum educators use dialogues and discourse as a regular teaching tool (Tran 2007). Can museums be open about their challenged museum identity (Di Domenico 2015; Tonner 2016) and use that struggle to reinvent themselves in the new cultural landscape as a place of discourse and reconceptualization? I think utilizing this framework of discourse in the larger museum context of informal education programs could build a pedagogy that moves a learner to a more open and inclusive worldview, where they can interact with and contribute to the conversation that is science. Brief, targeted interactions based on scientific discourse could be a way to initiate critical thinking about science. This conversational method focuses on creating a connection that allows meaningful dialogue between the public and the scientist that can tackle difficult subjects such as ethics.

Conclusions

Overall, on reflecting on my *Think and Drink with the Extinct* conversations, I recognize that they are short but often surprisingly deep. I think even these small interactions have the potential to change an individual's worldview. There is time in these interactions for learning and for remembering both the good and the bad that propels science. I work hard to make sure that I am presenting modern biological anthropology accurately and not hiding from uncomfortable truths about the history of the field. I view these events as opportunities to have conversations about history and ethics not just with colleagues and students but also with the public. Conversations are between individuals and result in learning by both participants. This has led me to a pedagogy of ethical conversation. This model encourages the unwilling student to embrace and challenge the ghosts surrounding scientific knowledge and knowledge creation. It can be challenging and difficult to discuss ethics or the ethical mistakes made by historical researchers. However, I find that the public—even a public attending a fun science-themed party—is, for the most part, willing to think critically and to engage with complex subjects. I want to confront the ghosts directly and help empower people to expect more from their cultural organizations, researchers, medical professionals, and policy makers. My job is not to hide complexity from the public. It is to help give them the tools they need to understand and evaluate.

Dr. Nicole M. Burt is the Curator of Human Health and Evolutionary Medicine at the Cleveland Museum of Natural History. Much of her recent work focuses on translating her research on diet, health, and human variation for the public in informal learning settings. She and her colleagues from the Louis Stokes Cleveland VA Medical Center's Center of Excellence in Primary Care Education Transforming Outpatient Care recently created the "Original Identify Program" taught in the museum galleries and classrooms to educate medical professionals on human variation, health disparities, and improve patient care.

Note

1. See Ellison (2018) for a short review of the history of the field and Turner, Wagner, and Cabana (2018) for a review of the evolution and current ethics in the field.

References

Archer, Louis, Emily Dawson, Amy Seakins, and Billy Wong. 2016. "Disorientating, Fun or Meaningful? Disadvantaged Families' Experiences of a Science Museum Visit." *Cultural Studies of Science Education* 11: 917–939.
Blakey, Michael L. 1987. "Skull Doctors: Intrinsic Social and Political Bias in the History of American Physical Anthropology with Special Reference to the Work of Aleš Hrdlička." *Critique of Anthropology* 7(2): 7–35.
Bernstein, Basil. 1999. "Vertical and Horizontal Discourse: An Essay." *British Journal of Sociology of Education* 20(2): 157–173.
Clementz, Laura, Megan McNamara, Nicole Burt, Mark Sparks, and Mamta Singh. 2017. "Starting with Lucy: Focusing on Human Similarities Rather Than Differences to Address Health Care Disparities." *Academic Medicine* 92(9): 1259–1263.
DeWitte, Sharon N. 2015. "Bioarchaeology and the Ethics of Research Using Human Skeletal Remains." *History Compass* 15(1): 10–19.
Di Domenico, MariaLaura. 2015. "Evolving Museum Identities and Paradoxical Response Strategies to Identity Challenges and Ambiguities: Changing Ethical Understandings in the Handling of Human Remains." *Journal of Management Inquiry* 24(3): 300–317.
Eckert, Julia. 2016. "Beyond Agatha Christie: Relationality and Critique in Anthropological Theory." *Anthropological Theory* 16(2–3): L241–248.
Ellison, Peter T. 2018. "The Evolution of Physical Anthropology." *American Journal of Physical Anthropology* 165(4): 615–625.
Fabian, Johannes. 2006. "The Other Revisited: Critical Afterthoughts." *Anthropological Theory* 8(2): 139–152.

Gazi, Andromache. 2014. "Exhibition Ethics—An Overview of Major Issues." *Journal of Conservation & Museum Studies* 12(1): 1–10.

Gordon, Avery F. 2011. "Some Thoughts on Haunting and Futurity." *borderlands* 10(2): 1–21.

Grenier, Robin S. 2010. "All Work and No Play Makes for a Dull Museum Visitor." *New Directions for Adult and Continuing Education* 127: 77–85.

Harris, Gardiner. 2010. "Journal Retracts 1998 Paper Linking Autism to Vaccines." *New York Times*, 2 February. Retrieved 24 September 2018 from https://www.nytimes.com/2010/02/03/health/research/03lancet.html.

Heimlich, Joe E., and E. Elaine T. Horr. 2010. "Adult Learning in Free-Choice, Environmental Settings: What Makes It Different?" In *Adult Education in Cultural Institutions: Aquariums, Libraries, Museums, Parks, and Zoos*, vol. 127, ed. E. J. Tisdell and P. M. Thompson, 57–66. San Francisco: Jossey-Bass.

MacFadden, Bruce J., Betty Dunckel, Shari Ellis, Lynn Dierking, Linda Abraham-Silver, Jim Kisiel, and Judy Koke. 2007. "Natural History Museum Visitors' Understanding of Evolution." *BioScience* 57(10): 875–882.

Marandino, Martha. 2016. "The Expositive Discourse as Pedagogical Discourse: Studying Recontextualization in the Production of a Science Museum Exhibition." *Cultural Study of Science Education* 11(2): 481–514.

Marks, Jonathan. 2012. "Why Be against Darwin? Creationism, Racism, and the Roots of Anthropology." *Yearbook of Physical Anthropology* 104: 95–104.

———. 2017. *Is Science Racist?* Cambridge UK: Polity Press.

Rogoff, Barbara, Maureen Callanan, Kris Gutierrez, and Frederick Erickson. 2016. "The Organization of Informal Learning." *Review Research Education* 40(1): 356–401.

Sandlin, Jennifer A., Robin Wright, and Carolyn Clark. 2011. "Reexamining Theories of Adult Learning and Adult Development through the Lenses of Public Pedagogy." *Adult Education Quarterly* 63(1): 3–23.

Schiller, Nina G. 2016. "Positioning Theory: An Introduction." *Anthropology Theory* 16(2–3): 133–145.

Tinning, Katrine. 2018. "Vulnerability as a Key Concept in Museum Pedagogy on Difficult Matters." *Studies in Philosophy and Education* 37(2): 147–165.

Tonner, Philip. 2016. "Museums, Ethics and Truth: Why Museums' Collecting Policies Must Face Up to the Problem of Testimony." *Royal Institute of Philosophy Supplements* 19: 159–177.

Tran, Lynn U. 2007. "Teaching Science in Museums: The Pedagogy and Goals of Museum Educators." *Science Learning in Everyday Life* 91(2): 278–297.

Turner, Trudy R., Jennifer Wagner, and Graciela Cabana. 2018. "Ethics in Biological Anthropology." *American Journal of Physical Anthropology* 165(4): 939–951.

CHAPTER 6

From Haunted to Haunting

Métis Ghosts in the Past and Present

KISHA SUPERNANT

Introduction: Encountering Ghosts

In the summer of 2011, I spent ten days living on a fishing boat doing archaeology off the northern coast of British Columbia. A month prior to the trip, I had graduated with my PhD after seven long years. A year before that, I had begun a tenure-track job in the Department of Anthropology at the University of Alberta in Edmonton, Alberta, Canada. It was an exciting and unsettling time. Still reeling from the challenges I had faced while trying to do community-based research for my dissertation (Supernant and Warrick 2014), I was adrift, seeking a future direction for my research, a signpost to direct me. Where to go next?

Close to the end of our long trip, I was standing on deck, near the bow. The sky was that special twilight of a midsummer evening, lingering long into the night as it does near solstice in the north. We were in a forested inlet, home to several sacred places of our hosts, the Gitxaala Nation. I was admiring the view, breathing in the briny sea air and the sharp smell of cedar forest before heading back to my new landlocked home, with its skinny, unfamiliar trees and big skies. Suddenly, the hair on my neck rose, a chill spreading through my body. A powerful feeling entered me, and I took a sharp breath in. As the feeling spread outward, filling me, I received a message: "Find your ancestors. It is your sacred responsibility. We have set you on the path. Now it is time for you to go home."

A few days later, I arrived back in Edmonton, my father's birthplace, located in my ancestral Métis and Cree homelands. The memory of the message from the Gitxaala ancestors still fresh, I wrote a note to myself, entitled "Remember," so I would never forget my responsibility. Over the next few months, I developed a grant application to study my own history through archaeology: the history of the Métis Nation of Canada. Working with the archaeology of my ancestors has brought me home to my Métis heritage and identity in ways I had not imagined and has compelled me to think about the impacts of studying heritage as an act of resistance to ongoing colonization and as subversions to erasure of my people. In this chapter, I share my journey from being haunted by my own history to using archaeology to haunt the present and the future. I draw on theories of haunting to manifest ghosts of the past in the present and expose the specter of erasure within history and archaeology (Garrison, Chapter 8; Surface-Evans, Chapter 9).

Archaeology Is Haunted

Archaeology is full of ghosts, but as in any good ghost story, they remain unseen, with archaeologists unwilling or unable to acknowledge them (Gustafsson and Karlsson 2011). I rarely tell stories about my own encounters with other-than-human beings in archaeology, and when I do, it is to a select audience: colleagues whom I interpret to be receptive to stories of what we might call the supernatural in Western terms but one that within many Indigenous contexts is simply part of a constellation of relations (V. Watts 2013). Many archaeologists have similar stories of their own, ranging from a particular "feeling" while in the field to specific encounters with other-than-human beings in archaeological contexts around the world. Archaeology is haunted, both by the people whose materials and remains we study and by the specter of our own past as a discipline and as part of settler-colonial society (Ferris, Harrison, and Wilcox 2014).[1]

Haunting as a theoretical framework emphasizes a refusal to be forgotten, a subversion to erasure, a persistent, forced remembering. Haunting implies a compressed temporality, as "it alters the experience of being in time, the way we separate the past, the present, and the future. These specters or ghosts appear when the trouble they represent and symptomize is no longer being contained or repressed or blocked from view" (Gordon 2008: xvi). As Tuck and Ree note, "Haunting . . . is the relentless remembering and reminding that will not be appeased by settler society's assurances of innocence and reconciliation. Haunting is both acute and general; individuals are haunted, but so are societies" (2013: 642). Haunting has been emerging in the discipline of Indigenous studies as a theory of Indigenous persistence in the face of erasure—a refusal to be forgotten in a society that wants to overlook our present or future and relegate us to the realm of ghosts (Gordon 2008; Tuck 2018; Tuck and Ree 2013). As Eve Tuck (2018) so poignantly says, "I do not want to haunt you, but I will."

Haunting implies a relational ontology, for to be haunted is to be made aware of the ghosts, the other-than-human beings who resist inanimacy, even when Western ontologies attempt to bound them as objects, places, or specimens without agency. Relational, or "flat," ontologies have become part of anthropological and social theories (C. Watts 2014), but their roots, whether acknowledged or not, are deeply tied to Indigenous ways of knowing and being in the world (Todd 2016). Archaeology is haunted by the discipline's past, present, and future. Many archaeologists have pointed out the complicity of our disciplinary ancestors in dispossessing Indigenous and other colonized peoples, robbing graves, excavating pasts not our own without engagement with the descendants of those pasts, and upholding settler colonialism. While changes have occurred in archaeology, our present actions are still implicated in late capitalism, settler colonialism, and an ongoing narrative about archaeologists as the rightful stewards of the past (Connaughton, Leon, and Herbert 2014). However, archaeologists are increasingly haunted, as Indigenous people assert their right to make decisions about the materials of their own past and their right to tell the stories of their ancestors using their own knowledge systems.

Archaeology can contribute, and has contributed, to the erasure of contemporary Indigenous peoples in North America. The original purpose of anthropology in the Americas was to record cultures that were vanishing, swept up in the inevitable wave of "progress" and assimilation into the modernity of settler-colonial culture. Indigenous people were supposed to die off, to become like everyone else, or to have our indigeneity erased through forced assimilation, perpetuated through colonial institutions such as boarding or residential schools and the child welfare system. Archaeology, as a remembering of the Indigenous past by people who are not us, became, at times, an erasure of the Indigenous present and future. We only existed "then," the lives of our ancestors a curiosity, a commodity to be consumed by settler-colonial institutions, ghosts to be studied and placed on display.

Archaeology has changed since its origins, partially in response to critiques from Indigenous peoples, and many archaeologists today work with and for Indigenous communities rather than on Indigenous pasts without involvement of living Indigenous people (Atalay 2006, 2008, 2012; Colwell-Chanthaphonh et al. 2010; Gonzalez et al. 2006; Martinez 2014; Nicholas and Watkins 2014; Silliman 2010; Smith 2013; Smith and Wobst 2005; Watkins 2005; Zimmerman 2005). In colonial contexts such as Canada, the United States, and Australia, new and emerging collaborations have engaged contemporary Indigenous people in archaeology, doing work that can transform how archaeology is done (Angelbeck and Grier 2014; Atalay et al. 2014; Bruchac, Hart, and Wobst 2010; Colwell-Chanthaphonh and Ferguson 2008; Gonzalez et al. 2006). However, some of the same patterns of erasure persist within the discipline today. Several recent archaeological news stories have demonstrated how archaeology can erase the present in studying the past. Whenever archaeologists are surprised to "discover" that people lived in places, we see the specter of erasure (de Souza et al. 2018). Whenever archaeologists do work on ancestral remains without permission, we can see the ghosts (Bhattacharya et al. 2018).

Haunting Canada: The Case of the Métis

In my own case, I am from a people that never fit comfortably in the racialized dichotomies at the foundation of settler colonialism, a people who defined themselves outside of the Canadian nation-state, resisted it, and were subsequently removed from the Canadian imagination, only later to be revived, brought back from the dead to haunt Canada. I am a member of the Métis Nation, a postcontact Indigenous people and nation in Canada. The Métis Nation emerged out of the crucible of the fur trade and the early contact era. Many of the first fur traders from France, England, and Scotland took wives *en façon du pays*, or "in the fashion of the country." The children of these unions, over time, married one another, formed communities, found economic niches, and were closely bound together through kinship networks. The Métis therefore arose as a distinct identity forged through colonial encounters between First Nations and European explorers, traders, and settlers (Macdougall, Podruchny, and St-Onge 2012; Peterson and Brown 1985; Sealey and Lussier 1975; Teillet 2008). Historical research has focused on where, when, and how the Métis Nation formed in what would become Canada, with an emphasis on how the Métis were a mixed people, "in-between" two worlds (Gaudry 2013; St-Onge and Podruchny 2012; Peterson and Brown 1985).

Métis politics and the role of the Métis in the formation of Canada have been the focus of considerable research and are often connected to the events at Red River (now Winnipeg, Manitoba) throughout the nineteenth century, culminating in the Northwest Resistances of 1869 and 1885, after which the hanging of Louis Riel as a traitor served as a turning point for Métis communities (Innis [1930] 1999; Payne 2004; Ray 1998). However, the Métis were not limited to the boundaries of the Red River Colony; they played a significant role in the opening of the Canadian west and forged a distinct cultural landscape stretching from the northern United States to the Northwest Territories (Figure 6.1).

Resisting the colonial nation of Canada had significant and dire consequences for the Métis community. To deal with the "problem" of the Métis in the aftermath of the Northwest Resistance of 1885, the government ran a scrip program that granted Métis either land or money to resolve any claims they had to territory (Augustus 2005). The scrip commission made its way through western Canada, leaving poverty and dispossession in its wake (Tough and McGregor 2011). Many Métis who took the land option were then swindled out

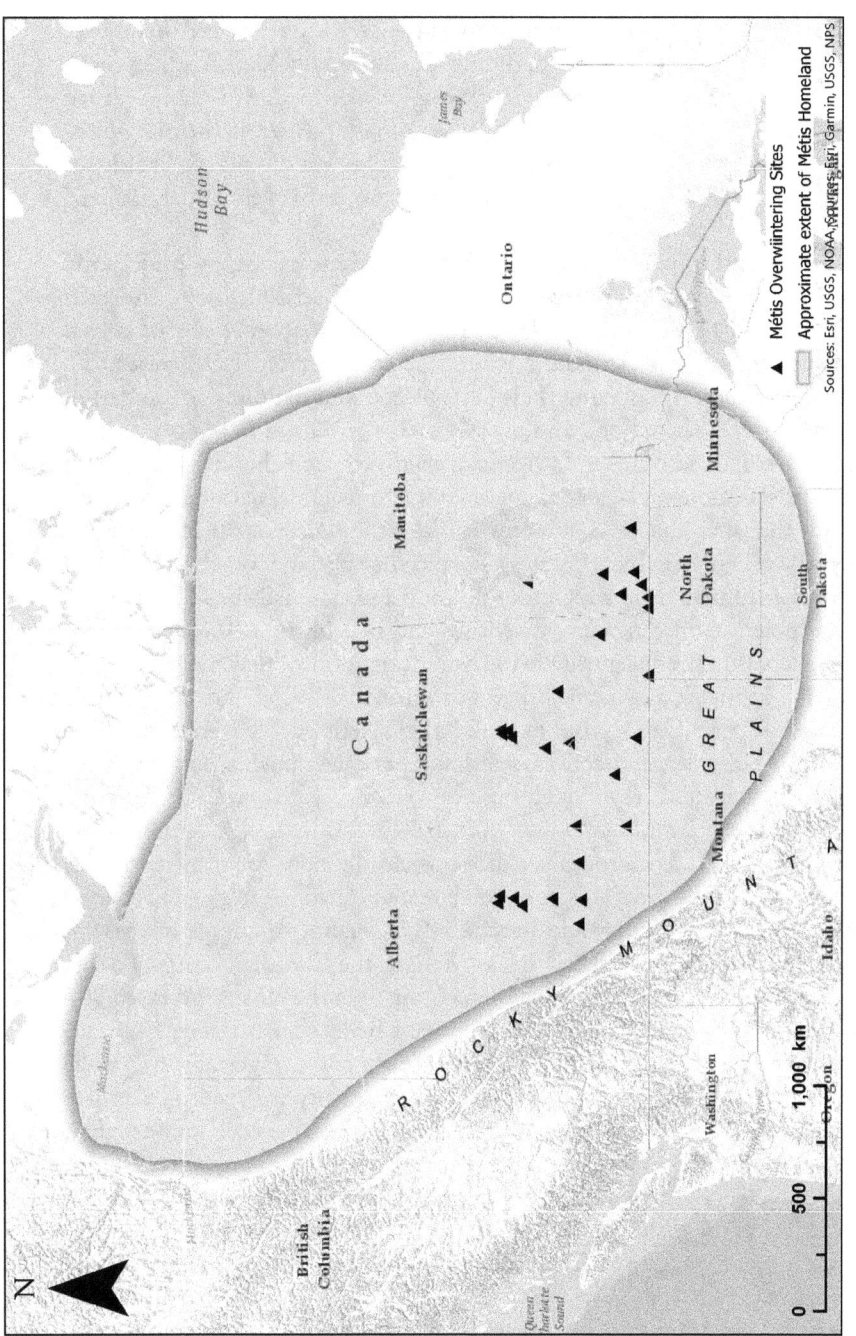

Figure 6.1. Map showing Métis homeland and known Métis wintering sites. Map by the author.

of their land by speculators, while those who took the money found themselves without a home or land base. Forgotten by Canada, many Métis families made their homes along road allowances, surviving off the land, and many learned to hide their Métis heritage. We were, quite literally, pushed to the margins of Canadian society, framed as a people in between two worlds with no identity of our own. Not quite settler, not enough First Nations, we were a marginalized people.

Historical and contemporary research on the Métis has begun to question the frameworks we use to understand the nature of Métis identity (Andersen 2008, 2011a, 2011b, 2014; Gaudry 2013), arguing that to center racialized definitions around mixed blood is to impose settler-colonial categories to a people, rather than recognizing their personhood and nationhood. Andersen argues that Métis nationhood and peoplehood is grounded in history, as "history is ... a crucial resource in Indigenous claims to peoplehood, as it is for all Indigenous claims, because it challenges dominant colonial national/historical narratives that marginalize or attempt to altogether erase our prior presence" (2014: 20). When mixedness defines a people, they become somehow less than either of the cultures from which they descend and can easily be forgotten.

The problem with centering mixedness and hybridity, *métissage* and creolization, is that these concepts belie the complexity of how new identities form and emerge, reducing a dynamic process to a primarily racial understanding of blood and ancestry (Gaudry and Leroux 2017). Métis people were a new people, with a set of cultural practices, politics, economies, kinship networks, and language that were and are uniquely ours, beyond merely a compilation of traits from our Indigenous and settler ancestors in some admixture. An emphasis on hybridity is, in fact, dangerous, as it has opened the door for some people in Canada to claim they are Métis based on a real or imagined Indigenous ancestor from the 1600s (Gaudry and Leroux 2017), leading to a huge increase in the number of people self-identifying as Métis in the Canadian census. For instance, the number of self-identified Métis counted in the census increased 900 percent in Nova Scotia and 450 percent in New Brunswick between 1996 and 2006 (Gaudry and Leroux 2017: 123). The rise of people (especially in Quebec and the Maritime Provinces) claiming a Métis identity is based on the idea that it is a long-ago First Nations ancestor that makes one Métis, rather than kinship and connection to a contemporary Indigenous community (Gaudry and Leroux 2017). Those claiming a Métis identity in these regions are disconnected from the historical Métis of western Canada and claim this identity based entirely on a racial understanding, undermining our rights and erasing our histories.

Over the past 150 years, historians have studied us, written stories about our political involvement in the formation of Canada's sense of national identity (Saul 2009), and tried to account for our position "between" the worlds of

First Nations and settlers through our racial mixedness (Burley 1989b; Chrétien 1996; Ens 1996; Foster 1978, 1994; Peterson and Brown 1985; Sealey and Lussier 1975). As for the Métis, the rhythm of our daily lives, the stories of our women, children, and elders, the expanse of our homeland, and the challenges of our experiences in the twentieth century tend to be left out of the historical accounts. When historical remembering erases us, where do we turn? What happens when a people are deliberately forgotten, when we are erased from memory? Do we become ghosts?

Helping Revive Métis History through Archaeology

My ancestors were ghosts, haunting me. I was never taught to remember them because the colonial nation of Canada interfered in my family's life, as it did in the lives of countless other Indigenous families: my father was taken away from his mother at his birth so he too could learn to forget. It took archaeology to help me remember, to find my way back to them, to begin the lifelong and intergenerational journey of healing my relations. Archaeology, as a means to bring the past into the present, can be a powerful way of haunting, a pushback against attempts to forget, a way to subvert the structures that seek to erase us. However, to fully realize archaeology's potential to bring a meaningful Indigenous pasts into the present requires approaches that are grounded in Indigenous ways of knowing.

Historical archaeology in Canada has tended to focus on the fur trade era (Doroszenko 2009), but with little consideration of Indigenous postcontact archaeology, including Métis-specific archaeologies. Research on the Métis archaeological record occurred primarily as salvage or regulatory projects in the 1970s and 1980s and focused on overwintering, or *hivernant*, sites dating from 1850 to 1880. Métis overwintering was a social practice of spending winters out on the prairies away from major settlements, echoing the summertime bison-hunting brigades, where large groups of up to sixteen hundred Métis people, often all related through extended kinship networks, would gather in structured communities to hunt bison (Figure 6.2). The winter equivalent saw groups of families following bison herds to protected, treed areas, building a collection of cabins, and spending the winter hunting the bison and socializing with their neighbors. Cabins were usually one room, made of logs, covered in mud or clay from local sources, with a thatched roof and a fireplace (Burley, Horsfall, and Brandon 1992; Carpenter 1977; Sealey and Lussier 1975). Overwintering sites are, therefore, distinctly Métis places on the landscape and provide a snapshot of a Métis way of life that may be harder to extricate from other fur trade–era sites (Burley 1989a, 1989b; Burley and Horsfall 1989; Burley et al. 1992; Doll, Kidd, and Day 1988; Weinbender 2003).

92 ❖ *Kisha Supernant*

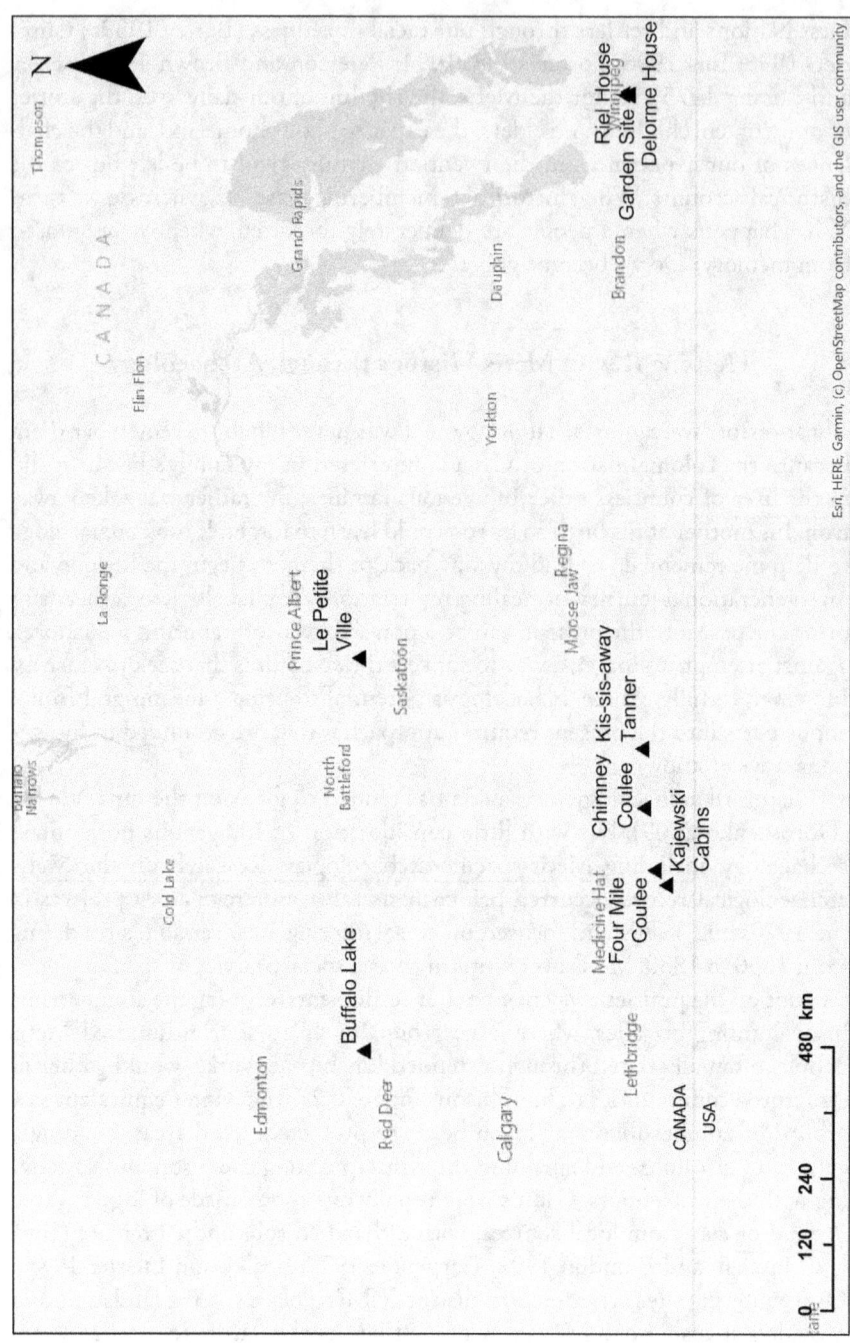

Figure 6.2. Métis archaeological sites in Canada. Map by the author.

Previous archaeological research at overwintering sites has tended to be of two types (Supernant 2018). First, several reports present the historical context, excavation methods, and basic results of material culture with limited interpretation (Burley, Horsfall, and Brandon 1988; Doll et al. 1988; Elliott 1971; Weinbender 2003). Analysis of the material culture and architecture, primarily done by David Burley (1989, 2000; Burley and Horsfall 1989; Burley et al. 1992), typically focused on either creolization and hybridity (e.g., in architecture) or emphasized how Métis people, especially women, used material culture to emulate their European kin and neighbors. There has also been a debate about whether Métis people used lithic technology at *hivernant* sites, with Burley and colleagues arguing that with the prevalence of European materials available, there was no reason for Métis winterers to use lithic material culture (Burley 1989).

The Exploring Métis Identity Through Archaeology (EMITA) project, of which I am the director, began by revisiting some of the sites of previous research, including a wintering site near Buffalo Lake, Alberta (Doll et al. 1988), to expand on what had previously been done but also to change the narrative of the sites to emphasize the experience of nineteenth-century Métis life. Instead of looking at data for ethnogenesis to provide insight into how the Métis *came to be*, we focused on data that moves us toward an understanding of a Métis *way of being*, three types of which I highlight below.

Métis Daily Life

Overwintering sites capture life on the prairies during harsh winters, demonstrating the resilience and ingenuity of Métis families while also showing the daily practices of eating, sleeping, dressing, and interacting with neighbors. Excavations at the Buffalo Lake Métis wintering site (Doll et al. 1988) reveal different types of activities happening inside and outside cabins, where more personal objects (e.g., beads) and kitchen objects are found inside the living spaces and more bone from processing bison and other fauna are found outside (Doll et al. 1988). For example, one of the largest artifact categories found at Métis sites, including Buffalo Lake, is drawn-glass seed beads of various colors. Beading is a well-known Métis tradition, wherein Métis women would bedeck their male kin in elaborately beaded moccasins, vests, jackets, gauntlets, leggings, and fire bags (Farrell Racette 2004). The traces of this practice are highly evident in the archaeological record, if the requisite care is taken to recover these tiny one- to three-millimeter beads, often numbering in the thousands (Figure 6.3). At Métis archaeological sites where excavation methods are designed to find beads, they consistently comprise the largest artifact category

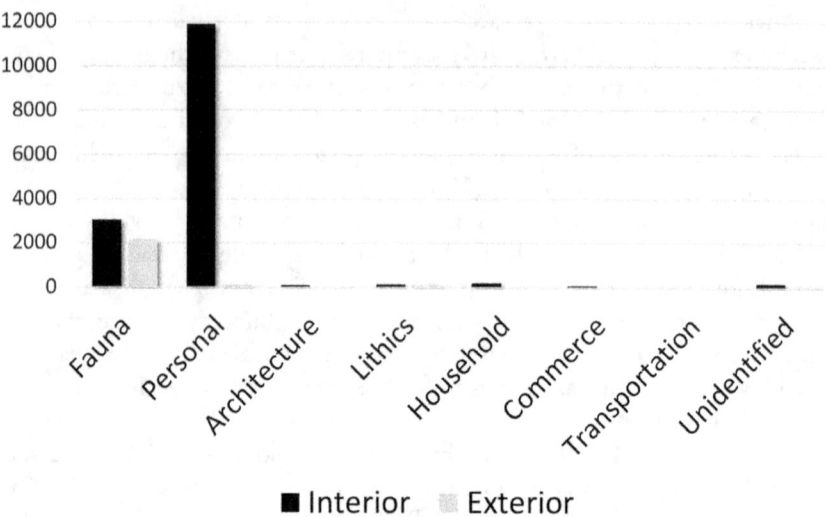

Figure 6.3. Artifact count from Cabin 3 at Buffalo Lake Métis wintering site, showing a high number of personal objects, 99 percent of which are beads.
Figure by the author.

found. This demonstrates the importance of modifying methods based on the history of the site, as one-quarter-inch or even one-eighth-inch mesh, more standard screen sizes, would miss every single one of these beads, erasing their presence from the archaeological record.

Métis Tracks and Trails

Métis people in the nineteenth century moved great distances, from wintering sites on the prairie to economic and social centers in and around fur trade posts such as Fort Edmonton, Qu'Appelle, Fort Carlton, and the Red River Colony. This movement, a hallmark of Métis lifeways, left marks on the landscape. The Métis were well known for an ingenious cart design, the Red River cart, which was often built entirely out of wood to ensure that a cart could always be repaired on the trail (Sealey and Lussier 1975). These carts, pulled by oxen or horses, were a major means of transportation throughout western Canada (Brehaut 1971–72) and left distinctive cart trails. Many of these trails were transformed into roads in the age of the automobile, but ephemeral traces of the former movement of Métis families remain in some places, as ghostly tracks on the prairie.

For many Métis, the paths of their travel were as significant as the nodes at which they joined, whether Red River, Fort Edmonton, or the wintering site.

I use trails recorded in early surveying and mapping of the region as a method to try to capture the material signature of Métis mobility. In previous work, I tested Geographic Information Systems (GIS)–based least-cost path models against the heuristic of these known historical trails, concluding that our current methods are unable to capture the complex and culturally specific landscape knowledge of the Métis across space in both short-term (e.g., seasons) and long-term temporal scales (Supernant 2017). I am working on refining GIS models to better capture a Métis perspective on mobility where rootedness and movement are not mutually exclusive and where the deep landscape knowledge of Métis peoples can be mapped more completely. Bringing these places back to life and telling the stories of how Métis people were deeply connected to the land and highly mobile is a powerful way of making our history visible in the present.

Métis Families and Kinship

Métis people were and are connected through complex webs of relations, or kinscapes (Macdougall et al. 2012), where families, ancestors, places, and other-than-human beings are understood as kin. Breathing life into the deeper relations can help bring them into the present in a world where settler colonialism has actively and passively disrupted these kinscapes.

At wintering sites, the remains of cabins tend to cluster in groups of three or four in one area, as marked on the surface by a collection of depressions from cellars, storage pits, or mudding pits, which were used for digging up mud to weatherproof the log cabin, and by mounds from collapsed chimneys. When I first began studying these sites, this pattern of clustering puzzled me, but the more I learned about Métis kinship, the more sense I was able to make of the pattern. My current hypothesis is that these show groups of closely related family members—parents and children, brothers and sisters, aunts and uncles—building their winter cabins close to one another, marking their kin relations in ways that are still visible on the landscape today.

Working in the historical time period also provides an opportunity to connect living people to specific ancestors in the past. At the Buffalo Lake Métis wintering site, we have demographic information, recorded by Catholic priests, about individuals who were baptized or married at this location between 1873 and 1878. These records contain the names of not just the individuals but also their parents and godparents, representing two types of kinship that were significant in the Métis kinscape. On a summer day in 2014, I took members of the Métis Nation of Alberta on tours of the wintering site just after we had finished a season of excavation, and almost every one of them wanted to know if their relatives were on the list. That day of tours, however, was also an important day for me to do my own personal work of reconnecting with my living family, because one of the participants asked if I had met a friend of theirs whose last name was similar to my own. Through my research, I made my first connection with my living family. My newly found cousin told me the tales of his childhood, raised in the bush, speaking Cree, learning to hunt and trap. He introduced me to my aunts and uncles, my kin. I received a picture of my great-great-grandparents (Illustration 6.1), and I heard family stories about

Illustration 6.1. Author's great-great-grandparents, Marie Flora Gauthier and Alexis Supernant.
Photograph provided by Cliff Supernault.

my ancestors. No longer were they mere ghosts haunting me from a piece of paper; they were part of who I was, connected across generations through story.

From Haunted to Haunting

Archaeology has taken me home. It is difficult to express how meaningful my journey has been; I am not the same person I was when I first came to my homeland. My archaeological work has brought me back to my ancestors, given me the opportunity to remember my family, and turned me from someone haunted into someone who haunts. I now use the practice of archaeology to remember my ancestors, to connect with my family, and to remind Canada of who we are as a nation. My research has allowed me to reclaim my heritage, to begin to learn my languages, to pass on cultural practices to my young daughter. While I have told a very personal story here, the implications of my archaeological research reach far beyond my own experience. Many of my kin have similar stories of their heritage having been either taken or hidden from them. I saw this firsthand when I took Métis people on the tour of the archaeological site. They were fascinated with the material we were finding, with the story of the place, and with their own family connections, which we were able to draw out using demographic data. They wanted to remember.

My work also matters in the context of Canada. Having tried, but failed, to erase the Métis, Canada is now grappling with our ongoing existence. Several recent legal battles have clarified our right to exist and to negotiate for our rights. Many settlers with a single long-distant Indigenous ancestor have begun to claim they are Métis, based on the false idea that we are only a people with Indigenous and non-Indigenous ancestry, rather than an Indigenous people with a shared history, culture, and identity (Gaudry and Leroux 2017). I have no doubt that my work will be used to continue to force Canada to reckon with our past, our present, and our future. In this way, archaeology matters to my whole community, and as the first Métis person to do Métis archaeology, I take my responsibility to help tell our stories very seriously. Instead of using archaeology to erase our present, I take the stories of our past and use them to imagine our future.

That day in 2011, when the Gitxxala ancestors spoke to me, I listened. I returned to my ancestral homeland and excavated the places of my relatives. Now, I use archaeology to tell a forgotten story about the day-to-day lives of Métis people in the past. I use archaeology to subvert our erasure, to persist in the face of settler-colonial society that would prefer to forget our existence. I use archaeology—a discipline of ghosts—to haunt Canada, to engage in relentless remembering and reminding through physical remains of the past. We will not be forgotten.

Dr. Kisha Supernant is Métis and Associate Professor in the Department of Anthropology and Director of the Institute of Prairie and Indigenous Archaeology at the University of Alberta. She is the Director of the Exploring Métis Identity Through Archaeology (EMITA) Project and has published widely in national and international journals, including *PNAS*, *Journal of Archaeological Science*, *Journal of Anthropological Archaeology*, and the *Canadian Journal of Archaeology* and is co-editing a forthcoming book entitled *Archaeologies of the Heart*. An award-winning researcher, teacher, and writer, she is actively involved in research on cultural identities, landscapes, collaborative Indigenous archaeology, Métis archaeology, and heart-centered archaeological practice.

Note

1. Throughout the chapter, I use "we" in two senses: as an archaeologist working in the discipline in an academic institution, and as an Indigenous person. There is a tension here, between these two ways of identifying, that indicates how challenging it is to be both Indigenous (the object of study) and archaeologist (those who do the studying) at times.

References

Andersen, Chris. 2008. "From Nation to Population: The Racialisation of 'Métis' in the Canadian Census." *Nations and Nationalism* 14(2): 347–368.
———. 2011a. "'I'm Métis, What's Your Excuse?': On the Optics and the Ethics of the Misrecognition of Métis in Canada." *Aboriginal Policy Studies* 1(2): 161–165.
———. 2011b. "*Moya `Tipimsook* ('The People Who Aren't Their Own Bosses'): Racialization and the Misrecognition of 'Métis' in Upper Great Lakes Ethnohistory." *Ethnohistory* 58(1): 37–63.
———. 2014. "*Métis*": *Race, Recognition, and the Struggle for Indigenous Peoplehood*. Vancouver: University of British Columbia Press.
Angelbeck, Bill, and Colin Grier. 2014. "From Paradigms to Practices: Pursuing Horizontal and Long-Term Relationships with Indigenous Peoples for Archaeological Heritage Management." *Canadian Journal of Archaeology* 38(2): 519–540.
Atalay, Sonya. 2006. "Indigenous Archaeology as Decolonizing Practice." *American Indian Quarterly* 30(3–4): 280–310.
———. 2008. "Multivocality and Indigenous Archaeologies." In *Evaluating Multiple Narratives: Beyond Nationalist, Colonialist, Imperialist Archaeologies*, ed. Junko Habu, Clare Fawcett, and John M. Matsunaga, 29–44. New York: Springer.
———. 2012. *Community-Based Archaeology: Research with, by, and for Indigenous and Local Communities*. Berkeley: University of California Press.
Atalay, Sonya, Lee Rains Clauss, Randall H. McGuire, and John R. Welch. 2014. *Transforming Archaeology: Activist Practices and Prospects*. Walnut Creek, CA: Left Coast Press.

Augustus, Camilla. 2005. "The Scrip Solution: The North West Métis Scrip Policy, 1885–1887." Master's thesis. Calgary, AB: University of Calgary.

Bhattacharya, Sanchita, Jian Li, Alexandra Sockell, Matthew J. Kan, Felice A. Bava, Shann-Ching Chen, María C. Ávila-Arcos, Xuhuai Ji, Emery Smith, and Narges B. Asadi. 2018. "Whole-Genome Sequencing of Atacama Skeleton Shows Novel Mutations Linked with Dysplasia." *Genome Research* 28(4): 423–431.

Brehaut, Harry Baker. 1971–72. "The Red River Cart and Trails: The Fur Trade." *MHS Transactions*. Historical and Scientific Society of Manitoba, Series 3(28).

Bruchac, Margaret M., Siobhan M. Hart, and H. Martin Wobst, eds. 2010. *Indigenous Archaeologies: A Reader on Decolonization*, vol. 2. Walnut Creek, CA: Left Coast Press.

Burley, David V. 1989. "Function, Meaning and Context: Ambiguities in Ceramic Use by the Hivernant Metis of the Northwestern Plains." *Historical Archaeology* 23(1): 97–106.

———. 2000. "Creolization and Late Nineteenth Century Métis Vernacular Log Architecture on the South Saskatchewan River." *Historical Archaeology* 34(3): 27–35.

Burley, David V., and Gayel A. Horsfall. 1989. "Vernacular Houses and Farmsteads of the Canadian Metis." *Journal of Cultural Geography* 10(1): 19–33.

Burley, David V., [Gayel] Horsfall, and John Brandon. 1988. *Stability and Change in Western Canadian Métis Lifeways: An Archaeological and Architectural Study*. Unpublished monograph. Burnaby, BC: Simon Fraser University.

Burley, David V., Gayel A. Horsfall, and John D. Brandon. 1992. *Structural Considerations of Métis Ethnicity: An Archaeological, Architectural, and Historical Study*. Vermillion, SD: University of South Dakota Press.

Carpenter, Jock. 1977. *Fifty-Dollar Bride: Marie Rose Smith, a Chronicle of Métis Life in the 19th Century*. Sidney, BC: Gray's Publishing.

Chrétien, Annette. 1996. "Mattawa, Where the Waters Meet: The Question of Identity in Métis Culture." Master's thesis. Ottawa, ON: University of Ottawa.

Colwell-Chanthaphonh, Chip, and T. J. Ferguson. 2008. "Collaboration in Archaeological Practice: The Collaborative Continuum." In *Collaboration in Archaeological Practice: Engaging Descendant Communities*, ed. Chip Colwell-Chanthaphonh and T. J. Ferguson, 1–34. Plymouth, UK: AltaMira Press.

Colwell-Chanthaphonh, Chip, T. J. Ferguson, Dorothy Lippert, Randall H. McGuire, George P. Nicholas, Joe E. Watkins, and Larry J. Zimmerman. 2010. "The Premise and Promise of Indigenous Archaeology." *American Antiquity* 75(2): 228–238.

Connaughton, Sean P., Mike Leon, and James Herbert. 2014. "Collaboration, Partnerships, and Relationships within a Corporate World." *Canadian Journal of Archaeology* 38(2): 541–562.

de Souza, Jonas Gregorio, Denise Pahl Schaan, Mark Robinson, Antonia Damasceno Barbosa, Luiz E. O. C. Aragão, Ben Hur Marimon Jr., Beatriz Schwantes Marimon, Izaias Brasil da Silva, Salman Saeed Khan, Francisco Ruji Nakahara, and José Iriarte. 2018. "Pre-Columbian Earth-Builders Settled along the Entire Southern Rim of the Amazon." *Nature Communications* 9(1): 1125.

Doll, Maurice F. V., Robert S. Kidd, and J. P. Day. 1988. *The Buffalo Lake Metis Site: A Late Nineteenth Century Settlement in the Parkland of Central Alberta*. Edmonton, AB: Historical Resources Division.

Doroszenko, Dena. 2009. "Exploration, Exploitation, Expansion, and Settlement: Historical Archaeology in Canada." In *International Handbook of Historical Archaeology*, ed. David Gaimster and Teresita Majewski, 507–524. New York: Springer.

Elliott, Jack. 1971. "Hivernant Archaeology in the Cypress Hills." Master's thesis. Calgary, AB: University of Calgary.
Ens, Gerhard. 1996. "Dispossession or Adaptation? Migration and Persistence of the Red River Metis, 1835–1890." *Historical Papers* 23(1): 120–144.
Farrell Racette, Sherry. 2004. "Sewing Ourselves Together: Clothing, Decorative Arts and the Expression of Metis and Half Breed Identity." Ph.D. dissertation. Winnipeg: University of Manitoba.
Ferris, Neal, Rodney Harrison, and Michael V. Wilcox, eds. 2014. *Rethinking Colonial Pasts through Archaeology*. Oxford: Oxford University Press.
Foster, John E. 1978. "The Metis: The People and the Term." *Prairie Forum* 3(1): 79–90.
———. 1994. "Wintering, the Outsider Adult Male and the Ethnogenesis of the Western Plains Metis." *Prairie Forum* 19(1): 179–192.
Gaudry, Adam. 2013. "The Métis-ization of Canada: The Process of Claiming Louis Riel, Métissage, and the Métis People as Canada's Mythical Origin." *aboriginal policy studies* 2(2): 64–87.
Gaudry, Adam, and Darryl Leroux. 2017. "White Settler Revisionism and Making Métis Everywhere: The Evocation of Métissage in Quebec and Nova Scotia." *Critical Ethnic Studies* 3(1): 116–142.
Gonzalez, Sara L., Darren Modzelewski, Lee M. Panich, and Tsim D. Schneider. 2006. "Archaeology for the Seventh Generation." *American Indian Quarterly* 30(3–4): 388–415.
Gordon, Avery F. 2008. *Ghostly Matters: Haunting and the Sociological Imagination*, 2nd edn. Minneapolis: University of Minnesota Press.
Gustafsson, Anders, and Håkan Karlsson. 2011. "A Spectre Is Haunting Swedish Archaeology—The Spectre of Politics: Archaeology, Cultural Heritage and the Present Political Situation in Sweden." *Current Swedish Archaeology* 19: 11–36.
Innis, Harold Adams. (1930) 1999. *The Fur Trade in Canada: An Introduction to Canadian Economic History*. Toronto: University of Toronto Press.
Macdougall, Brenda, Carolyn Podruchny, and Nicole J. M. St-Onge. 2012. "Introduction: Cultural Mobility and the Contours of Difference." In *Contours of a People: Metis Family, Mobility, and History*, ed. Nicole J. M. St-Onge, Carolyn Podruchny, and Brenda Macdougall, 1–21. Norman: University of Oklahoma Press.
Martinez, Desireé Reneé. 2014. "Indigenous Archaeologies." In *Encyclopedia of Global Archaeology*, ed. Claire Smith, 3772–3777. New York: Springer New York.
Nicholas, George P., and Joe Watkins. 2014. "Indigenous Archaeologies in Archaeological Theory." In *Encyclopedia of Global Archaeology*, ed. Claire Smith, 3777–3786. New York: Springer New York.
Payne, Michael. 2004. *The Fur Trade in Canada: An Illustrated History*. Toronto: James Lorimer.
Peterson, Jacqueline, and Jennifer S. H. Brown. 1985. *The New Peoples: Being and Becoming Métis in North America*. Winnipeg: University of Manitoba Press.
Ray, Arthur J. 1998. *Indians in the Fur Trade: Their Role as Trappers, Hunters, and Middlemen in the Lands Southwest of Hudson Bay, 1660–1870*, 2nd edn. Toronto: University of Toronto Press.
Saul, John Ralston. 2009. *A Fair Country: Telling Truths about Canada*. Toronto: Penguin Canada.
Sealey, D. Bruce, and Antoine S. Lussier. 1975. *The Métis: Canada's Forgotten People*. Winnipeg: Manitoba Metis Federation Press.

Silliman, Stephen. 2010. "Indigenous Traces in Colonial Spaces: Archaeologies of Ambiguity, Origin, and Practice." *Journal of Social Archaeology* 10(1): 28–58.
Smith, Claire, and H. Martin Wobst, eds. 2005. *Indigenous Archaeologies: Decolonizing Theory and Practice*. London: Routledge.
Smith, Linda Tuhiwai. 2013. *Decolonizing Methodologies: Research and Indigenous Peoples*, 2nd edn. London: Zed Books.
St-Onge, Nicole J. M., and Carolyn Podruchny. 2012. "Scuttling along a Spider's Web: Mobility and Kinship in Metis Ethnogenesis." In *Contours of a People: Metis Family, Mobility, and History*, ed. Nicole J. M. St-Onge, Carolyn Podruchny, and Brenda Macdougall, 59–92. Norman: University of Oklahoma Press.
Supernant, Kisha. 2017. "Modeling Métis Mobility? Evaluating Least Cost Paths and Indigenous Landscapes in the Canadian West." *Journal of Archaeological Science* 84(5): 63–73.
———. 2018. "Archaeology of the Métis." In *Historical Archaeology Oxford Handbook Online*, ed. Stephen Silliman. Oxford: Oxford University Press.
Supernant, Kisha, and Gary Warrick. 2014. "Challenges to Critical Community-Based Archaeological Practice in Canada." *Canadian Journal of Archaeology* 38(2): 563–591.
Teillet, Beverley-Jean. 2008. "The Metis of the Northwest: Towards a Definition of a Rights-bearing Community for a Mobile People." Master's thesis. Toronto: University of Toronto.
Todd, Zoe. 2016. "An Indigenous Feminist's Take on the Ontological Turn: 'Ontology' Is Just Another Word for Colonialism." *Journal of Historical Sociology* 29(1): 4–22.
Tough, Frank, and Erin McGregor. 2011. "'The Rights to the Land May Be Transferred': Archival Records as Colonial Text—A Narrative of Metis Scrip." *Canadian Review of Comparative Literature* 34(1): 33–63.
Tuck, Eve. 2018. "I Do Not Want To Haunt You but I Will: Indigenous Feminist Theorizing on Reluctant Theories of Change." Indigenous Feminisms Workshop, Edmonton, Alberta, 16 March.
Tuck, Eve, and C. Ree. 2013. "A Glossary of Haunting." In *Handbook of Autoethnography*, ed. Stacy H. Jones, Tony E. Adams, and Carolyn Ellis, 639–658. Abingdon: Routledge. Routledge Handbooks Online.
Watkins, Joe. 2005. "Through Wary Eyes: Indigenous Perspectives on Archaeology." *Annual Review of Anthropology* 34: 429–449.
Watts, Christopher, ed. 2014. *Relational Archaeologies: Humans, Animals, Things*. London: Routledge.
Watts, Vanessa. 2013. "Indigenous Place-Thought and Agency amongst Humans and Non-humans (First Woman and Sky Woman Go on a European World Tour!)." *Decolonization: Indigeneity, Education & Society* 2(1): 20–34.
Weinbender, Kimberley D. 2003. "Petite Ville: A Spatial Assessment of a Métis Hivernant Site." Master's thesis. Saskatoon: University of Saskatchewan.
Zimmerman, L. J. 2005. "First, Be Humble: Working with Indigenous Peoples and Other Descendant Communities." In *Indigenous Archaeologies: Decolonizing Theory and Practice*, ed. Claire Smith and H. Martin Wobst, 301–314. London: Routledge.

PART III

Identifying Ghosts within the Capitalist Landscapes of Late Modernity

CHAPTER 7

Rain on the Scarecrow, Blood on the Plow

Haunting, Trauma, and the Cruelty of the Agrarian Dream

LILIAN BRISLEN

Introduction

On a recent visit with a sixth-generation farmer, I walked with him through a grainfield laid out in tidy rows stretching almost to the horizon. Discussing his efforts to diversify production, the farmer observed, "We thought storage for barley would be a problem, but it turns out the old, small grain bins on this farm we bought are just about the right size." He gestured to three grain bins, their tops as tall as the nearby barn. In that moment I was struck by the fact that the farmhouse, the barn, and the grain bins were all remnants of a once thriving family farm that was likely wiped out during a past farm economic crisis.

Recognizing that the farm I stood on was, in essence, an empty grave sent a chill of the uncanny down my spine. Haunting, or the uncanny, occurs in deeply unsettling moments that threaten to upend our understanding of how the world works and our place within it (Gordon 1997). Avery Gordon describes the uncanny as the recognition of "the dead that are in the living" (1997: 52). Just as the presence of ghosts in mythological stories destabilizes the boundaries between life and death, reminders of our traumatic past threaten to smash the walls that we as communities or individuals erect to protect ourselves from unresolved pain and fear (Surface-Evans, Chapter 9). In that uncanny moment on the grain farm, I saw for the first time that graves and ghosts of the 1980s farm crisis cover the US countryside, standing as silent warnings of the dire stakes at play for farm families trying to "make it" in modern agriculture.

This chapter seeks the ghosts of the farm crisis and the impact of their specter on contemporary agrarian subjectivities, meaning farmers' sense of identity, beliefs, and motivations.[1] The search is driven by the paradox of why, despite the trauma of the 1980s, the majority of farmers continue on the same path of debt-driven intensification, consolidation, and reliance on global markets that dispossessed hundreds of thousands of farm families. Through the course of this ghost story, we will see the personal traumas caused by farm bankruptcy and farmer suicide were compounded by the generalized traumas of rural community disintegration, all of which were fueled by the machinations of "business as usual" for the expansion of global capitalism.

In this chapter, I suggest that the ghosts of the farm crisis pose an existential threat both to collective understandings of what it means to be a good farmer and to the conventional agrarian dream. The dire warnings of agrarian hauntings threaten the worldview and identity of those who continue to seek success through the business-as-usual model of conventional agriculture. This threat is so vast and terrifying that modern farming communities run away from an acknowledgment of past traumas, choosing instead to stick to the script of the modern capitalist fantasy, whistling in the graveyard that is the US countryside.

As a rural sociologist, I am interested in how social structures like economy and policy intersect with the lived reality and subjectivities of rural communities. Working from this perspective, I weave and assemble my ghostly narrative from a wide variety of sources both concrete and ephemeral, including historical analyses and seminal ethnographies of the farm crisis (Dudley 2000; Firerez-Remero 2005). I also look to the music of "heartland rock" and country songs, following a rich tradition in social theory of working with literature, poetry, films, and lyrics as cultural artifacts (Berlant 2011; Gordon 1997). Through a serious treatment of popular music, I follow Lauren Berlant's call "to see that in the affective scenarios of these works and discourses we can discern claims about the situation of contemporary life" (2011: 9). Similarly, Anthony Hutchisonsuggests that working with and through the emotional and symbolic content of music allows us to reconstruct the context from which those songs emerged, enriching our understanding of that moment in time and the "character of place"(2010: 270). He further argues that roots music created in the United States is "almost obsessively preoccupied with ghosts of the past" (272). As country music is the soundtrack to rural life, it has much to reveal about both the inner and outer lives of those living down on the farm and the ghosts that haunt them.

First as Triumph, then as Tragedy

Every semester I ask undergraduate students in our College of Agriculture, Food and the Environment—all of them now born after the year 2000—if they have heard of the 1980s farm crisis. Though most of the students come from farming families and rural communities, I am typically met with blank stares.

The erasure of this crucial piece of American agricultural history is shocking, but I have come to believe it is indicative of the subconscious and collective suppression of past trauma. The first step to any kind of reconciliation, with each other or with ghosts of the past, is truth-telling. Thus, telling the story of the farm crisis, reviving and reinscribing that history in our shared memory, is the first and a crucial step in allowing ourselves to be haunted by its ghosts.

This story takes place in two acts. In the first act, American farms were integrated into a new era of global commodity capitalism by embracing the debt-driven model of large-scale, export-oriented commodity production. In the second act, the triumph of boom markets turned into the seemingly inevitable tragedy of bust, resulting in the ruin of American farmers at the hands of both global market forces and their own friends and neighbors. These two dimensions of the crisis, one structural and one intensely personal, shook the foundations of American agriculture and left a countryside full of ghosts whose shadows of loss continue to haunt farmers.

To speak in generalization, which is a fraught proposition with something as vast and diverse as farming, American farmers prior to the 1970s valued self-reliance and thriftiness and had a strong aversion to debt (Bartlett 1993). Farms were typically diversified (producing multiple types of crops and livestock) and were essentially self-sufficient operations. Diversification allowed farms to produce their own inputs by saving seeds and utilizing manures and crop rotation to support soil fertility. Markets for farm products included a mix of regional sales to local processors and retailers and some national and international commodity exchange. Risk from both weather and market swings was partially mitigated through diversification of production and markets; if the corn crop was bad, the hog sales would likely carry the farm through the season. While farm incomes were modest, and significant regional and racial disparities in farmer welfare existed (Cowan and Feder 2012; Egan 2006), farming was generally a stable and multigenerational way of life.

While the forces and logic of capitalism were certainly present in agriculture before the 1970s, the rate of capitalist rationalization of farm production increased significantly following technological advances from World War II and differed by region and farm type (Fitzgerald 2003). During the 1970s, a boom in demand for grains by the Soviet Union and other nations of the then "third world" greatly expanded the role of US agriculture in supporting US geopolitical strategy (Buttel 1989). Seizing the opportunity, government and university agents advocated for American farmers to move away from diversification toward specializing in two or three commodity crops that would be sold to global markets. This required chemically and mechanically intensive production methods and extensive land investments, with production expanding "fence row to fence row." Farm expansion required capital, which federal and private lenders were eager to provide during the low-cost credit conditions that prevailed in the 1970s (Strange 1988).

With the reassurance that land never loses value, many farmers embraced equity financing (borrowing based on collateral) for the first time and mortgaged their family lands in order to expand (Friedberger 1993). Expansion and intensification also meant shiny new tractors on farms that had previously prided themselves on the ability to fix anything with duct tape and baling wire. As Kathryn Marie Dudley summarizes, "In addition to the 'push' [farmers] received from lenders hawking easy money ... they were also 'pulled' by the lure of new technology" (2000: 27). The general excitement over rising farm profitability led to a social environment where performing the new model of "progressive" farming through the purchasing of new trucks, machinery, and outbuildings became an important measure of success (Dudley 2000). Competition between farmers increased as success in farming shifted from who brought home the most blue ribbons from the state fair to who financed the largest land purchases, and the stakes were much higher.

As all financial swings do, the boom of commodity sales and high prices of the 1970s came to an end as the Soviet Union and other nations expanded production, and the Federal Reserve adopted new policies to reduce inflation and restrict credit (Bartlett 1993). Loan payments with higher real interest rates ate up an increasing share of income for farmers leveraged to the hilt from rapid expansion (Buttel 1989). By 1984, conservative estimates held that between 40 and 50 percent of midsized family farms were overleveraged and were unlikely to remain financially solvent (Strange 1988). The downswing in the commodity markets caused farmland value to drop precipitously, reaching nearly a 60 percent reduction in land values in some parts of the Midwest between 1981 and 1985 (Dudley 2000).

Nervous over the state of the farm economy, federal and private lenders who had previously served as cheerleaders of farm expansion called in farm loans, setting off a cascade of farm bankruptcies (Dudley 2000; Ramírez-Ferrero 2005). News articles from that time describe the crisis unfolding in once prosperous rural counties: multiple bank failures and major business closures, runaway farm bankruptcies, and even declining enrollments in schools and churches (Barnett 2018). Some counties in the agricultural region of Kansas studied by Eric Ramírez-Ferrero (2005) lost between 16 and 24 percent of their population over the course of the 1980s. Heffernan (1991) estimated that 600,000 families left their farms during that decade.

Dying like a Scarecrow in the Rain

"Rain on the Scarecrow" is the first track on John (Cougar) Mellencamp's 1985 album *Scarecrow*, released at the height of the US farm foreclosure crisis. Hailing from Seymour, Indiana, Mellencamp is a son of the rural Midwest whose music speaks directly to the experiences of his community during that time and place. The lyrics and music video of "Rain on the Scarecrow" capture the ghost-in-the-making of the farm crisis, both reminding us of what was lost and speaking dark omens of the yet-to-come.

At the opening of the music video, three young men speak to the camera while leaning against a seeding rig. They wear plain T-shirts, one with his sleeves torn off, tucked into worn blue jeans and seed company hats, the sound of blackbirds interspersed through their conversation. Speaking to us now as ghosts from the past, the men address the camera and comment on the financial crisis facing US farmers: "They want to keep giving more loans and more loans. . . . We don't need another loan; we need a good price." Their exchange reflects their frustration with the lack of public concern for the welfare of farmers and their dismay at the dissolution of farming as a way of life. With a wry gallows humor, the first man offers to the camera, "You want to buy a farm?" The three men laugh heartily, the bitter edge to the joke almost concealed.

As the music begins, the sounds of a driving guitar and drum beat are matched with shots of farm country that capture both the material and emotional ethos of that haunting moment in history: worn pickup trucks, crowds gathered at farm foreclosure auctions, hand-lettered "for sale" signs propped on farm equipment, and abandoned barns sinking back into the landscape. The lyrics lay plain the raw emotions the young farmers' laughter tries to cover.

Voiced from the perspective of a farmer who has lost his family's land, the song speaks to the anguish of both individual and collective loss. The singer is haunted not only by the memories of working alongside his father and grandfather but also by the loss of neighboring families, represented by "ninety-seven crosses planted in the courthouse yard." Overwhelmed by the scope of loss and the depth of trauma being inflicted on his family and his community, the farmer in Mellencamp's song confesses that he sometimes feels like "dying like a scarecrow in the rain" (Mellencamp and Green 1985).

Mellencamp's grim sentiments reflect a stark reality: during the peak of the crisis the suicide rate among farmers was 58 suicides per 100,000 farmers (Gunderson et al. 1993). Summarizing the situation succinctly, a farmer's wife told Dudley, "There were farmers, they took [bankruptcy] as a sign of failure. . . . You know men don't cry. Well some of them couldn't cry. They ended up down in the barn and hung themselves. That's just the plain old gospel truth" (2000: 126). As Gordon tell us, haunting occurs when we experience abstract social forces or structures in our everyday life, feeling ourselves to be objects within society and "vexed by the phantoms of modernity's violence" (1997: 19). Those farmers who "ended up down in the barn" were haunted by both gendered and cultural expectations of what it means to be a good man and a good farmer, and failure in the face of those phantoms rendered life unbearable.

In the song Mellencamp regularly references the farmer's relationship to parents and grandparents, referring to the invaluable nature of intergenerational legacies within agrarian communities and the terror instilled when those legacies are threatened. The connection between a farmer and their land extends far beyond simple means of production; ties between the person and place are both visceral and spiritual. Many farmers describe themselves as having "dirt in their veins" (Ramírez-Ferrero 2005: 78), and spectral ties to past generations are experienced and maintained through the land. As an example, a Kansas farmer confessed that he believed "the spirits of my parents and grandparents probably dwell in the place they loved. . . . I feel like my granddad's spirit is still right here with that old land" (79). Thus, the loss of family land enacted a second death of loved ones by severing the connection to their benevolent ghosts that resided in that place.

Farm bankruptcy enacted a dual trauma, first by capitalism and then at the hands of friends and neighbors. At the thousands of foreclosure auctions that took place across the heartland, farm families watched as their multigenerational legacies (equipment, livestock, homes, land) were sold by bank auctioneers for pennies on the dollar to their former neighbors. Farmers understood that the farm crisis was caused by "larger forces at work" (Dudley 2000: 136), or large-scale swings of global capitalism and politics; they were wounded more deeply by their community's complicity in the on-the-ground enactment of the crisis. As Dudley notes, "If the global market inflicts the initial blow, then it's the local market that adds insult to injury" (2000: 127). It is one thing to be angry at the government or tear your hair out over "the markets"; it is quite another to watch a former neighbor take advantage of your darkest hour for their personal gain.

When farms were foreclosed, the families left, but the empty barns and rusting machinery remained. Foreclosed farmsteads were assimilated into surviving operations, their fields animated by the zombie powers of global capitalism. As undead farms, the heart of the family is gone but the motions of planting and harvest continue to funnel commodities into the global capitalist system. Writing about ghostly absence, Lars Frers argues that "haunting exists as an eerie undercurrent that threatens to destabilize established categories of self as well as place" (2013: 433). Thus, as rural communities were abandoned and fell silent, the American countryside was transformed into an uncanny memorial, the silence as unsettling as the absence of the farmers themselves.

The Face of the Nation

While accounts of farmer suicides and foreclosures are heartbreaking, our ghost story must also recognize the suffering of those who survived and their struggle to make sense of the world in the wake of the crisis. An article published in the *Des Moines Register* in 1985 told the story of three farmers who took their own lives in a single week and included interviews with those left behind. One farmer spoke of a friend and neighbor he had once employed as a farmhand and whom he had helped to get a farm of his own: "It makes me feel bad 'cause I started him up in farming, and I carried him to his grave." Another surviving farmer spoke of his tormented feelings at the loss of his brother: "I'm angry for farming being the way it is," he said. "And I'm angry at [him] for doing what he did. I'm angry at myself for not tending to my own brother" (Kamin 1985). In these farmers' confessions of being "angry at farming" we see an anguish that cannot find a target, a confession of a feeling of powerlessness in the face of invisible forces. If we listen carefully, we can also hear personal torment: Why did I make it and he didn't? What if my survival is to blame for my brother's death? They are truly haunted by the loss.

If farmers could no longer count on the old ways of farming or norms of community to carry them through a crisis, a new model of success or "good farming" had to arise. Peggy Bartlett's (1993) study of Georgia farmers found that even among "successful" farmers, the stress and financial instability of the crisis era instilled resentment of the failed promise of upward mobility through modern farming. Speaking directly to the question of the agrarian dream, she writes that "this sense of failure—in the midst of success by the agrarian definition—reflects [the farmer's] unfulfilled dreams of a middle or upper-middle-class life" (178). Farm families who resisted or resented the enrollment of agriculture into global industrial capitalism noted how it "increasingly stripped away any social or cultural factor that could not be represented on a balance sheet" (Ramírez-Ferrero 2005: 169). As one mode of coping with tectonic shifts in farming culture and economy, Ramírez-Ferrero argues that "the concept of 'farmers' was itself transformed, linked now much more to management science and rationality and less to family, community, and the notion of stewardship" (2005: 169). This shift marked the transition from farming as an identity and a way of life to a world where agriculture is just another industry and farming just another job.

Government and academic analysts reinforced the transformation of agrarian culture by global capitalism. In their postcrisis assessment of the state of farming, the US Department of Agriculture suggested that "the decline of farming employment is, in many ways, a consequence of success" (USDA ERS 1995: 5). The implication was that the loss of midsized family farms was, in fact, a natural outcome of the increasing economic and productive efficiency of modern, scientific agriculture. Even from the standpoint of critique, Buttel (1989) argued that the farm crisis and loss of farm numbers generally can be attributed to both "long swings" of expansion and contraction in the world economy and inherent dynamics of capitalist growth in industrial-country agriculture. If the loss of family farms is a desirable outcome of progress, or at least of the inevitable swings of global commodity capitalism, how are farmers to make sense of the explicit pain and trauma that inevitable progress-via-dispossession inflicts? Are the survivors dupes or laudable champions?

While there was sympathy for the losses of those who were forced out of farming, the predominant narrative at the time was that those who failed must have been "bad farmers" or "poor managers" (Ramírez-Ferrero 2005). This collective hardening of hearts against the suffering of former neighbors reflects what Berlant (2011) calls an impasse: a moment of crisis where foundational beliefs about the world and how it works are thrown into question. As terrifying as any individual ghost or zombie farmstead, the threat to the promise of an agrarian good life was the truly horrifying specter. By ascribing both success and failure to individual merit rather than to structures of economy outside of individual control, farmers were able to keep alive the dream that you can get ahead if you play the commodity game right. Today's farmers subsume the trauma of the 1980s into a cruel optimism, an anti–ghost story that promises that smart, hardworking farmers will succeed, serving to erase the trauma wrought by global capitalism. Just as Mellencamp's music tells the story of how the crisis unfolded across the heartland, through contemporary country music we can trace the subsumption and erasure of those memories and the enforcement of a different narrative.

Handshake Money

In 2016, thirty-one years after the release of *Scarecrow*, a new farmer-centered anthem hit the country music scene: "Here's to the Farmer." The lyrics, penned by Luke Bryan, son of a Georgia peanut farmer and mill operator, reflect the ethos of contemporary farming and an utter lack of recognition of past trauma. While the opening stanza references the "uphill battle" of farming life, Bryan's ode to the contemporary American farmer paints that struggle as noble and necessary. Gone is the four-hundred-acre farm of Mellencamp's time, replaced by at least two thousand acres of commodity production that "turn from green to that harvest honey" (Bryan, Carter, and McGill 2016). The narrative of emotional struggle and critique of the agricultural economy found in Mellencamp's lyrics is replaced by a farmer who doesn't complain, doesn't question or "get rattled," and works himself into the sunset.

Unlike the three farmers gathered together at the opening of "Rain on the Scarecrow," in this music video we see Bryan by himself in a barn. Footage of Bryan sitting on a woodpile and strumming his guitar is interspersed with shots of workers setting up a concert stage next to an out-of-use silo, in an unplowed field where young couples play cornhole and wave American flags. Heavy equipment moves across the fields, but instead of tractors or seeders, we see forklifts and semitrucks emblazoned with Bryan's face. While the song professes an admiration for "the farmer," throughout the nearly four-minute video we do not see a single identifiable farmer, only enthusiastic concertgoers.

Bryan's concert takes place on a zombie farmstead, a space formerly filled with the vibrant life of a family farm but now animated only by the empty activities of commodity capitalism. The false face of the empty barn and silos (from the outside we do not know they are hollow) are co-opted as a means to prop up the imagery of a crumbling agrarian dream and hide the skeletons of past crises. In the image of the fallow field turned patriotic playground, we see evidence of Dudley's argument that "the depopulation of the rural landscape has created a new, ghostly version of the pastoral ideal" (2000: 9). Our modern farmer is lauded for his technological and entrepreneurial mastery over the forces of nature and global commodity markets alike. The ghost towns of rural America and empty grange halls serve as a memorial to their triumph, and the farmer's isolation is a testament to the merits of self-reliance.

The contrast in attitudes between Mellencamp and Bryan is startling. Mellencamp is explicit in his description of the disastrous spiral of crashing commodity markets and compounding debt ending in foreclosure. His lyrics are dripping with disdain, rejecting the banker's claim that foreclosure was "just his job" and snidely offering to pray for his soul. With an ominous and disturbing play on the song's chorus, Mellencamp suggests that when a man's livelihood is taken from him, so goes his dignity, and "there'll be blood on the scarecrow, blood on the plow" (Mellencamp and Green 1985). In contrast, Bryan's lyrics are obsequious in their adoration of both the farmer's noble struggle and the banker's handshake money. The farmer's idyllic nuclear family gathers every evening to send their praise to God, and despite the hardships they encounter, "somehow they get closer when times get harder" (Bryan et al. 2016).

Bryan's Panglossian adulations place this song within the class of melodrama, which Berlant calls "the supreme genre of ineloquence." As she observes, "In melodrama, the soundtrack is . . . what tells you that you are really most at home in yourself when you are bathed by emotions you can always recognize and that whatever dissonance you sense is not the real, but an accident you have to clean up after, which will be more pleasant if you whistle while you work" (2011: 34). In this vein, Bryan's catchy tune soothes away any dissonance one might feel when riding one's tractor past abandoned farmsteads or listening to the grim news from the latest commodity price report.

To be possessed by a cruel optimism is to desire something that is itself the obstacle to your flourishing, to cling to fantasies of attaining "that moral-intimate-economic thing called the good life" and to the conviction that this time things will be different (Berlant 2011: 2). In Bryan's ode to farming, we see a resolute (cruel) optimism that denies any doubt or worry, to "[defend] against losing emotional shape entirely" (Berlant 2011: 44). Whistling a pop-country tune, Bryan's imagined farmer "don't ever get rattled" by the ghosts of past failures that surround him. He does not question the wisdom of his banker or the Father and finds comfort in familiar feelings of patriotism and his identity based on entrepreneurial individualism. Bryan's contemporary farmer ignores both the dissonance caused by the haunting of the farm crisis and any suggestion that the odds of the agriculture game are stacked insurmountably against him. The lyrics belie a naively optimistic belief that we live in the best of all possible agricultural worlds—a worldview founded in neoliberal ideals that reassures us that the farmers who endure are the farmers who "deserve" to remain, through their hard work and astute management.

"Here's to the Farmer" was released in the midst of another boom-and-bust cycle in US agriculture, which began in 2008. As the United States and the world entered the great recession, weak global commodity production spurred high prices and strong exports for US farmers. Commodity agriculture enjoyed a "golden period" with net farm income hitting a record high of $123.7 billion in 2013 (Schnepf 2018). Simultaneously, investors desperate for a refuge for their capital in the midst of the global financial crisis poured money into farmland both as a hedge against inflation and as a form of profit speculation (Fairbairn 2014). Consequently, the average price per acre for farmland soared from $2,640 in 2009 to $4,100 only five years later (USDA NASS 2018a).

As Bryan acknowledges, times will someday "get harder," and that someday is now. Rather than sustaining a robust class of midsized farms, the boom years served only to continue the drive to intensification and consolidation, with fewer and fewer farms working ever-larger swaths of land. At the end of the 1980s, very large farms (more than $1 million in sales) contributed 31 percent of all US farm production; by 2015, more than half (51 percent) of farm production came from such farms (MacDonald, Korb, and Hoppe 2013). In a familiar pattern of events, farmers who used the boom of the golden years to leverage readily available debt financing to make needed repairs or expand operations are now faced with plummeting prices and robust overseas competition. Projected farm income for 2018 was down 47 percent from its record high of $123.7 billion in 2013, with projected farm incomes dipping into the negative numbers (Schnepf 2018). The financial strain caused by down markets is further compounded by an unfolding trade war with China in which retaliatory tariffs target soybeans, pork, and other commodities (Eller 2018).

Recognition of the new farm crisis has been slow among farm analysts, but farmers are feeling the stress. The grain and dairy sectors are in a tailspin, locked in a rapidly accelerating crisis of overproduction, industry consolidation, and market prices that are below farmers' cost of production (Chrisman 2018; Kinney 2018). Dairy has been hit particularly hard. In 1970 there were 650,000 dairy farms in the United States, but only 40,219 remained at the end of 2017 (USDA NASS 2018b). In one example of the trends in dairy, Walmart, the number one grocery retailer in the United States, announced in early 2018 plans to further consolidate and open its own fluid milk operation, cutting existing processors and farmers out of the loop (Reuters 2018). Now without a buyer, Dean Foods canceled contracts with more than one hundred dairy farmers across seven states. With no buyers left to turn to, and in a bitterly ironic turn on past admonitions to get big or get out, these farmers are being counseled to "sell out as fast as you can" (McCausland 2018). A dairy cooperative in New England went so far as to enclose suicide-prevention flyers in payment checks to farmers. With these warnings, the phantoms of failure and loss arise once more from the graves of empty farmsteads, sending a familiar shiver of the uncanny down the backs of those of us paying attention.

Living with Ghosts

Why are we afraid of ghosts? They unsettle our worldview; they violate our understanding of the absolute division of past and present, of the dead and the living. The ghosts of the 1980s farm crisis haunt the countryside with memories of specific losses (this family's land, her father, our neighbors) but also threaten the dream of the American agrarian good life. This existential threat is indicative of a paradox at the heart of American agriculture wherein the dominant ideas and practices of good farming and good farmers are themselves partially responsible for dismantling the family farm–centered system of agriculture upon which the agrarian dream depends (Burton 2004). Discussing what she calls the "pastoral paradox," Dudley argues that agrarians have allowed themselves to "entertain the illusion that any family with the right combination of skill, ambition, and luck can make a decent living on the land," when in fact this dream is no longer credible (2000: 9). We convince ourselves that if we run from ghosts, they might not catch us.

Farmers who held on through the crisis did not come out unscathed and bore financial, emotional, and subjective scars. Recognizing how the timescapes between farming's past and present blend in complicated ways, Lia Bryant and Bridget Garnham observe that "refractions of the historical image of the hardy [farmer] carry forward to infect contemporary farmer subjectivity even as modern neoliberal discourses reshape ... farming and notions of farming" (2014: 68). In other words, farmers are aware of the paradoxical position they inhabit, simultaneously exalting the ideals of self-reliance and the market supremacy from neoliberal capitalism while also mourning the loss of the agrarian culture and security that it destroys (Dudley 2000).

Today's farmers are haunted by the ghosts of the 1980s crisis, which stand everywhere in empty barns and on vacant farmsteads. Both memories and landscape are grim reminders that even the best-intentioned farmer can be materially and subjectively undone by structural forces outside of their control—the very forces over which they are supposed to be masters. Caught between their dreams of good farming and the lived reality of the modern agricultural economy, today's farmers are embroiled in a situation of not only economic crisis but also affective precarity (Berlant 2011). Both the future of the farm and how they understand and evaluate their life as a farmer are at stake.

What can listening to the ghosts of the farm crisis offer us? Donna Haraway observes that "mourning is about dwelling with loss, and so coming to appreciate what it means, how the world has changed, and how we ourselves change and renew our relationships if we are to move forward from here" (2016: 38). Thus, living with ghosts requires agrarian communities to both mourn what was lost and recognize how farmers and farming have changed. Gordon further suggests that we might allow ghosts to "help us imagine what was lost that never existed" (2008: 57). For US farmers, recognizing what "never existed" requires questioning the cruel optimism of the modern agrarian dream. It requires abandoning faith in promises that they can find success if they just work hard enough and play the commodity markets right. Such a transformation would require farmers to allow themselves to be possessed by the ghosts of failed farmers and to recognize that there is no guarantee they will not meet the same fate.

The fear engendered by the haunting of the farm crisis arises from an abyss of uncertainty: If not this world, then what? The haunting caused by commodity capitalism is predicated on the erasure of past trauma and present doubt, as we see in Bryan's melodramatic tune. The lack of readily articulated vision as to how to move away from the current mode of global commodity agriculture leaves farmers, both the living and the departed, in limbo. The loans are on record, the expensive machinery is in the barn, and, as we see with today's dairy farmers, there are few markets to turn to if you want to try something different. However, whispers of change are emerging from the countryside. Farmer-led efforts to opt out of global grain markets and re-regionalize grain production (Halloran 2015), locally operated food hubs distributing food for the benefit of their own farming communities (Brislen 2018), and other postglobalist efforts work to address the structural forces of consolidation and rapacious profit-seeking that have shattered the countryside.

In the end, our ghost story is unresolved. There is no exorcism, no releasing of earthbound spirits. By residing in this moment of impasse, recognizing the ongoing unfolding of the present crisis, there is an opportunity to radically reimagine a new world and a new dream (Berlant 2011). A new agrarian dream requires a new song, one that creates space for the mourning of past traumas and lost dreams while also looking to an uncharted future beyond the abyss. A new dream must fully inhabit the haunted countryside, reckon with the costs (emotional, social, environmental) of past agrarian lives, and allow for new birth to arise from zombie farmsteads. Such a dream requires the courage to invent "new practices of imagination, resistance, revolt, repair, and mourning, and of living and dying well" (Haraway 2016: 55). Living with ghosts, allowing their stories of loss and redemption to sing through our hopes for the future, is crucial to finding that path.

Acknowledgments

I owe Dr. Christopher Oliver of Tulane University a debt of gratitude for referring me to "Rain on the Scarecrow" during the early days of my conceiving this chapter. His deep knowledge of 1980s popular music is to thank for the analytical lynchpin of this chapter.

Dr. Lilian Brislen is the director of The Food Connection at the University of Kentucky. She is a Rural Sociologist whose work focuses on issues affecting mid-sized family farms, and the development of just and sustainable agro-food systems. Her previous research includes explorations of gendered and generational dimensions of farmer identity (*Rural Sociology, Journal of Extension*), an in-depth case study of a failed food hub (*USDA Rural Development*), and the challenges faced by traditional farmers transitioning (scaling-over) into alternative food networks (*Culture, Agriculture, Food and Environment*).

Note

1. As we live in a digital age, I strongly encourage you, the reader, to use the resources at your disposal to view the two music videos discussed in this chapter. They are readily available online and will provide another affective dimension to our ghostly exploration of the past and present.

References

Barnett, Barry J. 2018. "The U.S. Farm Financial Crisis of the 1980s." *Agricultural History* 74(2): 366–380.
Bartlett, Peggy F. 1993. *American Dreams, Rural Realities: Family Farms in Crisis*. Chapel Hill: University of North Carolina Press.
Berlant, Lauren Gail. 2011. *Cruel Optimism*. Duke University Press.
Brislen, Lilian. 2018. "Meeting in the Middle: Scaling-Up and Scaling-Over in Alternative Food Networks." *Culture, Agriculture, Food and Environment* 40(2): 105–113.
Bryan, Luke, Michael Carter, and Chase McGill. 2016. "Here's to the Farmer." Track 2 on *Farm Tour*. Capital Records.
Bryant, Lia, and Bridget Garnham. 2014. "Economies, Ethics, and Emotions: Farmer Distress within the Moral Economy of Agribusiness." *Journal of Rural Studies* 34: 304–312.

Burton, Rob. 2004. "Seeing through the 'Good Farmer's' Eyes: Towards Developing an Understanding of the Social Symbolic Value of 'Productivist' Behaviour." *Sociologia Ruralis* 44(2): 195–215.

Buttel, Frederick H. 1989. "The US Farm Crisis and the Restructuring of American Agriculture; Domestic and International Dimensions." in *The International Farm Crisis*, ed. David Goodman and Michael Redclift, 46–83. London: Palgrave Macmillan.

Chrisman, Siena. 2018. "Is the Second Farm Crisis upon Us?" *Civil Eats*, 10 September. Retrieved 5 November 2018 from https://civileats.com/2018/09/10/is-the-second-farm-crisis-upon-us/.

Cowan, Tadlock, and Jody Feder. 2012. "The *Pigford* Cases: USDA Settlement of Discrimination Suits by Black Farmers." CRS Report for Congress 7-5700, 29 May. Washington, DC: Congressional Research Service.

Dudley, Kathryn Marie. 2000. *Debt and Dispossession: Farm Loss in America's Heartland*. Chicago: University of Chicago Press.

Egan, Timothy. 2006. *The Worst Hard Time: The Untold Story of Those Who Survived the Great American Dust Bowl*. Boston: Houghton Mifflin.

Eller, Donnell. 2018. "Low Prices, Trade Disputes Sow Fears of '80s-Style Farm Crisis." *Des Moines Register*, 4 June. Retrieved 20 October 2018 from https://www.desmoinesregister.com/story/money/agriculture/2018/06/04/trade-war-tariffs-farm-iowa-economy-low-prices-dispute-interest-rates-debt-worries-crisis-1980-s/661905002/.

Fairbairn, Madeleine. 2014. "'Like Gold with Yield': Evolving Intersections between Farmland and Finance." *Journal of Peasant Studies* 41(5): 777–795.

Fitzgerald, Deborah Kay. 2003. *Every Farm a Factory: The Industrial Ideal in American Agriculture*. New Haven: Yale University Press.

Frers, Lars. 2013. "The Matter of Absence." *Cultural Geographies* 20(4): 431–445.

Friedberger, Mark. 1993. "Women Advocates in the Iowa Farm Crisis of the 1980s." *Agricultural History* 67(2): 224–234.

Gordon, Avery F. 2008. *Ghostly Matters: Haunting and the Sociological Imagination*, 2nd edn. Minneapolis: University of Minnesota Press.

Gunderson, Paul, Doris Donner, Raymond Nashold, Linda Salkowicz, Samuel Sperry, and Beverly Wittman. 1993. "The Epidemiology of Suicide among Farm Residents or Workers in Five North-Central States, 1980–1988." *American Journal of Preventive Medicine* 9(3): 26–32.

Halloran, Amy. 2015. *The New Bread Basket*. White River Junction, VT: Chelsea Green.

Haraway, Donna J. 2016. *Staying with the Trouble: Making Kin in the Chthulucene*. Durham: Duke University Press.

Hutchison, Anthony. 2010. "'Following the Ghost': The Psychogeography of Alternative Country." In *Popular Ghosts: The Haunted Spaces of Everyday Culture*, ed. Maria del Pilar Blanco and Esther Peeren, 268–281. New York: Continuum International.

Kaimn, Blair. 1985. "Anguish Forecloses on Lives of 3 Farmers." *The Des Moines Register*. 13 October, 1.

Kinney, Jim. 2018. "Information on Suicide Prevention Arrives with Checks for Agri-Mark's Dairy Farmers; Milk Prices Expected to Keep Dropping." *Mass Live*, 7 February. Retrieved 20 October 2018 from https://www.masslive.com/business-news/index.ssf/2018/02/agri-mark.html.

MacDonald, James M., Penni Korb, and Robert A. Hoppe. 2013. "Farm Size and the Organization of U.S. Crop Farming." Economic Research Report No. 152. Washington, DC: United States Department of Agriculture, Economic Research Service.

McCausland, Phil. 2018. "Best Advice to U.S. Dairy Farmers? 'Sell Out as Fast as You Can.'" *NBC News*, 30 June. Retrieved 5 October 2018 from https://www.nbcnews.com/news/us-news/best-advice-u-s-dairy-farmers-sell-out-fast-you-n887941.

Mellencamp, John Cougar, and George M. Green. 1985. "Rain on the Scarecrow." Track 1 on *Scarecrow*. Riva Records.

Ramírez-Ferrero, Eric. 2005. *Troubled Fields: Men, Emotions, and the Crisis in American Farming*. New York: Columbia University Press.

Reuters. 2018. "Wal-Mart Jumps into Milk Processing, Hits Dean Foods' Stock." *Reuters Business News*, 22 March. Retrieved 11 November 2018 from https://www.reuters.com/article/us-wal-mart-stores-milk/wal-mart-jumps-into-milk-processing-hits-dean-foods-stock-idUSKCN0WO37R

Schnepf, Randy. 2018. "U.S. Farm Income Outlook for 2018." CRS Report. Washington, DC: Congressional Research Service. Retrieved 5 October 2018 from https://fas.org/sgp/crs/misc/R45117.pdf.

Strange, Marty. 1988. *Family Farming: A New Economic Vision*. Lincoln: University of Nebraska Press.

USDA ERS (United States Department of Agriculture, Economic Research Service). 1995. "Understanding Rural America." Agricultural Information Bulletin No. 710, February, 5. Washington, DC: USDA.

USDA NASS (United States Department of Agriculture, National Agricultural Statistics Service). 2018a. "Land Values 2018 Summary." August. Washington, DC: USDA. Retrieved 19 October 2019 from https://www.nass.usda.gov/Publications/Todays_Reports/reports/land0818.pdf.

USDA NASS (United States Department of Agriculture, National Agricultural Statistics Service). 2018b. "Milk Production." February. Washington, DC: USDA. Retrieved 19 October 2019 from https://release.nass.usda.gov/reports/mkpr0218.pdf.

CHAPTER 8

Boneyard Quiet
A Ghost Story

A. E. GARRISON

Boneyard Quiet: a ghost story

A.E. Garrison

There is a care to be taken in remembering. Some scholars insist that once an event has a story—a retelling—it is no longer "true," no longer a happening, but a story of a story, through time.1 Still others would suggest that our memories are complicated understandings, inscribed or written by those in our social worlds, into our own experiences.2

But remembering a place that has never been is wholly something else. And I don't mean that any "social figures" I might conjure in the telling of this story did not exist, but that in my time, I have never seen them.3

Their forms are with me nonetheless. I find, however, that the space is essential for a haunting that moves forward through the fogginess of scattered pasts. What can be seen from a distance is not always the clearest vision. What seems most likely is not always what happens.

In the spring of 2016, I began to explore the city of Lansing, Michigan on foot. I lived in the heart of the city, in a neighborhood referred to as Moores Park. The neighborhood rests on the edge of REO Town, affectionately and appropriately named by the city's residents for its history in a mammoth automotive past.

It was not my intention to "find" anything, necessarily. I set out on a hot summer day along the Grand River. The Lansing River Trail recreation park system provides an asphalt path that leads along the river, across from the behemoth Otto C. Eckert Municipal Power Plant, across the water to buttress the city's only remaining GM plant–Lansing Grand River Assembly. Makers of Camaros.

I had never been so close to a factory.

These walks would take me all over the city, walking over ground I later discovered was the predictable trace of the Lake Shore & Michigan Southern Railroad–under pavement, under concrete, under more asphalt, under traffic. Under Interstate 496, which ripped its way neatly through the heart of the city, making all around it a blur of irrelevance. Roofs and tree tops peeked over its concrete shoulders, the river invisible to anyone strange to the town.

This trail would take me along the bank, sometimes busy with people and their pursuit of fitness. Often solitary. Never quiet.

The trail snaked along the banks all the way downtown, revealing secrets along the way. Empty, partial concrete foundations, half-submerged in the current. Curious, chain-laced dead-end streets with no beginning, whose edges were jagged asphalt drops into the Grand River.

Painted buildings with no windows. Repurposed structures with empty parking lots. And a heaviness that told nothing—a silence around a noise that was unidentifiable to me.

. . . a buzzing of ghosts. A cacophony of whispers from a time I could not know.

The heavy breath of a past is a hard thing to unpack in an unfamiliar place. Stories were sitting on the surface at every turn. Every street corner, every rise of a hill. A pile of rubble in the middle of an empty field. But, so much of what I could see told me nothing, other than *something* had been there. Something larger that bloomed in the weight of the busy quiet.

It was not as though The Past of Lansing was not documented. I take much of my knowing and telling here from the works of Lisa Fine,4 a gifted socio-historian, and from the generous librarians working throughout the Michigan library system to protect and preserve these documents of times that never were, were it not for photos. The only visible markings of Lansing's past are historic signs, created and erected by the federal Department of the Interior that note the site of the Diamond REO factory, detailing in brief the life of Ransom E. Olds and the history of the auto industry in the city's heart. Along the main street in REO Town, signs told anyone interested about the history of the Oldsmobile-Lansing's claim to a place in the story of Michigan, of Rust Belt cities, of the car in the United States. And then, of course, the names of the streets were quick impositions of what residents and visitors would take for granted: someone who no longer mattered, in some other time, but who no longer mattered to anything but navigation.5

Haunting nonetheless. Ghosts of spaces. Ghosts in places.6

Avery Gordon (2008) describes haunting as "a particular way of knowing what has happened or is happening." 7 In pieces, we discover the lives we fictionalize to tell a story of social realities, "fictions of the real.8 Haunting as uncovering a time when the names of the streets were living people, making their money, leading the city, while their fortunes fueled the policy and practice of Michigan's capital.

These are all markers to conjure the curiosity of some other time—a beginning. Authenticity, after all, is important to US culture. Originality and invention. Individuality embodied, so that the genius belongs to one, and not many.

There are other hauntings, however, other ghosts, whose shadows aren't dissolved by the bright lights of historic relevance. Not directly. Markers are rarely dedicated to everyday life. The lives of those who go unremembered by the powers of history's telling are fundamental elements of the "progress" of a future under control.

These hauntings and their boneyards, where the surface of a foundation still grips the barbed wire, secured there once by someone invested in protecting whatever it was, in wait for nothing. Crumbled bits of other times, made by other hands-troubled by the troubles of their lives.

But there is a danger in remembering something that never happened.

As I continued to walk through the city every day of that summer, my curiosity became consumed with piecing together a past of a place that was the proto-type of the American Dream.

Labor. *Unions.*

Democracy. *Public good.*

Equality. *Sidewalks. Swimming pools.*

Or what I imagined a dream like that would look like . . . here . . . at the bottom of the peninsula.

Public works projects, funded by the monies of the tycoons at the local and national levels, in conjunction with the federal government, fueled other growth. Workers lived down the hills or across the river from their bosses and local capitalists. And while it would be reductive to assume that all of the folks in the heart of Lansing at the turn of the 20th century were white, the variation among labor resided primary in ethnicity.9

The houses in my neighborhood and the neighborhoods I walked through were all close together. There were some empty lots next to houses, not quite big enough to fit another house. Curbs broke in curves to nowhere, and sidewalks from the street went right to nothing.

There were collective movements as the white residents of the city fled it-around the same time the federal government opened the floodgates on cheap property just outside city limits.10 The city did not "die," even if wounded-and it was not immune to the seismic waves cracking the earth of urban spaces all along the Rust Belt. Thousands lost their jobs, whole neighborhoods emptied out, the temperature of Lansing dropped. But there was everyday life nonetheless. People walked to work, bought houses, had children, mended broken hearts, and struggled under the consequences of policies made by those looking out from somewhere else. Familiar tellings of one past make for a silencing of the justice that would be served to those whose stories disappear in the murky waters of power's heroic tales of itself.11

Federal programs would allow the government to claim residents' property, buying their rights for less than the property was worth in many cases.12 The building of interstate connectors through cities was subsidized by the federal government's slum clearance/urban renewal projects.13 The interstates allow us to drive over boneyards of neighborhoods not long gone. The city's landscape sits on thin layers of other times.

It is impossible for any of us to know the everyday lives of the people who walked through this city in the time of its beginning. As a trusted friend and colleague asked me: "Why would anyone save these things?" Neighborhoods, parks, pools, and bridges. It is precisely because we would not know to ask about these spaces that they are important. And not only the story of the bridge, or pool, but the people around those spaces-the people who used them, the people who planned them, the people who wrote the check, and the people who destroy them. In the end, they are just a bridge, and just a pool. It matters, however, that they mattered.14

I can only claim that a bridge mattered because it crossed a river. I can only say it matters because it provided a way for people to get across this part of the Grand River, in this part of the city, for a very long time. And then, like the city itself, it was forgotten and left to rot.

Unlike the city, however, the bridge disappeared- and with it, the shared experience of its crossing. The changes to the cityscape are only captured in time only by photographs. These captive seconds show a different world than the horizon of the present.

And yet, I can't help but want to see what was seen in those moments. Postcards from a time that looked so different, but not unfamiliar to me. Archived photographs of bridges, neighborhoods, city streets whose bricks lie under layers of layers of repair, repave, resurface, and repeat.

What follows is a story of obsession, haunting, and ghosts. I place myself in different times in form only, and to ask questions that incite the ghosts I have seen to emerge and show themselves to anyone who would seek them out, even as they evade notice in dreams of a past that never happened. If they whisper from the shallows and materialize in opacity to tell their stories, what would they tell us?

Would they tell us that they saw the slow decomposition of themselves in the neglect of "the public"...? Would they tell us that their rememberings disappointed their realities, sharing the struggles of achieving the impossible in the American Dream? A warning, perhaps, to remember intentionally? To proceed with critical caution? Or, most likely, a whole symphony of other stories, unrelated to anything but the very real doings of everyday life?15

Demolition by neglect makes for treacherous footing.

It is in this uncertainty that we begin . . .

*Souls are mixed with things; things are mixed with souls.*16

17

"... the ghost is just the sign ... that tells you a haunting is taking place. The ghost is not simply a dead or missing person, but a social figure, and investigating it can lead to that dense site where history and subjectivity make social life. The ghost or the apparition is one form by which something lost, or barely visible, or seemingly not there to our supposedly well-trained eyes, makes itself known or apparent to us, in its own way, of course. The way of the ghost is haunting, and haunting is a very particular way of knowing what has happened or is happening. Being haunted draws us affectively, sometimes against our will and always a bit magically, into the structure of feeling a reality we come to experience, not as cold knowledge, but as transformative recognition."18

I-496

the Grand River

the bones

River Street

follow me . . .

I lived in the neighborhood closest to the power plant. **Moores Park**

The power plant sat on land that was donated by General Motors in the 1920s.19 The houses in my neighborhood had been there longer than that.

Luckily for the automaker, its main city plant sat adjacent to the location of the giant municipal power station. Before that, Oldsmobile had reigned over Lansing.

At the time the power plant was constructed, the population of Lansing was 57,327. A great portion of the population worked in automotive manufacturing.20

The power plant was haunting, but not in the ways that reveal a spectre.

The plants stacks were shorter and more numerous. Environmental protections in the 1970s and '80s required a distancing of the stacks from the ground.21

By design, surrounding neighborhoods housed the supervisors-the feet of the workers would touch the same cement as those of the company's middle managers. And they all lived down the street from the richest men in the city.22

...footsteps of everyday life

The rhythm of the city's hea palpitated often. Pieces of dissolved into fields, into unnamed buildings, and ye others held the gauzy haze its ghosts close.

I drew the stacks over and over - they cast their spell on most of us living in the capital. They enchanted my imagining

Glimpses of another time. Sightings of different evaluations of governance, of the state, of the corporation... of capitalism in practice and motion.

The fascination spread out.   ...and already, the romance thinly covers the truths I might find.

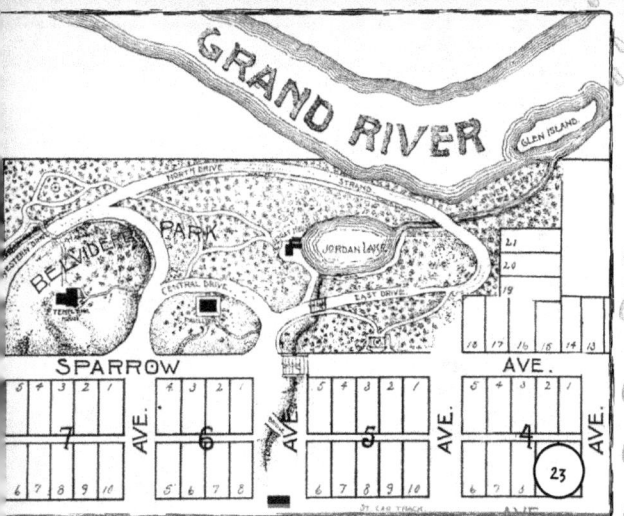

Every day that was warm enough, young people from the neighborhood gathered on the basketball courts ... in the river valley of Moores Park. I could hear their contests from the front porch of my house.

I found an old park plan in an archive of the Capital Area District Library. It transformed the way I saw and thought about this century-old neighborhood and city heart.

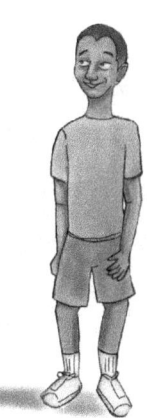

is this everyday life ... ?

... where a milestone, historic "natatorium" sat a few feet away.

A pool for the public.

ores Park, a public park, undulated with the sts of a time that was, mixing with the energies he living ... in the present.

But no two people's experiences are identical–nor are the tellings of those life stories. Realities of our social worlds are created by an order–a modernized life. Stratification. Hierarchies. Toxic dangers produced by power.

... and yet, power produces these public spaces ... where people come together who might be strange to one another. That is a "hope" in and of "public."

The neighborhood had changed since the 1920s, when the park, the power plant, and the school were built. But th changes, as in so many other neighborhoods in the United States, did not suit *all* of the residents.24

People from the area shared their stories with me. Often the secrets of the public park politic of the neighborhood flashed themselves in these conversations.

The flash disguised itself, and softened as stories of stories. The context of "community," where not all present are invited.

They said they didn't want 'more RATS' in the park . . . .

"The public" is taken for granted, as ideal "inclusion" is only a theory.

Practice is different.

Manifestations of expectations: Who was "the public," and who would be a spectator to a privileged "progress" in the chlorinated waters? Outside, looking in . . . always.

Municipal swimming pools provided a space for white men and women to meet. Access was denied to Black folks beginning in the 1920s as the complications of sexuality, future ("progress"), as ever-present exercise of racism tied up the tangles of segregation.26

he power plant, the pool and the school (forgotten)...

Public endeavors.

Is this everyday life?

I am both a part of and apart from these worlds. A spectator on the edge of what I can imagine but never see. At the same time, I know elements of the past that linger here. The moment the photo of the pool was snapped in 1935, it never happened again. Just that one time. Just for that second of exposure.

The jewels of Moores Park faced threats at the turn of every year. Their half-century-and-more-year-old structures were crumbling, in the heart of a city where the powerful remembered them only when money arose as a question of upkeep, and obligation. Only the west entrance of the pool and the natatorium itself are historic landmarks registered with the federal Department of the Interior.28 The pavilion is not protected under the same guidelines and policies that would require its "owners" to maintain its historic condition. At the same time, even the protection of federal agencies in policy can't make for preservation in practice.29 The pool's mortar weathers every season in the Great Lakes state. The urgency of repairs, however, goes unheeded.

It is not easy or accurate, to say that a city simply stops doing maintenance on its public spaces. Proving intention is difficult. Rather, the connection of revenue to the funding of projects is complicated-the allocation of those funds, the quantifiable proof of need over waste. Everyday life in and of bureaucracies. Such hopes in process. Such anticipation for a "return" to a moment that has never really been. Or that was . . . *just that one time*. Politics have their own romance-their own shrouds of the mythic: when history can point to "what worked" and when, while still only making clear the truth it seeks to show. The days of yearning behind us are days to lament only if our imagination of power's past deceives us with a void for "equality." The "public good" has never been "equal." 30

In the spring of 2017, the radio and local newspapers were scattered with stories of the park's pavilion, its base all fieldstone, its concrete and mortar cracking. The city and its contracted engineers determined that the structure was unsafe, and boarded up all access to the picnic platform.32 This pavilion was a neighborhood gathering place–the only place to sit and eat with other people in the whole park.

Demolition was one of its five fates. The city deferred to the contractors for estimates and learned quickly that the repairs would be more expensive than simply tearing it down.33

The *City Pulse*, another of Lansing's news outlets, reported that the inspection done by city officials had revealed "...a state of sheer failure" in the structure of the pavilion.34 Questions loomed about the cost, versus the benefit. Technocracy can be subtle. The benefits versus the cost of preserving the only shaded structure that provided enough seats for large groups of people from the community to gather. Renovation or reconstruction would overrule complete demolition if "the public" was considered. But demolition was cheapest.35 At the same time, the justification for its care and rejuvenation would be balanced with the promise of revenue. This city property had not generated revenue since it was closed over a year earlier.36

The city waits. The pavilion sits still . . . waiting . . . wetting, drying, wetting, drying, and weathering away further.

A slow creep toward demolition by neglect.

A slow disintegration of "public" pieces.

"We won't take the next step until we finish gathering input from residents,"[Parks and Recreation Director, Brett] Kaschinske said, adding that there is a possibility that the pavilion could be demolished, repaired or a new one could be built altogether.

Lansing State Journal, Wednesday, July 26, 2017 31

DEMOLITION BY NEGLECT:

". . . a term used to describe a situation in which a property owner intentionally allows historic property to suffer severe deterioration, potentially beyond the point of repair. Property owners may use this kind of long-term neglect to circumvent historic preservation regulations." 37.

In order for a structure to be subject to this classification, it must be registered as a "historic landmark" with the US Department of the Interior or state governments.

"Context in Which Demolition by Neglect Arises: . . . neglect is an affirmative strategy used by an owner who wants to develop the property."38 Develop for whatever reason.

What is this practice called when done by a government–a city, state or municipality?

...but that is only a part of the story.

On this particular day in January, I set out to document a mystery.

There were these bones, you see...

We animate [place] in our imaginations, we construct it in our minds...

sticking out from the river bank... with no marker, no gravestone, no presence of a memory to tell the story of its living.

The place possesses us, and we possess it; we belong to the place, and the place belongs to us.39

I had to find out more.

"Somewhere between the Actual and the Imaginary ghosts might enter without affrighting us." 40

As I made my way through the slushy, icy streets of REO Town, questions of the public "demolition by neglect" only flickered. The weather made being outdoors nearly unbearable, spitting and freezing in a subtle, numbing wind. I had to alternate hands in coat pockets; the wind bit my fingers through my gloves.

I did not know exactly where to go. The strange made itself big and looming, at the same time that I could not resist its calling.

I hoped to find bones. I hoped to catch a ghost, walking over the landscape, from the corner of my eye. To glimpse what Michael Mayerfeld Bell calls "the aura of our web of social relations." 41

follow me...

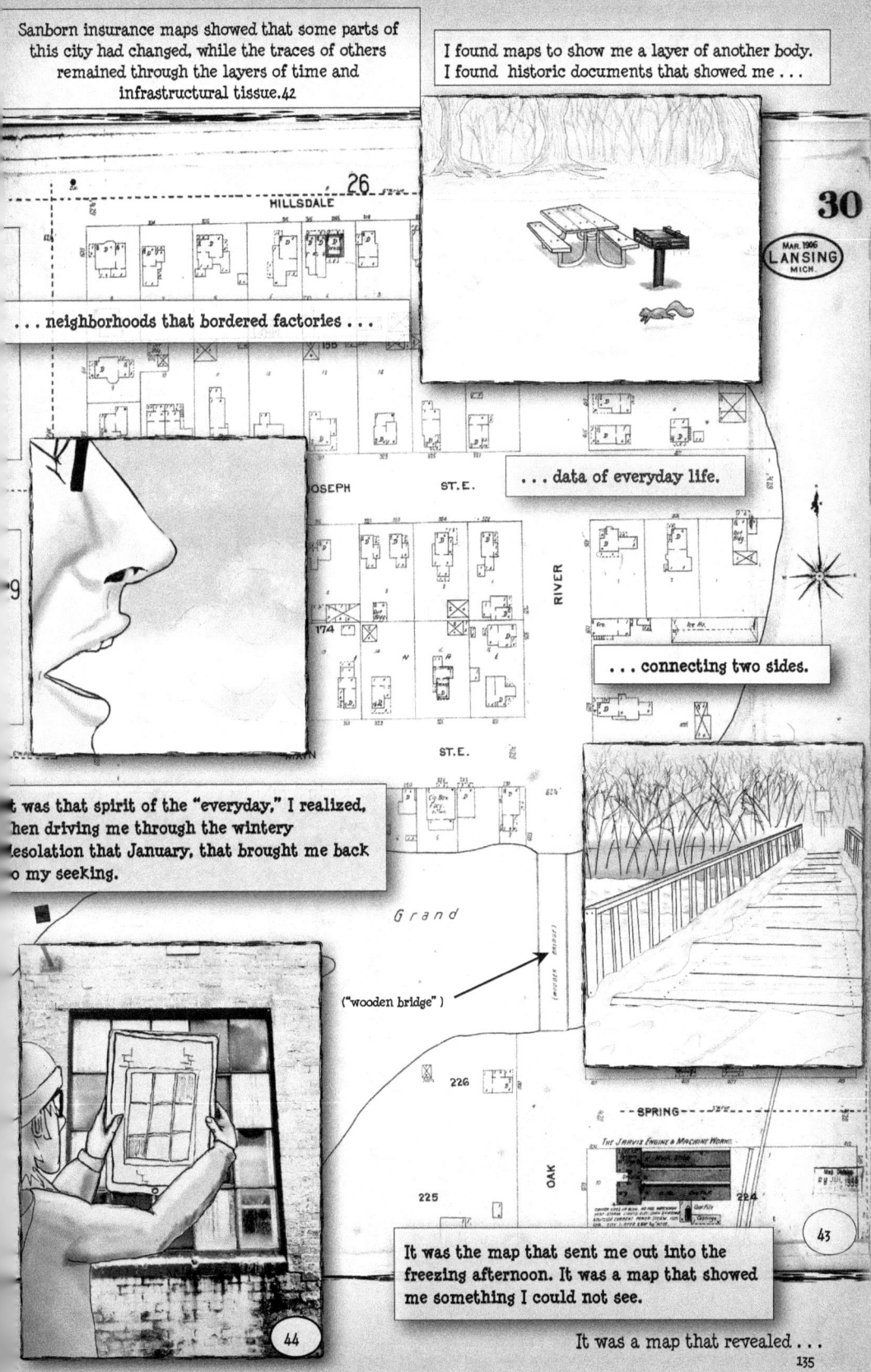

fictions of the real . . .

. . . and the *[ghost]* of a bridge at the end of River St.

transformative recognition . . . 46   Neglect that would predict demolition.

This is not merely the story of this ghostly form ... disappeared, with its traces of concrete bone matter, left behind. No, for we are not haunted by the materiality of our everyday lives *because* of the brick, or the rebar, or the pebbles in the pavement. Indeed, we are haunted, *if* we are haunted, as Heather Van Wormer also states in her chapter, *by* each other.47 We are haunted by the humanity that connects us to one another over time through the meaning we share in objects. Connected through the stories we tell, the lives we live, and the technologies we make to progress these lives forward. River banks, connected. *Furniture without memories.*48

I return to my friend's question of "Who cares about this bridge?" as one whose answer could lie in truly sociological principles. *"The story is about haunting and about the crucial way in which it mediates between institution and person, creating the possibility of making a life, of becoming something else, in the present and for the future."* 49 Imagining experiences connected to history, and to the very real institutional policies and practices that organize our lives. The birth and death of this bridge are regulated by governing bodies, just as the slow dismemberment of public space comes from decisions made elsewhere.

50

... ghosts might enter without affrighting us ...

The bridge serves as a node in structures of social relations.51 The strands connect all those living in various social worlds. As a sociologist on foot, it is not only the bridge I search for, but the traces of everyday lives, past and present, in the structure and boneyards of this city. I search for how those lives cross, down the cracked sidewalks of this city. Just as Brigitte Bechtold describes, the doing of building together matters to everyday life.52 The sidewalks, just like the bridges, were often contracted by cities across the country.53 To the "cheapest bidder," with the best connections. There is a process to the bid, a process to the application, a process preceding action, done by people in positions to make decisions for everyone else.

The pool and the pavilion are also nodes, places on the steely webs of our relations to capital, labor, and the rest of the world. But the pool and the pavilion remain in the spots where they were built so long ago–when the park was the paradise between the river and a different time. The bridge was gone, and with it the access to which people had who used it (to work and back, or wherever) had. Its use became itself a problem for some residents of the neighborhood–even as its use in decades before had been a consideration the city had to take in its maintenance.54 Its building was unremarkable: history does not tell its story, as it would of its sisters. The Kalamazoo Street bridge, the Washington Street bridge, the Grand River bridge all had their notice and commemoration in time, frozen for the memories of those who had never seen iterations of these public structures in the past. The River Street bridge did not have the same fate.

It was this discovery, the connections between the document of history, of an intentional telling, that drove the obsession of finding its image—and this bridge's life that connected two sides of the Grand River. I captured the absence of the bridge in my own photographs. It was not there, but I imagined its narrow shoulders, the slow putter of cars over time, crossing it, crossing it again. The cracking of the wood in the cold ice of the winter when first it provided crossing to people on horses, in carriages, on foot. The bridge began to take shape in my imagination as not only a structure, now missing, but a touchstone for whole neighborhoods, truck routes, bus routes, bike rides-and get-aways. I imagined the responses of people familiar, coming back to this spot-once crossable-only to find it closed . . . impassable.

When I finally found the images of the River Street bridge, the puzzle's picture was clear. But it was just a bridge. The pictures revealed an abandoned body-one crumbling, forgotten, ignored.

Neglected.

I imagine the "traumascapes" theorized by Maria Tumarkin (2005) to be much as Sarah Surface-Evans suggests in her chapter, the spaces we come to know demolished, destroyed or closed off to us, when access used to be unlimited.57 Could traumascapes be just as easily considered in the slow decomposition of a public structure? A restriction of funding? A slow disintegration of "investment" in what would be "the public"?

Traffic changes when the bridge is gone. What was once a through street becomes a "dead end." River Street runs into both the Cedar (at its south) and the Grand (on its north side). I am the only one out here-at least, the only one visible. The only one in the spitting freezing rain. Standing on parts of a sidewalk that were laid in 1923, blocks from the power plant, the pool, and down the street from where this ghost was once real. The Department of Public Works stamped this panel of concrete and moved on. How many feet have rested here for only seconds in stride, where my booted feet, frozen inside socks, now stand?

I see the feet touching this pavement . . .

everyday life in the pavement.

everyday life in our steps.

everyday life in the walk to work.

everyday life in the walk back home again.

So what of the disruptions to everyday life by the absence of this bridge? Untangling the complications of "demolition by neglect" in practice by governing, or "owning" participants in public life, yielded frustration and discouragement. Impossible to prove, if the definition applied to literal property of historic value. "The public" was a "structure of historic value," but not of property and profit. Social gain costs money. "Progress" is expensive.

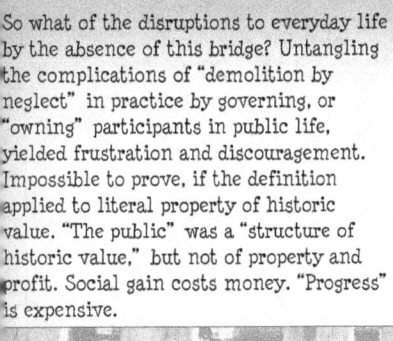

colleagues were curious but not mystified ... not like me.

"So, wait ... the city stopped maintaining it, and people still used it?"

"There was a weight limit set, but heavier trucks crossed it nonetheless. It was not designed for the weight, and it just broke.59"

"Even if the city had wanted to keep up the bridge, though, the communities most affected by its demolition were not crucial voters. Harsh but true."

Bridge must be replaced

By Debra Cassidy
Staff Writer

"The bridge should be closed for the safety of everybody. . . .

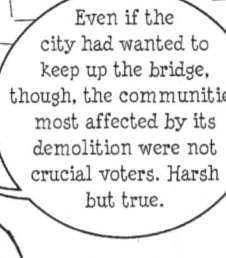

I sabotaged every conversation to talk about the end of the bridge . . .

Otherwise vandals will be able to escape by foot across the bridge-while police cars will be unable to follow them." -Meg Getz, Cherry Hill resident.

I heard something else in this talk ... I heard "vandals" and "escape" echoing from the top of Cherry Hill. I recognized the language. The bridge was already in its death throes. It had permitted only pedestrians for years.61

"they said they didn't want 'more RATS' in the park . . ."

displaced...

I read about Interstate-496, opened in 1970, and how it changed the lives of the people who were displaced by federal policies and practices.62 It changed the lives of commuters... making their time between work and home shorter and faster. *comfort...*

I could not stop thinking about it...

But there was no replacement, as the headline suggested. The bridge at the end of River Street had a long life of uncertainty that ended quite fatefully for a city pinching its pennies.

From its early beginnings as a wooden bridge, it seemed to serve its purpose for only a moment.

By 1924, its fate was under discussion-traffic did not warrant the sinking of resources into its upkeep.65 Many factories moved from the banks of the Grand to other places around the city, and with the progression of transportation and other technologies, not to mention the social movements that nearly 100 years inevitably unfold over a hundred years, the fate of the River Street bridge might have been its inevitable destruction.

It lasted until 1987 before it was disappeared by the city.66 The city contracted out the labor to take it down. Pieces of it loom greenish-gray just below the surface of the river, scattered on its banks.

We watch the bridge die, and our
memories of its life-or of the life of any
ject we share in our social *public* worlds-
nnect our experiences. These reference
ints are merely pieces of the world we
are. It is the relationship that people
ve with one another around these spaces
at makes the spaces matter.67
With its death, trauma. Not debilitating
uma, not like that of direct violence.
ther, the slow, painful departure of
mething, of an object, of meaning.

o cares, indeed.

This is not the story of the bridge as it
nds alone, or once did. This story is a
ry of people, and of those lives shared
ough connections to and through the
cial figures" in our physical, public
rlds.
These spaces of sharing are contentious
the United States. The knowledge people
p and the stories people share connect
in ways that laws and policies cannot.
, at least, restrictive power has a more
ficult time administering control and
er when communities come together
share space and experience. When
ormation/knowledge is exclusive
imming in a resort-like swimming pool
sus standing on the other side of the
ce, looking in),68 the boundaries that
efit power to keep remain in place.
ologies (racism, misogyny, homophobia)
their keepers, maintain their grips.
is is the danger nestling in "the public,"
at least, history shows the
sequences, sometimes fatal, of what
pens when people separated, come
ether for a common reasons.69
ategies of alienation are just that:
ctices within ruling relations that
anize everyday experiences.70
Demolition by neglect as a practice
anized the experiences of those whose
ryday lives involve or include these
ects of meaning.
f we walk over it everyday, we watch it
roach and it is familiar.
f we are afraid on it, and dread crossing
but can't take the time to go around to a
rdier bridge, blocks and traffic away,
t fear might linger there.

veryday life.

m my return to my warm house, down
street from the power plant that cold
uary day to these years after, the
steries of that bridge and the everyday
s that knew it, haunts me still. "*The
d as yet remains an enchanted place.*" 71

Whatever our experience,
if demolition by neglect
is in motion, how does
the "neglect" process
make a traumascape
from everyday
encounters with that
"social figure" ?72, 72a
People reported great
sadness over the razing
of their homes for the
installation of the
interstate.73 And over the
razing of the REO Plant
in the center of the
city.74 The loss of these
spaces resonates with
people, not necessarily
because of the structures
themselves, but because
of the people (the
meaning) associated with
the memories of those
spaces. We haunt one
another with the objects
that we make. We remain
when we have gone
through the structures
and pieces of the world
we share.

It is within reach, the
vision that would expose
the ghosts that most don't
remember. It is within
grasp, a different way to
see the decisions made in
the past, "*between
institution and person,
creating the possibility of
making a life, of becoming
something else, in the
present and for the
future.*"75

. . . a ghost story.

Acknowledgments

Special acknowledgment and thank you to Heidi Butler of the Capital Area District Library/Forest Park Library & Archives for her tireless work on and enthusiasm for this project. Also, to Nathan Holt of historicbridges.org, whose curiosity and interest in this project took me in directions I would not have found on my own. Without the curiosity and interest of the Clarke Historical Library, I would not have discovered the structures that made the bones of this work: maps. John T. Fierst retrieved endless old documents and provided challenging questions and suggestions all along the way of this project. Librarians are essential as the keepers of our stories—the records of our lives—especially so we can remember one another. I am grateful for their service.

Dr. A. E. Garrison is Assistant Professor of Sociology at Central Michigan University. She earned her doctorate in Rural Sociology from the University of Missouri in 2011. Her work focuses on the development of graphic sociological methodology for scholarship and pedagogy. Her graphic work includes "Ghosts of Infertility: Haunted by Realities of Reproductive Death" (2016). Garrison's research interests also include social consequences resulting from urban planning policies, impacting urban infrastructure in Rust Belt cities. Her work in this subject area includes "Boneyards of the *Sortatropolis*: Exploring a City of Industrial Secrets – Lansing, Michigan (Part 1)" (2017).

Notes

Page 121
"Original Olds Factory Site." n.d. Courtesy of Capital Area District Library (CADL)/Forest Park Library & Archives (FPLA), Lansing, MI.

Page 124
1. Butler, *Undoing Gender*, 154.
2. Hirsch, "Generation of Postmemory."
3. Gordon, *Ghostly Matters*.
4. Fine, *Story of REO Joe*.
5. The original posting detailed biographical information about the city's early capitalists/philanthropists and politicians, posted by the Lansing Regional Chamber (Chamber of Commerce). This particular page for the website is no longer available. Originally retrieved 10 September 2018 from https://www.lansingchamber.org/page/Leaders1263.
6. Bell, "Ghosts of Place."
7. Gordon, 8.
8. Gordon, 11.

Page 125
9. Fine.
10. Rothstein, *Color of Law*.
11. Surface-Evans, Chapter 9, this volume.

12. Rothstein, 127.
13. Rothstein, 131.
14. Bell, 816. A series of newspaper articles in the *Lansing State Journal*, published between 1930 and 1970, feature the bridge as a marker for various occurrences, including recreational tourism (mineral springs), car accidents, boat races, suicides, and assaults. The bridge is not the central focus but the mediator of these exchanges. It mattered.
15. Gordon, 18.

Page 126
16. Bell, 819.
17. "River Street Bridge." 1987. Caterino Postcard Collection. Courtesy CADL/FPLA.
18. Gordon, 8.

Page 128
19. "Hold Rite at Power Plant," 1.
20. Forstall, "Population of States and Counties."
21. Albright, 96.
22. Fine, 33–36.

Page 129
23. "Belvedere Park." 1890. *Lansing State Republican*, 6 December. Courtesy of CADL/FPLA.

Page 130
24. Rothstein, 139–48.
25. I had several conversations with different members of the community. This "flash" represents a "glomming" together of conversations had, casually, over one year.
26. Wiltse, *Contested Waters*.

Page 131
27. This is a multilayered illustration. The postcard (populating the pool; c. 1935) is from the Caterino Postcard Collection, courtesy of the CADL/FPLA. The postcard is layered over a digital photograph I took with my iPad mini. Finally, the figure of "me" sitting on the bench is done in pencil and ink on newsprint, digitally added to the other two layers to create the effect.
28. "River Street Bridge."
29. "[S]he or he is concerned with learning from their experience and with tracing how their everyday lives and doings are caught up in social relations and organization concerting the doings of others, although they are not discoverable from within the local experience of anyone." Smith, *Institutional Ethnography*, 61.
30. Kemp and Lowe, "Fabric of Historic Bridges," 6.

Page 132
31. Gabbara, "Bikers Ride in Solidarity," 5A.
32. Mikolajczyk and Zargara, "Moore's Park Pavilion."
33. "Moores Park Pavilion Update."
34. Heywood, "Our Crumbling City."
35. "Moores Park Pavilion Update."
36. Schor, *2018 State of the City Report*, 28.

37. National Trust for Historic Preservation, "Demolition by Neglect," 1.
38. National Trust for Historic Preservation, 1.

Page 133
39. Bell, 824.

Page 134
40. Gordon, 139.
41. Bell, 819.

Page 135
42. According to the Library of Congress, Sanborn Fire Insurance Maps are a "uniform series of large-scale maps, dating from 1867 to the present and depicting the commercial, industrial, and residential sections" of cities all over the United States (and Mexico). The maps were intended to provide insurance companies with a sense of the liability of properties, as a way to assess worth and risk. "Sanborn Maps: About This Collection," Library of Congress, retrieved 18 November 2018 from https://www.loc.gov/collections/sanborn-maps/about-this-collection/.
43. Sanborn Fire Insurance Map: Lansing, MI. 1906. Sanborn Fire Insurance Maps. Courtesy of Clarke Historical Library, Central Michigan University, Mount Pleasant, MI.
44. I have included this image with the intention of showing the thin line between what is "true" (photograph) and what is "interpreted truth" (the drawing). The number of panels in the window drawn is intentionally inaccurate, only to show the subtle, yet seemingly blurry lines between truths.

Page 136
45. "The River Street Bridge."
46. Gordon, 8.

Page 137
47. Van Wormer, Chapter 3.
48. Gordon, 3.
49. Gordon, 142.
50. "The River Street Bridge."
51. Bell, 825.
52. Bechtold, Chapter 10.
53. Cushing, "Sidewalk Stamps."
54. McGrayne, "River Street Bridge Replacement Urged," 1.

Page 138
55. "On Eve of Automotive Age, Michigan's Capital City Was a Sturdy Community of Homes and Industries." Drawn and Published by C. J. Pauli & Co. Courtesy of Clarke Historical Library.
56. "The River Street Bridge."

Page 139
57. Surface-Evans, Chapter 9.
58. Personal photograph, taken 26 June 2018 on River Street, Lansing, Michigan. This sidewalk panel is nearly overgrown with grass and is quite uneven. It is badly cracked,

but the stamp itself is very clear. This sidewalk panel would not be visible from a car. Exploration by foot is a required aspect of summoning ghosts and welcoming a haunting.

Page 141
59. "Bridges Unsafe Says Engineer," 1.
60. Direct quotations, and inspiration for this drawing, from McGrayne, "River Street Bridge Replacement Urged." Please see the newspaper for the record.
61. "River Street Bridge for Pedestrians, Plan," 26.

Page 142
62. Miller, "Looking Back: I-496 Construction."
63. "River Street Bridge." 1948. Carl Dalrymple Collection. Courtesy of CADL/FPLA.
64. This drawing was inspired by Grose, "Old Bridge in Limbo," 11. See this reference for the record.
65. "Bridges Unsafe Says Engineer";
66. "Place South Span of River Street Bridge," 1.

Page 143
67. Bell, 816.
68. Wiltse, 2.
69. Wiltse, 123–24. Social controls enforced by police officers or other appointed officials work to maintain boundaries, preventing intimacy that might otherwise undo the privileges that exist in white supremacy.
70. Smith, *Writing the Social*, 73–95.
71. Bell, 832.
72. Tumarkin, *Traumascapes*; Surface-Evans, Chapter 10.
73. Miller, 8A.
74. White, "Reo Plant Coming Down," 1.
75. Gordon, 142.

References

Albright, John B. 1978. "Stack Project to Change Skyline." *Lansing State Journal*, 14 July, 96.
Bell, Michael Mayerfeld. 1997. "The Ghosts of Place." *Theory and Society* 26(6): 813–836.
"Bridges Unsafe Says Engineer." 1919. *Lansing State Journal*, 24 September, 1.
Butler, Judith. 2004. *Undoing Gender*. New York: Routledge.
Cushing, Lincoln. n.d. "Sidewalk Stamps." Docs Populi website. Retrieved 9 June 2018 from http://www.docspopuli.org/articles/Stamps/Presentation.html.
Dozier, Vickki. 2018. "Project Will Tell the Story of How I-496 Construction Impacted Lansing's Black Community." *Lansing State Journal*, 4 December. Retrieved 2 January 2019 from https://www.lansingstatejournal.com/story/news/2018/12/04/interstate-496-black-communityhistorical-society/2154723002/.
Fine, Lisa. 2004. *The Story of REO Joe: Work, Kin, and Community in Autotown, U.S.A.* Philadelphia: Temple University Press.
Forstall, Richard L. 1996. "Population of States and Counties of the United States: 1790–1990." Report No. PB96-119060, March. Washington, DC: Department of Commerce, US Bureau of the Census, Population Division. Retrieved 1 July 2013 from

https://www.census.gov/population/www/censusdata/PopulationofStatesandCountiesoftheUnitedStates1790-1990.pdf.

Gabbara, Princess. 2017. "Bikers Ride in Solidarity to Save the Moores Park Pavilion." *Lansing State Journal*, 26 July, 5A.

Garrison, A. E. 2017. "Boneyards of the *Sortatropolis*: Exploring a City of Industrial Secrets: Lansing, Michigan—Part I." *Michigan Sociological Review* 31: 27–54.

Gordon, Avery F. 2008. *Ghostly Matters: Haunting and the Sociological Imagination*, 2nd edn. Minneapolis: University of Minnesota Press.

Grose, Tom. 1981. "Old Bridge in Limbo." *Lansing State Journal*, 5 May, 11.

Heywood, Todd. 2017. "Our Crumbling City: Picnic in the Pavilion? Not at Moore's River Park." *City Pulse*, 17 May. Retrieved 18 May 2017 from https://lansingcitypulse.com/article-14798-Ourcrumbling-city.html.

Hirsch, Marianne. 2008. "The Generation of Postmemory." *Poetics Today* 29(1): 103–128.

"Hold Rite at Power Plant: Cornerstone Laying Is Directed by Masons." 1922. *Lansing State Journal*, 5 August, 1

Kemp, Emory L., and Jet Lowe. 1989. "The Fabric of Historic Bridges." *Journal of the Society for Industrial Archeology* 15(2): 3–22.

McGrayne, Sharon. 1982. "River Street Bridge Replacement Urged." *Lansing State Journal*, 13 September, 1.

Mikolajczyk, M. T., and Zargara, C. M. 2017. "Moore's Park Pavilion – Inspection Summary of Finding and Recommendations." Mannik Smith Group, Inc. correspondence to Mitch Whistler (assistant city engineer), City of Lansing, Michigan. Retrieved 20 December 2019 from http://mooresparkneighborhood.com/moores-park-pavilion-updates.

Miller, Mark. 2009. "Looking Back: I-496 Construction, a Complicated Legacy." *Lansing State Journal*, 22 February, 1, 8A.

"Moores Park Pavilion Update." 2017. Moores Park Neighborhood Organization website, 29 June. Retrieved 12 July 2018 from http://mooresparkneighborhood.com/moores-park-pavilion-updates.

National Trust for Historic Preservation. 2009. "Demolition by Neglect." Preservation Law Educational Materials. Washington, DC: National Trust for Historic Preservation.

"On Eve of Automotive Age, Michigan's Capital City Was a Sturdy Community of Homes and Industries." 1890. Drawn & Published by C.J. Pauli & Co. Courtesy of Clarke Historical Library.

"Place South Span of River Street Bridge." 1919. *Lansing State Journal*, 24 September, 1.

"River Street Bridge for Pedestrians, Plan." 1924. *Lansing State Journal*, 20 June, 26.

Rothstein, Richard. 2017. *The Color of Law: A Forgotten History of How Our Government Segregated America*. New York: Liveright.

Schor, Andy. 2018. *2018 State of the City Report*. Lansing, MI, 22 January.

Smith, Dorothy E. 2004. *Writing the Social: Critique, Theory, and Investigations*. Toronto: University of Toronto Press.

———. 2005. *Institutional Ethnography: A Sociology for People*. Lanham, MD: AltaMira Press.

Tumarkin, Maria. 2005. *Traumascapes: The Power and Fate of Places Transformed by Tragedy*. Melbourne: Melbourne University Press.

White, Otis. 1979. "Reo Plant Coming Down for (Pretty) Sure." *Lansing State Journal*, 4 January, 1.

Wiltse, Jeffrey. 2007. *Contested Waters: A Social History of Swimming Pools in America*. Chapel Hill: University of North Carolina Press.

CHAPTER 9

Traumascapes
Progress and the Erasure of the Past

SARAH SURFACE-EVANS

By their very nature, cityscapes are haunted landscapes. Cities are the accumulation of memories, lives, and the assorted material culture left behind by many generations, both inhabitants and visitors. This complex accumulation of artifacts, memories, and material culture is what archaeologists would refer to as a palimpsest: a thing with many layers or stories beneath the surface. The traces of those who came before us are often quite literally buried beneath our feet, to be remembered or forgotten. In a sense, ghosts can only exist because of the living. Our minds, memories, and artifacts act as the repository for what happened or existed in the past. Perhaps it is this notion of persistence that attracted me to archaeology in the first place; I experienced the death and loss of many family members as a child and young adult. Throughout my life, I have carried their ghosts with me and feel their ghosts remaining in the places of my childhood. They are comforting ghosts. But not all ghostly hauntings are positive—many specters are created by trauma—and it is a form of negative haunting that I consider in this chapter. I seek to uncover the specters of gentrification—a very specific type of haunting that I propose is created by and perpetuates trauma.

The cities of the American Midwest are relatively young in comparison to some of the world's cities, but they are haunted nonetheless. They are haunted by progress. They are haunted by the machinery of capitalism and the inevitable classism and racism that accompanies capitalism. American cities are imagined as places of newness, innovation, and progress (Mallach 2018), leaving no space for grieving what is lost. Many programs and policies throughout the twentieth century and the beginning of the twenty-first century have sought to refresh and remake American cities, often with disastrous consequences for minorities and the working poor (González 2017; Mallach 2018). In urban landscapes across the United States, federal, state, and local policies have favored the "growth machine" model, which places the goals and needs of bankers and businesses over middle-class and poor city dwellers (González 2017). Such policies include urban renewal, redlining, spatial deconcentration, and White Flight, all of which had the cumulative effect of decreasing the overall housing available to low-income families and increasing the racial segregation of urban spaces. In recent years, neoliberal policies coupled with disaster capitalism have accelerated gentrification of regions hard hit by the 2008 Great Recession (González 2017; Mallach 2018).

City leadership is often complicit in hastening gentrification in marginalized communities by divesting public properties and placing them into private ownership for development (Mallach 2018). Typically, such development is claimed to be an investment and revitalization of so-called blighted areas. But as Alan Mallach points out, the application of such investment is piecemeal and has led to increased "economic sorting" and the "hollowing out" of the middle class within urban spaces (2018: 37). New York mayor Bill De Blasio described this phenomenon as America's "tale of two cities" (González 2017: 3). Gentrification is the deliberate control of land and transformation of place, to suit the desires of wealthy white elites. Often another consequence of gentrification is the erasure of memories of the past and control of the narrative of the present and future (Epstein 2016). This process effectively seeks to silence diverse histories, ignore dissenting voices, and whitewash the past.

As an archaeologist living the last twenty years in the postindustrial landscape of Lansing, Michigan, I came to know the history and character of the various neighborhoods and communities that make up this city. As gentrification slowly began to take root I was haunted by the forced erasure of the past and dislocation of personal and community memories that were once found within the cityscape around me. One day while on a run along a familiar path, I was struck by the devastation that surrounded me (Illustrations 9.1a through 9.1c). All the trees had recently been cut down in a park that the city was selling for development. Construction of a new condo loomed above, towering disproportionately over the rest of the neighboring buildings (Illustration 9.1a). Meanwhile, an artist had been commissioned to paint pleasant murals in the highway underpass. While the new mural covered graffiti and might be thought of as an improvement, the project displaced the homeless individuals who had once sheltered here. This action further harmed the already displaced and forgotten members of our community.

A few blocks away, the familiar edifices of historic community shops and restaurants had been torn down to make way for more condos (Illustration 9.1b). In the process, the developer and local business were trying to rebrand the Eastside neighborhood as "East Town" (Illustration 9.1c) (Ross 2014). Residents saw this rebranding as an attempt to erase the sense of place that longtime community members maintained for themselves. Meanwhile, many

Illustrations 9.1a to 9.1c. Aspects of gentrification (construction, demolition, and rebranding) I pass by regularly while walking and running in my neighborhood. Photos by the author.

houses in the neighborhood have remained empty and abandoned since the 2008 Great Recession (Hinkley and Mencarini 2017).

While some might welcome these changes and call them "progress," they transformed the neighborhood without the consent of those who live here. None of these improvements provided relief for those in need in the community. I felt these changes as a deliberate erasure of community memory and identity. Every time I walked or ran in my neighborhood, I had a profound sense of loss. The ghosts of what was erased now lingered in the back of my mind as I moved through my neighborhood day to day. Walking provides the perspective and time for contemplation—in these moments, the change around me felt traumatic and I felt powerless. It was in this space that I realized the violence of gentrification to create traumascapes.

Defining Traumascapes

For my purposes, "trauma" is perhaps best defined from the psychological or emotional perspective: a disorientation of experience or memory. Social worker Laura van Dernoot Lipsky further defines the concept of "trauma exposure response" as "the transformation that takes place within us as a result of exposure to suffering," leading the "world to look and feel like a different place to you as a result" (2009: 41). This underscores the realization that trauma is cumulative, that repeated exposure to traumatic events or sights can fundamentally alter how we experience the world around us.

Psychologists and social workers have also noted the temporal and social nature of trauma and how it can be transmitted through generations as "historical trauma." Historical trauma has been recognized in the cases of the Holocaust, the Vietnam War, and Federal Indian boarding schools, to name just a few (Caruth 1991; Faimon 2004; Hirsch 2012; Schönfelder 2013; Sheffield 2011). Another way to conceptualize historical trauma is as "postmemory." As defined by Marianne Hirsch, "postmemory describes the relationship of the second generation to powerful, often traumatic, experiences that preceded their births but that were nevertheless transmitted to them so deeply as to seem to constitute memories in their own right" (2012: 29). In other words, traumatic memories can be transferred intergenerationally.

I became familiar with the phenomenon of historical trauma when I began community-based archaeology with the Saginaw Chippewa Tribe of Michigan, on the Mount Pleasant Indian Industrial Boarding School in 2011 (Surface-Evans 2016; Surface-Evans and Jones n.d.). The colonizing program of Federal Indian boarding schools was immensely traumatic for Native American communities throughout the United States (Adams 1995; Fear-Segal 2007). It produced a legacy of historical trauma that Native American communities are still struggling to heal from (Sheffield 2011). During my research, I witnessed the powerful ability of community-based archaeology to generate healing from this trauma by empowering communities to take control of the historical narrative of the boarding school era. It was this memory work and consideration of colonialism as a form of haunting (Surface-Evans and Jones, forthcoming) that led me to draw parallels between historical trauma and the gentrification I experienced in my own community. As gentrification intensified, I increasingly felt my neighborhood transformed into a traumascape.

Maria Tumarkin (2005) defines traumascapes as places that have been marked by traumatic events. This phenomenon is significant to me as an archaeologist who studies how people interact with their landscape and environment. In other words, trauma can become associated with or embedded in places. Tumarkin's examples are primarily related to places that have experienced traumatic death or violence associated with acts of terrorism. However, I argue that traumascapes can encompass a wider variety of places. The common theme and defining characteristic of traumascapes is their historical significance as a consequence of the trauma that people experience and/or witness at these places and the haunting specters that such trauma leaves behind on the landscape (Gordon 1997; Starzmann and Roby 2016; Tumarkin 2005). In other words, places become associated with and defined by their traumatic past (Bell 1997). Through witnessing or experiencing the trauma and the social and personal transference of these memories, places can become traumascapes. Therefore, it is possible to understand that a range of traumascapes can exist, some more harmful than others.

For example, many of the Great Lakes lighthouses where I conduct archaeological work are often defined by traumatic events, such as shipwrecks near their shores or the untimely deaths of lighthouse keepers or their family members (Surface-Evans 2015). Such traumatic happenings frame the historic narrative of these sites and, in the case of lighthouses, create a sense of nostalgia that is often capitalized on by heritage tourism. (Everyone knows that lighthouses are haunted places. I will save my own ghost stories from a rainy October stay in the oldest lighthouse on the Great Lakes for another time.) These sites are a category of traumascape defined by a traumatic moment or moments, but the nature of this trauma is not fundamentally contested or complicated. Rather, these happenings create real or imagined drama that empathetically connects visitors to these spaces and places through storytelling (see Beisaw, Chapter 1). Nostalgia, as discussed by Brigitte Bechtold in Chapter 10, is a mirage that simplifies our vision of the past. I am not taking up the discussion of nostalgia here; rather, I hope to demonstrate that some types of traumas leave behind unsettled specters on a landscape.

In my archaeological work I have also encountered a second type of traumascape, which is the result of systematic violence and oppression. I have found this type of traumascape often associated with institutions, such as Federal Indian boarding schools, prisoner-of-war camps, and even Civilian Conservation Corps (CCC) camps and company-owned lumber camps. In these cases, structural violence imposed by colonialism, capitalism, racism, and classism create contested experiences of trauma that are defined by the complexity of individual experience and identity. Put another way, the memories emplaced in these traumascapes are contested or even dangerous. Michalinos Zembylas and Zvi Bekerman define dangerous memories as "those memories that are disruptive to the status quo, that is, the hegemonic culture of strengthening and perpetuating existing group-based identities" (2008: 125). Narratives of memory at such traumascapes are complicated by the suppression of some voices and the erasure of power for communities to maintain their own identity. The intentional silencing of certain narratives of the past leads to a different sense of haunting—that which is missing. As defined by sociologist Avery Gordon, a contested haunting occurs when "the oppressed past or the ghostly will shock us into recognizing its animating force" (1997: 66). Gentrified places fit within this "dangerous" type of traumascape because of the contested nature of these haunted landscapes.

In one aspect the "sense" of haunting prevents erasure, even when some stories are actively erased by structural oppression and power. Yet there is violence in forgetting. Once communities lose their physical connection to their past and their identities through gentrification and demolition, trauma becomes embedded in the landscape. Extra burdens are placed on those who are left to do the work of remembering, especially if that remembering is a narrative of the past that is different from that of those in power. According to social worker Mary Beth Faimon, "remembering and mourning are critical" in "addressing the historical trauma" (2004: 241). This is why the intentional destruction and disorientation of community places through gentrification is so damaging. As the features of the landscape in which personal and community memories are embedded are eroded away, people become dispossessed of their identity and memories. They are haunted by what was but can never be again.

For example, one evening not so long ago, my eldest son was having a hard time. To help him process his day and feelings, we went for a walk. During this walk, we explored a courtyard between two old buildings in a block near our house. We goofed around taking pictures of the way the light and shadow played off the old bricks (Illustrations 9.2a and 9.2b) and took selfies. This space represented a moment of creativity, sharing, and unwinding. It was a passing moment, but because of the emotions connected to this place, my son remembered it and talked about it often. Sometime later, those buildings were demolished to make way for a four-story mixed-use development (Illustrations 9.2c and 9.2d). We both mourn the loss of that special place to which we can no longer return. It exists only in our minds now and preserved in a few random pictures—the meaning and importance of which is only known to us. The

Illustrations 9.2a to 9.2d. Photos of an old building, taken while on a walk with my son; and the demolition of the same building.
Photos by the author.

ghosts of those moments are now displaced from the landscape and wandering restlessly.

Now imagine this phenomenon magnified and amplified over the space of a city, in all of the spaces and places important to people for various reasons. Many of these places might be intimate, like houses; others might be public or shared with others, like parks, churches, factories, and workplaces (Bechtold, Chapter 10). These are the spaces in which we live our lives and to which we have personal connections, where we make our memories (Halbwachs 1992). As these places disappear, so too do our physical connections to our memories and ourselves, in both the individual and collective sense. Places often represent mnemonic devices that help us recall the past and connect us to others. As Bechtold discusses in Chapter 10, these cultural resources represent an "intellectual commons," storing memories for a community.

Public parks, perhaps more than other types of spaces, are integral for building community identity and cohesion—what city planners call "place making." What makes these places important, are their connections to people and memory. During the era of civic capitalism, when industrial entrepreneurs were more invested in the communities where they lived and owned factories, they also funded the construction of civic projects, such as parks, pools, and museums (Garrison, Chapter 8; Mallach 2018). Often, the establishment of public parks was tied to paternalistic views by the wealthy elite of caring for the health and well-being of the working class (Jordan 1994). Parks, especially gardens, were seen as a means to "refine" and improve the morality of the working class (Jordan 1994: 86; Loukaitou-Sideris and Stieglitz 2002). While such public improvement of urban spaces appears altruistic, it was also tied to the growing union movement and seen as a way to curb their power (Mallach 2018). These trends speak of whom the "public" were conceived to be: white, working-class citizens of the city (see Garrison, Chapter 8).

The intersections of race and class are equally important today, when examining inequalities in park location and maintenance. The "shrinkage and privatization of the public realm" has decimated parks in urban settings (Loukaitou-Sideris and Stieglitz 2002: 472). The perception of parks by public planners has changed, such that they now view urban parks as a breeding ground for "urban pathology" (471). The consequence is a ready-made justification for the privatization of public parks. Class and race are factors that determine which public spaces are valued, protected, and remembered. This brings me to the story of a particular traumascape: a public park birthed by industrialization (Hasbrook 2016) and ultimately destroyed by deindustrialization and gentrification. It is the story of a traumascape that continues to haunt me and the Lansing community.

The telling of this story is difficult for me, because it is not complete but still evolving. As a disorienting experience, where do you start in the telling? In the past, the present, or the future? Somewhere in the middle? Time is compressed in trauma (Tumarkin 2005). And how do I tell the story of this particular trauma without reference to the many traumas that exist within this cityscape? As in many cities in America today, those who remain within the urban core of Lansing have been repeatedly traumatized by the erasure of community memories and meanings in the name of progress. While I could talk about how highways bisected neighborhoods, or how housing policies displaced and marginalized communities, or how the loss of industrial employment and other aspects of deindustrialization continue to economically isolate the urban landscape, the greatest recent assault on Lansing community identity has come in the form of park privatization and destruction.

In the past decade Lansing leadership has eroded the public assets of the city by selling off or demolishing numerous park spaces, typically after a period of intentional neglect and often under a cloud of suspicion (Alusheff 2017; Balaskovitz 2014; Heywood 2016a, 2017; Kaminski 2018). The privatization and divestment of parks has primarily affected working-class and minority neighborhoods, where people have less access to cars or other transportation out of the city to enjoy State Parks or private recreation facilities. Yet research shows that urban parks are more heavily used and valued by neighboring communities than are parks in suburban or rural settings (Loukaitou-Sideris and Stieglitz 2002). Various community stakeholders attempted to halt demolition of public spaces in Lansing and formed grassroots organizations to amplify their collective voices. Despite these efforts, public parks have been repeatedly divested or destroyed. The final straw for many was the proposed demolition of Scott Park for the Board of Water and Light Central Substation project.

Trauma, Haunting, and Gentrification: A Lansing Case Study

In February of 2016, while the rest of the country watched the US presidential election heating up, people in Lansing were just learning about a plan to demolish a prized historic garden to make way for an electrical substation ("BWL Announces" 2016). Scott Park, which included a landscaped sunken garden and adjacent historic home, was used by Lansing residents as a quiet oasis in the midst of industrial development (Illustration 9.3a). The land was owned by the City of Lansing, given in trust by the Scott family in the 1960s (Lee 2010). The park contains many ghosts. The specters of Lansing and Michigan history touch this place in many ways. There are specters of industrialization and capitalism and specters of racial injustice and justice. These ghost stories are woven over 150 years of history.

In 1930, the sunken garden was commissioned by Richard Scott, who owned a house adjacent to the parcel. Scott's importance to Lansing history is significant, as he was an engineer who worked alongside Ransom E. Olds to create the REO Motor Car Company. It is impossible to think of Lansing without REO: the history of the city is the history of the auto company (Bray and DuShane 2009). Scott went on to serve as president of REO Motors from 1923 to 1945 (Christensen 2016; Lee 2010). A local Lansing artisan, Nick Isaac Willem Kriek, designed the garden for Scott (Christensen 2016). The sunken garden itself was designed on the limestone foundation of the former home of Michigan Supreme Court Justice Edward Cahill ("The Scott House" 2016). While Cahill has many notable achievements, he is best known in the community for his role in supporting African American civil rights in the nineteenth century. Cahill raised and led the first African American infantry unit in Michigan during the Civil War. He is also linked to a Michigan Supreme Court decision in 1890 that prohibited racial discrimination in public spaces ("Photo Gallery" 2016; Putnam 2016b).

The Scott family demolished their mansion and donated the land containing the sunken garden to the city when Interstate 496 was built mere feet from their property in the 1960s (Lee 2010; Garrison considers the politics and racial undertones of the highway construction in Chapter 8). The historic house in the park today is not the Scott home but that of local businessman Orien A. Jenison. His Tudor-style house was built in 1918 and relocated to Scott Park by the City of Lansing in 1978 (Illustration 9.3b) (Cosentino 2017). The Jenison house originally served as the Art and Garden Center for the community but was left to fall into disrepair in the early 2000s. Despite this complicated past, many in the Lansing community view Scott Park as a symbol of Michigan's civil rights history (Putnam 2016b). The community reaction to the proposed demolition of the park for the Board of Water and Light (BWL) substation project shows that this place is an important anchor for community memories.

The substation was part of a multiyear plan to phase out the aging Otto E. Eckert coal plant and shift to a new natural gas power plant ("BWL Announces" 2016). The three stacks of the Eckert plant, affectionately called "Wynken, Blynken, and Nod" by Lansing locals, can be seen from anywhere in the city and are iconic of the Lansing skyline (more so than the dome of the state capitol) (see Garrison, Chapter 8). The community was told that the substation could not be built on alternative locations owing to existing infrastructure limitations, costs, and needs of businesses located downtown ("Alternate Location" 2016; Nelson 2016b). Rather than selling the property to the utility company, which would require a ballot vote, the city aimed to change the park's zoning by a special land-use permit to allow the substation, effectively side-stepping the democratic process. The Lansing Parks and Recreation Board and Development and Planning Board both voted in favor of the special permit (Nelson 2016a). City officials and BWL justified the decision in terms of the park being "under-utilized" (Palmer 2016). This determination ignored

Illustrations 9.3a and 9.3b. The Scott Garden and Jenison House. Photos by the author.

the fact that three African American communities were located within walking distance of this park—Cherry Hill, Moores Park, and REO Town (Figure 9.1)—and that Scott Park is located in an otherwise industrial area with few green spaces. Additionally, the primary beneficiaries of the substation were not the residential neighborhoods in which it would be situated but local industry (primarily General Motors) and state government.

The plan put forth by BWL was to demolish the historic sunken garden and Jenison house to build the substation ("BWL Announces" 2016). The utility tried to soften the blow by arguing that it was beautifying the community and offering a place for public art on the wall that would surround the substation. This was particularly offensive to community, as nearby REO Town is known for its vibrant tradition of homegrown street art (Associated Press 2018; Paisley 2017). Before city council voted on the permit and accompanying zoning change, public backlash against the project was immediate (Dozier 2016; Illitch 2016a, 2016b; Putnam 2016b; Stanaway 2016).

Community activism developed among the neighborhood associations nearby. Historical societies, environmental groups, and gardening organizations were all outspoken opponents of the park destruction (Nelson 2016a, 2006b; Schwartz 2016). Michigan universities and experts from the State Historic Preservation Office went on record in support of the historic and ecological significance of the site (Carrington 2016; Christensen 2016; Donnelly 2017). Advocates from the Historical Society of Michigan and the Cultural Landscape Foundation got the story into the regional and national news (Nelson 2016a, 2016b). Descendants of the Scott family, seen often in tears at city council meetings, spoke out about the fact that their gift to the city had been

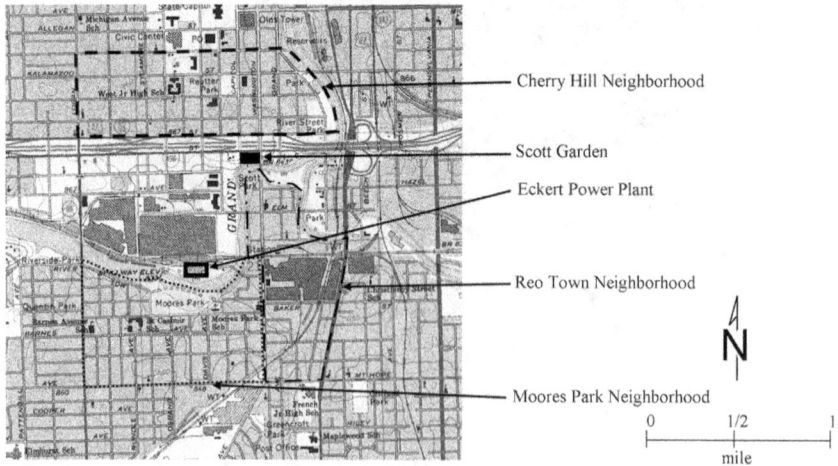

Figure 9.1. Map of neighborhoods near Scott Garden.
Map by the author.

betrayed (Donnelly 2017; Gracia-Wing, McClurken, and O'Brien 2016; Putnam 2016b; Rosado 2016). Activists held multiple rallies and protests and circulated petitions.

All of the different stakeholders were united through social media and their love of the park. To counteract the notion that the park was not utilized, several social media campaigns highlighted the various ways the community used the park. Thousands of community members shared photographs showing their relationship with the garden through the memories created there and special occasions marked in this intimate space: birthdays, graduations, weddings, and just quiet moments of contemplation. For several months, every time the substation was on the agenda at a city council meeting, hundreds of citizens would show up and give hours of public comment in allotted three-minute chunks of time (Illitch 2016b). Pain and desperation were palpable in many of their voices.

A coalition of diverse stakeholders formed the Friends of Scott Sunken Garden in an attempted to negotiate with the city and BWL to halt the project. They also spearheaded a letter-writing campaign to persuade General Motors, which owns all the land surrounding the park, to offer a portion of its unused land for the substation (Nelson 2016a). You would think that with all the vocal opposition to the park's destruction, this story would have a happy ending. Unfortunately, this is not the case for Scott Park, like many gentrified traumascapes.

When it became clear that the project was a "done deal," the coalition of stakeholders shifted their approach from stopping the project to mitigating its effects on the park. An attempt was made to find land to which the Jenison house could be moved, with community stakeholders working with Habitat for Humanity. In May of 2016, Mayor Virg Bernero announced a deal in which the city would sell land to Habitat for one dollar, provided that the organization paid to move the house (Heywood 2016b; Parker 2016; Putnam 2016a). Unfortunately, city council never approved this plan. Even if they had, the $90,000 price tag to move the house caused Habitat to walk away from the plan (Putnam 2016a). Ultimately, the failed plan resulted in the house being destroyed, to the outrage and grief of the community, in December 2016. Ironically, the city demolished it after having gone to much effort to save the home less than forty years prior (Donnelly 2017; Smith 2017). My research of newspapers uncovered prior discussion of the costs related to maintaining the house, in 2010. The city's prior strategy was simply demolition of the historic house through neglect (McNamara 2010).

When it came to saving the garden itself, the community was deeply divided. Many were unwilling to work with the city or BWL to minimize the impact on the garden simply out of principle—because of the lack of public accountability and transparency. Trust between the people of Lansing and city officials had been broken. However, a contingent of stakeholders, including gardening clubs and neighborhood organizations surrounding the park, decided to find a compromise ("Preliminary Meeting" 2016). They worked with BWL leadership to create plans for the removal and reconstruction of the garden in another Lansing park, the nearby Cooley Gardens (Schwartz and Omeish 2016). BWL agreed to front the costs for this move and create a $40,000 endowment for the long-term care of the garden. While many viewed this as a sellout, some saw it as a victory ("Editorial" 2016). Certainly, BWL used this agreement to its own political advantage, touting the plan as an "innovative design to capture [the] area's history and to link downtown Lansing with Reo Town" ("BWL Announces" 2016). Sadly, it is the community's own history that is being destroyed by this project.

Those against the plan worried about whether BWL would follow through with its pledge and note that the plan still contributes to a reduction of park space in Lansing as well as destroying the historic setting of the original garden. Seeing both sides of the argument, I attempted to inject a component of salvage archaeology into the proposed garden move and offered to conduct the work on BWL's timetable with student and community volunteers; however, I was ultimately unsuccessful in this bid, as neither the city nor BWL would consent to the investigations.

Demolition of the garden started with cutting down hundred-year-old trees on the property in the spring of 2017. These trees had born witness to the past. They had shaded and comforted many a Lansing resident. Community reaction to this loss was shock and sadness. Images of the destruction, along with expressions of trauma, quickly circulated through social media. In response, BWL erected screens around the property to prevent the community from being able to see the demolition of the garden. Since then, BWL has attempted to sanitize its assault on the community ("Scott Center House Demolished" 2017). BWL's general manager, Dick Peffley, was quoted as saying, "We're pleased to be able to help contribute to building the gateway to REO Town" ("Lansing BWL" 2018). The BWL website describes the project as an "upgrade to Scott Sunken Garden" that was approved by all community partners ("Project Overview" 2016). BWL held multiple design charettes; although poorly attended by the community, the utility used these meetings to claim there was community engagement in the design process (Rzepecki 2016).

As the walls of the substation emerged in 2018, along with the towers of the electrical infrastructure behind it, the community was continually reminded of the destruction of the park that had once existed (Illustration 9.4a). In the spring of 2018, BWL announced a request for proposals to install murals surrounding the substation walls in partnership with the local arts council. This "community art" project, touted as an "investment in the community" (Hillman 2018), has the effect of invalidating the existing grassroots and local arts in the community. While the murals have not yet been installed, the "three stacks" of the Eckert power plant were reproduced as a sculpture on the substation wall (see Illustration 9.4b). The stacks, which are a powerful symbol of Lan-

Illustrations 9.4a and 9.4b. The substation and walls during construction. Note the "three stacks" motif in Illustration 9.4b, with the actual stacks in the background. The blank panels on either side of the "three stacks" sculpture are meant for artist-commissioned murals. Photos by the author.

sing identity, will eventually be removed by BWL. Their reproduction on the substation wall forever ties together the destruction of these two important community touchstones.

Here we see how this substation project creates a traumascape of gentrification. The defining characteristics are the presence of structural inequality and the forced dislocation of memory from the landscape. The needs of city and business leaders outweighed those of the community, leading to the destruction of a prized public space in a majority minority neighborhood. The plans to destroy the park were initially made with no public oversight, and later, minimal compromise was made even in the face of overwhelming and coordinated community criticism.

The community is traumatized repeatedly over a period of several years, during the controversial decision, during demolition, and now during construction of the substation. The last insult is the deliberate erasure of the memory of Scott Park and the recent public struggle to preserve that history via public art projects. As Griffin Epstein (2016) discusses, public art is often a tool of gentrification used to legitimize and reinforce structural inequality and erase dissenting voices. The burden of remembering is placed on the affected community who lost the physical connection to their past and identity. As of the writing this chapter, the murals have not yet been painted or announced to the public. Nor has the reconstructed garden been unveiled. Many in the community are skeptical that BWL will uphold its promise to provide any green space.

Protecting the Past for Communities

Memory has a material component that is significant for all societies and communities to connect to their past and their identity (Begun, Chapter 2; Halbwachs 1992; Sabloff 2008; Van Wormer, Chapter 3). Objects, buildings, and their traces are important triggers for shared identity and experiences (Bechtold, Chapter 10). We must also acknowledge that the past is contested: not all voices are heard equally, because social inequality forces some stories to be forgotten or hidden (Lawton, Chapter 4; Starzmann and Roby 2016; Supernant, Chapter 6). It is in this contested experience and traumatic past that some ghosts are manifested. As Lilian Brislen discusses in Chapter 7, running from the ghosts of trauma only intensifies their power.

Our perspectives as social scientists allow us to turn our gaze upon and confront these specters (see also Lawton, Chapter 4; Supernant, Chapter 6). Much of my recent archaeological work has focused on bringing the voices of children, women, and the working class—those whose stories are not told by dominant narratives—to the forefront (Surface-Evans 2016; Surface-Evans and Jones n.d.). This research takes an activist stance, attempting to subvert the narratives of the powerful and allow the telling of alternative narratives of history by the powerless. In essence, community-based research seeks to reanimate and expose minority experiences hidden or forgotten through hegemony. This work facilitates healing and empowerment for communities and decolonizes our discipline.

Such a perspective about the past can also play a role in protecting relatively recent landscapes of trauma from erasure. Like Barbara Little and Paul Shackel (2007), M. Jay Stottman (2010), Edward González-Tennant (2018), and others, I argue that archaeologists can promote social justice through critical engagement with the past. For me, this means bringing my skills as an archaeologist into my community. During the Scott Park controversy, I testified before city council, wrote letters to city leadership, and even offered to conduct archaeological testing at the park before its demolition. Unfortunately, this was not enough to save the garden this time. But since the loss of Scott Park, I have played an even more active part in helping my community heal from this trauma. I joined the county historical commission and became a board member of Preservation Lansing. In my role in these positions, I can collaborate with other stakeholders and create links with natural allies such as neighborhood associations, historical societies and commissions, preservation organizations, parks organizations, and environmental groups. Together we work to heal from the trauma of gentrification and protect community memory on their own terms.

For example, we help to increase homeownership rates of historic houses in Lansing through providing small grants and working with the county land bank. We work with and support progressive developers who seek to restore and repurpose historic structures for low- and moderate-income housing. We collaborate with local Native American tribes and community organizations on issues of preservation advocacy and develop education and outreach programming. Together, we support a shared vision for social justice through heritage and environmental preservation. Only through collaboration do we have the potential to subvert the notions of "progress" that create ghosts.

As those affected by historical trauma have learned, telling and sharing stories—keeping memories alive—is vital for healing from trauma (Faimon 2004). It will be interesting to see how Lansing moves forward from the Scott Park incident. Will Lansing choose to forget and hide the wound, allowing gentrification to fester and create yet another Lansing ghost story (Bray and DuShane 2009; Carpenter 2018)? Or will Lansing residents fight to keep the memories alive and reclaim the voice of the people? At least for now it appears that the community refuses to let the struggle be forgotten. For my own part, my family and I still share stories about our time spent in the Scott Park garden and mark its passing like we would the loss of a good friend.

Dr. Sarah Surface-Evans is Associate Professor of Anthropology at Central Michigan University. Her community-based archaeological research investigates cultural landscapes in the Great Lakes region of the United States. Her recent publication "A Landscape of Assimilation and Resistance: The Mount Pleasant Indian Industrial Boarding School" in the *International Journal of Historical Archaeology* examines the gendered and powered components of institutional design at Federal Indian Boarding Schools. This ongoing research was recognized for a Michigan Governor's Award for Historic Preservation in 2016. She has a forthcoming publication that utilizes "haunting" as a way conceptualize the trauma of colonial landscapes.

References

Adams, David W. 1995. *Education for Extinction: American Indian and the Boarding School Experience, 1875–1928*. Lawrence: University Press of Kansas.

"Alternate Location for Central Substation Too Costly." 2016. Media release. Lansing: Board of Water & Light, 13 April. Retrieved 30 June 2016 from https://www.lbwl.com/...BWL/News/BWL—Alternate-Location-for-Central-Substation-Too-Costly.

Alusheff, Alexander. 2017. "Why Red Cedar, Park District Projects Could Get a Boost." *Lansing State Journal*, 27 February.

Associated Press. 2018. "Lansing Murals Share Stories, Connect Community." *WILX News*, 17 September. Retrieved 15 November 2018 from https://www.wilx.com/content/news/Lansing-murals-share-stories-connect-community-493493461.html.

Balaskovitz, Andy. 2014. "Frandor Owner Suing City over Red Cedar Project." *City Pulse*, 3 April. Retrieved 30 June 2016 from http://lansingcitypulse.com/article-10061-Updated-Frandor-owner-suing-city-over-Red-Cedar-project.html.

Bell, Michael Mayerfeld. 1997. "The Ghosts of Place." *Theory and Society* 26(6): 813–836.

Bray, Nicole, and Rev. Robert DuShane. 2009. *Paranormal Lansing*. Atglen, PA: Schiffer.

"BWL ANNOUNCES NEW SUBSTATION PROJECT." Board of Water and Light (BWL), 10 February 2016, Retrieved 30 June 2016 from lansingenergytomorrow.com/news/bwl-announces-new-substation-project/.

Carpenter, Jenn. 2018. *Haunted Lansing*. Charleston: The History Press.

Carrington, Peter. 2016. "Sunken Garden Can't Be Relocated." *Lansing State Journal*, 12 September.

Caruth, Cathy. 1991. "Introduction." In "Psychoanalysis, Culture, and Trauma," special issue, *American Imago* 48(1): 1–12.

Christensen, Robert. 2016. Email to Friends of Scott Sunken Garden, 25 April. Retrieved 30 June 2016 from https://www.facebook.com/notes/scott-sunken-garden-friends/national-register-coordinators-recommendation-of-scott-sunken-gardens-historical/1027945290586784/.

Cosentino, Lawrence. 2017. "End of the Line: A Surrogate Bears the Fate the First Scott House Avoided." *City Pulse*. 15 March. Retrieved 15 March 2017 from https://www.lansingcitypulse.com/stories/end-of-the-line,2431.

Donnelly, Colin. 2017. "Demolition of Lansing's Scott House Causes Uproar from Local Preservationists." *State News*, 23 March. Retrieved 15 November 2018 from http://

news.jrn.msu.edu/2017/03/demolition-of-lansings-scott-house-causes-uproar-from-local-preservationists/.

Dozier, Vickki. 2016. "Scott Sunken Garden Supporters Speak out." *Lansing State Journal*, 14 August 14. Retrieved 15 September 2016 from https://www.lansingstatejournal.com/story/news/local/2016/08/14/scott-sunken-garden-supporters-speak-out/88718244/.

"Editorial: Scott Park Plan Good Enough." 2016. *Lansing State Journal*, 16 June. Retrieved 30 June 2016 from https://www.lansingstatejournal.com/story/opinion/editorials/2016/06/16/editorial-scott-park-plan-good-enough/85940892/.

Epstein, Griffin. 2016. "Remembering Right, Remembering White: Public Art, Colonial Memory, and Gentrification in Toronto's Parkdale Neighborhood." In *Excavating Memory: Sites of Remembering and Forgetting*, ed. Maria Theresia Starzmann and John H. Roby, 64–85. Gainesville: University of Florida Press.

Faimon, Mary Beth. 2004. "Ties that Bind: Remembering, Mourning, and Healing Historical Trauma." In "Empowerment through Literature," special issue, *American Indian Quarterly* 28(1–2): 238–251.

Fear-Segal, Jacqueline. 2007. *White Man's Club: Schools, Race, and the Struggle of Indian Acculturation*. Lincoln: University of Nebraska Press.

Gordon, Avery F. 1997. *Ghostly Matters: Haunting and the Sociological Imagination*. Minneapolis: University of Minneapolis Press.

González, Juan. 2017. *Reclaiming Gotham: Bill De Blasio and the Movement to End America's Tale of Two Cities*. New York: The New Press.

González-Tennant, Edward. 2018. *The Rosewood Massacre: An Archaeology and History of Intersectional Violence*. Gainesville: University Press of Florida.

Halbwachs, Maurice. 1992. *On Collective Memory*, trans. and ed. Lewis A. Coser. Chicago: University of Chicago Press.

Hasbrook, M. A. 2016. "100 Years of Lansing's Environmental Protection." Scott Sunken Garden Friends. 24 April 2016.

Heywood, Todd. 2016a. "Red Cedar Kerfuffle." *City Pulse*, 7 December.

———. 2016b. "Scott Center's New Home? BWL, City and Habitat Offer Plan to Save House from Bulldozer." *City Pulse*, 31 May.

———. 2017. "How Did the Ormond Park Road Proposal Get into the Master Plan?" *City Pulse*, 7 June.

Hillman, Sarah. 2018. "Solar-Powered Metal Murals Planned for the New BWL Substation." *Capital Gains – Lansing*, 30 May. Retrieved 15 June 2018 from http://www.secondwavemedia.com/capitalgains/innovationnews/SolarPoweredMurals1204.aspx.

Hinkley, Justin A., and Matt Mencarini. 2017. "It's Been 10 Years since the Great Recession: Is Lansing Housing Market Back to Normal?" *Lansing State Journal*, 11 September. Retrieved 15 June 2018 from https://www.lansingstatejournal.com/story/news/local/watchdog/2017/09/11/its-been-10-years-since-great-recession-lansing-housing-market-back-normal/646832001/.

Hirsch, Marianne. 2012. *The Generation of Postmemory: Writing and Visual Culture after the Holocaust*. New York: Columbia University Press.

Illitch, Alexandra. 2016a. "Lansing City Council Votes In Favor of Building New BWL Substation on Historic Scott Sunken Garden Site." *WLNS News*, 26 September. Retrieved 26 September 2016 from https://www.wlns.com/news/lansing-city-council-votes-in-favor-of-building-new-bwl-substation-on-historic-scott-sunken-garden-site/999977376.

———. 2016b. "Public Weighs In on Plans to Replace Scott Sunken Gardens with BWL Central Substation." *WLNS News*, 22 August. Retrieved 15 September 2016 from https://www.wlns.com/news/public-weighs-in-on-plans-to-replace-scott-sunken-gardens-with-bwl-central-substation/1078939510.

Jordan, Harriet. 1994. "Public Parks: 1885–1914." *Garden History* 22(1): 85–113.

Kaminski, Kyle. 2018. "City Council Votes to Sell Red Cedar Property: Sale Price Discounted $5M after Talks." *City Pulse*, 26 July.

"Lansing BWL and Arts Council of Greater Lansing Announce Central Substation Mural Project." 2018. Media release. Lansing Regional Chamber of Commerce, 19 March. Retrieved 15 November 2018 from https://www.lansingchamber.org/news/391551/Lansing-BWL-and-Arts-Council-of-Greater-Lansing-Announce-Central-Substation-Mural-Project.htm.

Lee, Marilyn. 2010. "History of Scott Sunken Garden and Its Restoration." *The New Citizens Press*. 26 September 2010. Retrieved 15 December 2019 from http://www.tncp.net/Articles/tabid/1800/articletype/ArticleView/articleID/2475/Default.aspx.

Little, Barbara J., and Paul A. Shackel, eds. 2007. *Archaeology as a Tool of Civic Engagement*. Lanham, MD: Alta Mira Press.

Loukaitou-Sideris, Anastasia, and Steglitz, Orit. 2002. "Children in Los Angeles Parks: A Study of Equity, Quality, and Children's Satisfaction with Neighbourhood Parks." *Town Planning Review* 73(4): 467–488.

Mallach, Alan. 2018. *The Divided City: Poverty and Prosperity in Urban America*. Washington, DC: Island Press.

Gracia-Wing, Veronica, James McClurken, and Rita O'Brien to Lansing City Council. 2016. "Re: Minority position regarding amendment of the City's Master Plan allowing the Board of Water and Light to build on Scott Park," 11 May. Retrieved 20 June 2016 from https://www.facebook.com/PreservationLansing/posts/1176873178998878.

McNamara, Neal. 2010. "A House with No Name: City Aims to Close 92-Year-Old Scott House to Save $7,000." *City Pulse*, 28 April. Retrieved 15 November 2018 from http://lansingcitypulse.com/article-4250-a-house-with-no-name.html.

Nelson, Cassandra. 2016a. "Lansing City Council Approves Demolition of Historic Scott Park Sunken Garden." Cultural Landscape Foundation website, 6 October. Retrieved 15 November 2018 from https://tclf.org/lansing-city-council-approves-demolition-historic-scott-park-sunken-garden.

———. 2016b. "The Scott Sunken Garden Faces Relocation." Cultural Landscape Foundation website, 22 August. Retrieved 15 November 2018 from https://tclf.org/scott-sunken-garden-faces-relocation.

Paisley, Jamie. 2017. "REO Town's 'Art Attack' Bends the Rules Making Public Art." *WKAR*, 27 August. Retrieved 15 November 2018 from http://www.wkar.org/post/reo-town-s-art-attack-bends-rules-making-public-art.

Palmer, Ken. 2016. "BWL Gets Go-Ahead for Substation near Downtown Area." *Lansing State Journal*, 26 September. Retrieved 15 November 2018 from https://www.lansingstatejournal.com/story/news/local/2016/09/26/bwl-gets-go-ahead-substation-near-downtown-area/91146658/.

Parker, Dawn, and Eric Lacy. 2016. "Historic Home in Lansing to Be Saved, Moved by BWL." *Lansing State Journal*, 31 May. Retrieved 30 June 2016 from https://www.lansingstatejournal.com/story/news/local/2016/05/31/scott-house-bwl/85186538/.

"Photo Gallery: Scott House History." 2016. *City Pulse*, 6 April. Retrieved 30 June 2016 from http://lansingcitypulse.com/galleries-53-Photo-Gallery-Scott-House.html.

"Preliminary Meeting: Central Substation Project." 2016. Media release. Lansing: Board of Water & Light, 15 November. Retrieved 15 November 2018 from http://lansingenergytomorrow.com/news/central-substation-preliminary-meeting/.

"Project Overview: Central Substation." 2016. Media release. Lansing: Board of Water & Light, 12 November. Retrieved 15 November 2018 from http://lansingenergytomorrow.com/news/central-substation-project-overview/.

Putnam, Judy. 2016a. "Backers Appear to Be Dangling Carrots to Lessen Resistance to the Plan." *Lansing State Journal*, 6 June. Retrieved 30 June 2016 from https://www.lansingstatejournal.com/story/opinion/columnists/judy-putnam/2016/06/05/putnam-pulling-up-roots-lansing-history/85351054/.

———. 2016b. "Lansing Hidden Garden Faces Controversial Uprooting." *Lansing State Journal*, 6 June. Retrieved 30 June 2016 from https://www.freep.com/story/news/local/michigan/2016/06/06/lansing-garden-scott-sunken-garden/85477390/.

Rosado, Alexis. 2016. "A Fight for Lansing's Sunken Garden." *WLNS News*, 2 April. Retrieved 30 June 2016 from https://www.wlns.com/news/a-fight-for-lansings-sunken-garden/1078957865.

Ross, Allan I. 2014. "Welcome to East Town: Eastside Businesses Transform Neighborhood into Cultural Hub." *City Pulse*, 25 June. Retrieved 15 November 2018 from https://www.lansingcitypulse.com/stories/welcome-to-east-town,6209.

Rzepecki, Annie. 2016. "First Design Charette Successful!" 8 December 8. Retrieved 15 November 2018 from http://lansingenergytomorrow.com/news/first-design-charette-successful/.

Sabloff, Jeremy A. 2008. *Archaeology Matters: Action Archaeology in the Modern World*. New York: Routledge.

Schönfelder, Christa. 2013. "Theorizing Trauma: Romantic and Postmodern Perspectives on Mental Wounds." In *Wounds and Words: Childhood and Family Trauma in Romantic and Postmodern Fiction*, 27–86. Bielefeld, Germany: Transcript.

Schwartz, Berl. 2016. "Preservationists Make Gains Despite Loss to Bernero, BWL." *City Pulse*, 23 November. Retrieved 23 November 2016 from http://lansingcitypulse.com/article-14045-Jaws-of-defeat.html.

Schwartz, Berl, and Nasein Omeish. 2016. "BWL Asked to Shift Substation to Create New Riverfront Access." *City Pulse*, 27 April. Retrieved 30 June 2016 from http://lansingcitypulse.com/article-13094-Updated-Making-lemonade.html.

"Scott Center House Demolished." 2017. *Greater Lansing Business Monthly*, 20 March. Retrieved 15 November 2018 from https://lansingbusinessnews.com/business-news-today/2017/03/scott-center-house-demolished/.

Sheffield, Carrie Louise. 2011. "Native American Hip-Hop and Historical Trauma: Surviving and Healing Trauma on the 'Rez.'" *Studies in American Indian Literatures* 23(3): 94–110.

Smith, Mathew Dae. 2017. "Scott House Coming Down Today in Downtown Lansing." *Lansing State Journal*, 13 March. Retrieved 15 November 2018 from https://www.lansingstatejournal.com/story/news/local/2017/03/13/scott-house-coming-down-today-downtown-lansing/99125522/.

Stanaway, Loretta. 2016. "Opinion: Don't Tear Down the Jenison House." *New Citizens Press*, 20 March. Retrieved 30 June 2016 from http://www.tncp.net/Articles/ta

bid/1800/articleType/ArticleView/articleId/4827/Opinion—Dont-Tear-Down-the-Jenison-House.aspx.

Starzmann, Maria Theresia, and John H. Roby, eds. 2016. *Excavating Memory: Sites of Remembering and Forgetting*. Gainesville: University Press of Florida.

Stottman, M. Jay, ed. 2010. *Archaeologists as Activists: Can Archaeologists Change the World?* Tuscaloosa: The University of Alabama Press.

Surface-Evans, Sarah. 2015. "Archaeological Investigations of the Barn Structure at McGulpin Point Lighthouse (20Em140)." *Michigan Archaeologist* 55: 1–74.

———. 2016. "A Landscape of Assimilation and Resistance: The Mount Pleasant Indian Industrial Boarding School." In "Colonial Institutions: Uses, Subversions, and Material Afterlives," ed. Laura McAtackney and Russell Palmer. Special issue, *International Journal of Historical Archaeology* 20(3): 574-588.

Surface-Evans, Sarah, and Sarah J. Jones. Forthcoming. "Discourses of the Haunted: An Intersubjective Approach to Archaeology at the Mount Pleasant Indian Industrial Boarding School." In special issue, *Archaeological Papers of the American Anthropological Association*, ed. Tiffany Cain and Teresa Raczek.

"The Scott House." 2016. Lost Lansing website, 23 February. Retrieved 30 June 2016 from http://www.lostlansing.org/?p=367.

Tumarkin, Maria. 2005. *Tramascapes: The Power and Fate of Places Transformed by Tragedy*. Melbourne: Melbourne University Press.

van Dernoot, Laura and Connie Burk. 2009. *Trauma Stewardship: An Everyday Guide to Caring for Self While Caring for Others*. San Fransico: Berrett-Koehler Press.

Zembylas, Michalinos, and Zvi Bekerman. 2008. "Education and the Dangerous Memories of Historical Trauma: Narratives of Pain, Narratives of Hope." *Curriculum Inquiry* 38(2): 125–154.

CHAPTER 10

Brickwork, Capitalism, Collective Memory, and the Commons

BRIGITTE H. BECHTOLD

For many of us, ghosts linger in aspects of the human-built environment. To me, brickwork is a source of such fascinating specters. Brick connects me with my childhood and with the many generations that came before me. Brick captures and stores events, such as a mortar holes from war, and it accumulates the changes made by those who adapt old buildings to new causes. Ultimately, brickwork may be demolished altogether and the leftover broken bricks used as filler and gravel. In their various incarnations, brickwork and the bricks themselves invoke many ghosts. Aided by observations made during numerous walks—in the suburbs of Brussels, in London and Kettering, in Pittsburgh, and along the lonely banks of the Firth of Forth near Edinburgh—I summon ghosts to help explore the connections between bricks, different conceptualizations of time, collective memory, and the commons. The bricks themselves and the things erected from them leave traces and a presence of many ghosts: ghosts of workers and families in past generations, of bricklayers and workers in brick kilns, of capitalist entrepreneurs, and of those they employ. Placing brickwork in the context of alternative ways of measuring time, of ghosts, of collective memory, and of the commons leads to some inferences about nostalgia, social action, and walking.

Childhood Walks

Growing up in Belgium in the 1950s, I was continually fascinated by bricklayers and their work, observing them either from a window in my home or by means of sideways glances on my way walking to school. In those times, the mortar was often still mixed manually without mechanical tumbler, by pouring sand in a circle on the ground, adding a bag or more of powdered cement and a measure of water in the middle, and mixing the lot by pulling the outside dry material into the wetness of the inner circle. While this could be accomplished by one man, most often it was done by a twosome in what seemed like a duet, producing harmonic movements and satisfying sounds of scraping, blobbing, slurping, and patting. Of course, I never saw women doing this and could not help but feel a silent envy that I would so often experience as I moved through childhood and adulthood: Why can't I do this? But this is another sort of ghost story. As the duet rapidly unfolded, more water was added until the slurry was just right. The brick workers always knew when it was just right.

There were separate and sometimes parallel teams of brickmakers who were paid for digging the brick-clay, molding it, and firing it. As a child, I also saw this activity in areas that were off the beaten path but where it was safe for children to roam about—and I did so frequently. A stacked and aerated set of clay shapes could be left within a kiln with the correct amount of heat and would become solid, hardened bricks. The dark red bricks that were produced at the open-air kiln were easily recognized around the small town where I lived, as they contained sharp light-gray bits of ash. I saw the houses constructed with these very bricks, and I realized that the duplex house my parents rented nearby had also been constructed from them. I felt that I was somehow "connected" to the brick kiln, my home, my small town, my family, the bricklayers, and their families. The connections crisscrossed and became part of my own memories as well as the collective memory of the groups of people I belonged to in the community. Even as a child I sensed a collective memory that was distinct from history, prescient of what I would learn in my future life as a sociologist. Later I read the work of Maurice Halbwachs, who explains how collective memory differs from history, in that the collective memory is not like a clearly delineated "play in several parts" and society is "like the cloth woven together from many strands" (1992: 143).

The bricklaying I observed in midcentury was typically accomplished by small teams in which an older, more experienced worker showed the ropes to the younger and less experienced ones. "Pointing" (the finishing of the mortar seams between rows of brick) was typically done by those with more years on the job, as it involved not just the use of the narrow-bladed trowel but the application of sufficient pressure for the seams to stick and be properly sealed. Lunchtime was an opportunity for easy camaraderie among the workers, who sat on upturned buckets, eating similarly dull bread and cheese or ham sandwiches, drinking coffee from dented tin canteens with ceramic stoppers, and telling stories. The day did not end before the last of the mortar was used up—seemingly miraculously, the right amount for the day had been mixed—and every bucket and trowel was meticulously rinsed for the next day, often by the lower-ranked apprentices. The workers left for their homes filled with a sense of community, camaraderie, fulfillment, and pride in their work, and they shared these feelings with the family at home, providing ingredients for family stories, family history, and the community's collective memory. Occasionally, a bricklayer's younger siblings who were schoolmates of mine would tell anecdotes related to this fascinating craft. Invisible strings connected me to the brick buildings, the bricklayers, their families, and the ghosts of those who had done such tasks in earlier generations, even though I did not have personal memories of them. The accumulation of physical brick-related evidence around me and the feeling of permanence evoked by the buildings and the generations of bricklayers became like ghosts who, in a sense, guarded this labor and existence. Ghosts are mixed with spaces, as Michael Mayerfeld Bell carefully explains in his article "The Ghosts of Place" (1997: 819) and the brick spaces and communities of my childhood manifested the four types of ghosts he describes.

The ghosts of the long dead were rather vividly evoked for me in the public school where I received my elementary education. The building had been a castle, constructed, primarily in the fifteenth century, out of sandstone and orange brick. Its previous occupants accompanied me in its classrooms, as I walked by its outside wall, and especially when I went with my classmates on teacher-escorted walks to the edges of the school grounds where a small two-story hunting pavilion stood. I felt the presence of the ghosts of the people who had rested, conversed, and held parties in that space, and several years later, in 1964, I felt a visceral personal loss that connected with the long-departed when the pavilion completely collapsed, allegedly due to vibration caused by a jet plane flying low overhead ("Kasteel Isque" 2013). This happened around the time when bricklaying and everything connected to it was also collapsing in a fashion, victim to market-driven capitalist decision making that drastically altered spaces and peoples' lives. Linda Clarke ([1992] 2011) describes the technical aspects of changes brought by capitalism in her classic work, *Building Capitalism*. One of these changes was the end of the artisanal system, where exchange relations were directly related to artisan production (81). Capitalism called for the architect's specifications and "for the work to be performed based on a schedule of prices for the number of bricks to be used in the construction, amounting to a lump sum for the total brickwork at given market prices" (82).

Reflections amid Rapid Changes

Moving from the localized spaces of childhood memories to the built spaces of towns and cities in Belgium, as I grew older I could see all around me edifices that had been erected by the hands of bricklayers throughout history. I saw numerous castles, many of them layered with bricks alternated with stripes of white sandstone. Roman ruins, factories and farms, and the houses in which the workers themselves lived were all part of this built landscape that housed ghosts of the past. In the late 1950s—hastened by the formation of the European Economic Community in 1957—and especially in the 1960s, the built environment increasingly became the product of corporate enterprises. Gone were the small gangs of bricklayers. Now came heavy equipment, including huge mortar mills mounted on the backs of lorries that efficiently mixed their contents while being driven to work sites. During this time, demolition became as visible as construction, leaving holes of nostalgia within myself and many of the older workers who had been self-employed or worked with friends and kin in small enterprises. We began to see the ghosts created by capitalism.

Gradually, and influenced by university education, travel, and a latent love of architecture and history, I inevitably noticed that certain brick buildings such as Roman ruins and medieval castles possessed sufficient historical, social, or profitable significance that their existence was not threatened with demolition. By contrast, everyday simple terraced (row) houses, obsolete factories, railway stations, and other utilitarian buildings were demolished without a second thought to the importance of the former inhabitants or workers. It became increasingly obvious that many decisions about the continued existence of buildings were made by corporate owners, on the basis of the market and expected profits. This shift was aided by government subsidies and policies related to building codes, safety regulations, and eminent domain. The bricklayers (or their descendants), their families, and communities had little say in the matter. More often than not, they were renters rather than owners. In my own mind, I began to see connections between urban brickwork and the social forces of capitalism. The ghost in these places was the ghost of capitalism.

The Bricks That Built Capitalism

It is undeniable that the evolution of early capitalism in Britain, some countries in continental Europe, and the United States has given rise to or "produced" numerous brick constructs: factories and workshops, housing for workers, viaducts, train depots, and more. While some were impressive railroad bridges and stations, factories, and roads, others were rows upon rows of standardized housing for laborers. These buildings have a social significance that goes well beyond their usefulness in terms of capitalist profit. Illustration 10.1 is a photo I took during walks along East Carson Street in South Pittsburgh to and from a sociology conference. Imposing factory buildings such as this are typical in this area, and not many houses are interspersed with the enormous buildings that often take up a whole street block. Many of the houses have since been demolished. They once were homes to families, and their layout and other

Illustration 10.1. Factory on East Carson Street, South Pittsburgh, 8 April 2018. Photo by the author.

characteristics entered the individual and collective memories of succeeding generations of families and communities. One has a sense of something lost when walking through neighborhoods such as this today. Neighborhoods are no longer convenient for walking. Sidewalks are in dismal shape or missing altogether in some places. I found that I was pretty much the only conference participant who walked the approximate mile to the hotel where many of us were staying. Automobile traffic on East Carson Street was busy, but pedestrians were rare. It was expected that we would take a taxi or the shuttle bus. As A. E. Garrison (Chapter 8) and Sarah Surface-Evans (Chapter 9) reveal in the methodology shaping their research, the activity of walking brings our awareness to built spaces that we could easily miss if we zoomed by them in automobiles.

While walking around the buildings between East Carson Street and the Monongahela River, I wondered how the built space in this neighborhood could still form strands in individual and collective memories for the people who lived there as well as for those whose families had moved away long ago. When built spaces are torn down, do holes appear in the fabric of the collective memory? Are these holes occupied by ghosts of those who once lived in these houses, and who are no longer "remembered" by their descendants? Is it just the factory that is retained in the collective memory?

It is not always the case that the houses built as homes for workers in capitalist industries get abandoned or bulldozed altogether. The better housing is often retained, as it can be sold profitably and modified with modern conveniences. Cities like Manchester, Liverpool, and London, to name a few, retain large swaths of the brick houses that capitalism built. Often these neighborhoods are now gentrified, with the result that the original inhabitants can no longer afford to live there. Much has been written about the terraced houses (called row houses in the United States) that characterize the manner in which employers accommodated the masses of people flocking to the cities at the beginning of the nineteenth century. To cram as many as possible into housing on a tract of land, the terraced houses shared walls with the adjoining houses, typically had no cellar, and in their smallest form might be just single-room houses or one-up one-down houses with a common courtyard that contained the single shared outhouse, cesspit, and standpipe for water provision. They had no yards and their fronts abutted the street (Calow 2007). Even the rather more comfortable version of the terraced housing complex shown in Illustration 10.2 has no front garden or walkway. The builders did not envisage leisure activity on porches or front stoops. The houses were erected just about flush with the street, and many presented dismal living conditions for the lodgers.

I got a feel for terraced working-class housing when I explored the old industrial area of Kettering, England, that was once the center of the shoe and boot industry.[1] There are several streets such as the one shown in Illustration 10.2, with side-by-side terraces, a sliver of sidewalk, and no greenery. Kathryn Morrison and Ann Bond, in their very detailed volume *Built to Last?*, describe the buildings of the Northamptonshire boot and shoe industry. Havelock Street, pictured in my photo, features in an aerial panoramic photograph in this book (2004: 24), which shows the street as part of the larger area, built in the second half of the nineteenth century and containing several parallel streets lined by terraced housing with boot and shoe factories between the rows. This particular alignment may be the reason why the neighborhood is still attractive to home buyers. In between Havelock and Wood Streets are narrow strips of gardens—some with small workshops—that make up for the missing street-side greenery. Plumbing is incorporated, where needed, by adding "espaliered" sewer pipes along the house's back—something that does not faze English homeowners but would probably be a building violation in the United States.

Today's housing prices are rather steep in this Kettering neighborhood owing to gentrification. While the factories have closed or have been readapted to new uses, housing has been preserved and gradually upgraded to middle- and upper-middle-class use, as attested by their well-tended facades and the fancy

Illustration 10.2. Terraced (row) houses on Havelock Street in Kettering, England, 25 November 2018.
Photo by the author.

cars parked on the narrow street. As I walked through these streets, I did not have the sense of something lost as I did on South Pittsburgh's East Carson Street. To me, the ghosts of past occupants may find a continuity of human existence in the lives of present occupants. However, the similarities may only be on the surface. There were no cars, no indoor plumbing facilities or central heating when the homes were occupied by the families of the shoe factory workers more than a century ago. What's more, present-day owners are often commuters who avail themselves of easy access to the train station or the expressway. While they build their own narratives and family memories of what it means to live in this community, they have picked up strands of past families' memories as well. They are happy to live in the rather stark-looking houses built by bricklayers of long ago and once occupied by laborers in the shoe and boot industry. Much remains of that physical brick environment. Therefore, in this neighborhood one has a sense that there is not an abrupt fissure between the passage of chronological time and what I will call *social time*, which coincides more or less with many individual and collective memories in the community.

Capitalist Time

I argue that alternative time frames come into existence with the construction, deconstruction, or destruction of buildings at the behest of capitalist entrepreneurs. First, *chronological time*, is the embodiment of brick constructs. Second, two social time dimensions are associated with the capitalist era. The first can be considered *capitalist time*, linked to return on investment and profit. In this time frame, buildings continue to exist as long as they enable profitability. *Social time* is when events and physical phenomena are measured by means of what is of social significance. The brick buildings erected under capitalism can be viewed as playing a role in all three of these time frames. However, the capitalist agenda relegates chronological and social versions of time to the margins. In families and communities of bricklayers, the narratives of "my grandfather helped build this" or "the factory at the end of town was built by people in this community" begin to lose their context and physical evidence. In the conceptualizations of time and social memory, bricklayers and other workers have chronologically constructed edifices of the eighteenth, nineteenth, and twentieth centuries by first making and then installing the bricks tediously, one by one, and most often with small groups of coworkers; the method of construction and teamwork makes the resulting built works the basis for social histories and the collective memories of individuals, families, and communities. Social time is of significance here, but what is viewed to be social is also directly influenced by decisions made by capitalists. The demolition of the old and the construction of a new plant will make it to the newspapers and the media. The feelings of workers in relation to significant events in their social time will not. This is one reason why a historical perspective is so important in social science research. Sociologists and archaeologists can bring these narratives of social time into the light.

Of course, not everything brick is demolished. Some of the constructions that are no longer of use in their original form are repurposed, refurbished, restored. A beat-up factory is a prime candidate for gentrification into lofts. For example, St. Pancras Station in London—now known as St. Pancras International—is a perfect example of a repurposed and refurbished railway station (Illustration 10.3). When it was originally built as a coal transport station, thousands of houses were demolished to make room for the project. Its resurrection as the destination for trains from the European continent required much labor, capital, and government spending. However, it is no longer what it once was. The flashy facades and inside features of the building no longer reveal the artful tile work and other hand-constructed features of the old station that have been callously destroyed, drilled through, or hidden. The station is now gentrified and the social time of the workers is lost. The station is home to upscale boutiques and restaurants and a hub for travelers who have the money to afford vacations abroad.

Brickwork, Capitalism, Collective Memory, and the Commons ❖ 179

Illustration 10.3. Restored passage in St. Pancras International, London, April 2018. Photo by the author.

What we often see with old buildings that have not withstood the test of usefulness or refurbishment is that they get neglected or torn down altogether. Illustration 10.4 shows the last remaining house in a series of row houses. Even this relic of a different era probably will not be there much longer. It has already

Illustration 10.4. The last of a set of row houses on S 5th and Cabot Way. South Pittsburgh, April 2018.
Photo by the author.

been graffitied, its brickwork is in disrepair, and the sliver of stoop and front sidewalk are crumbly and precariously tilted. A much larger piece of painted art awaits the walker in another section of Carson Street. What at first sight looks like a cheery set of row houses backgrounding happy activities, is in reality an immense mural. A person approaching this site walking from west to east on East Carson Street would see a huge apartment building apparently constructed of the same ochre brick as the nearby factories and warehouses. Once past the corner, on closer inspection, the walker would see a nostalgic mural painted over what is the sole remaining outside wall of a large building that has been all but demolished. The east side of the wall, displaying the elaborately painted trompe l'oeil mural, was skimmed with smooth mortar to receive the painted image.

Refurbished edifices like St. Pancras, and embellished ruins such as the muraled wall on East Carson Street, evoke nostalgia for the artifacts' collective memory. Does the cultivation and encouragement of nostalgia form a cultural practice that helps close gaps between chronological time and collective memory? Kathleen Stewart writes that nostalgia is everywhere and can be a rhetorical tool that orders events in time and "dramatizes" them; however, she argues that nostalgia results in mirages that have overly romantic simplicity (1988: 227). In other words, nostalgia is not so much a lens as a mirage.

Bricks *as* Time

Brickwork "tells time" in several ways. Even chronological historical time is complicated when we consider brickwork. For example, is a demolished building still an artifact that fits in time? Despite the actions and the influence of capitalist entrepreneurs, there are different interpretations of chronological "time" related to brickwork: a compressed instant and timeless view with regards to a completed project. At the same time, a long, extended view of time connected to *building* time-memory, and its disruption when capitalist progress calls for dismantling and destruction of the brick building, provides another interpretation. This is evocative of several theories related to time-space. Notably, Ehei Dōgen's thirteenth-century philosophy sees time-phenomena as noncontinuous, nonchronological. In much of his writings, he conveyed the fleeting/immediate, the changing/unchanging, the cycling of time and the timelessness of the moment, often using metaphors such as spring and cherry blossoms (e.g., "as usual cherry blossoms bloom in my native place their color unchanged spring" [Tanahashi 1985: 14]). While a brick is very different from a cherry blossom in its physical form, it too captures the changing/unchanging (brickwork constructions and their alterations), the fleeting/immediate (e.g., the way a brick wall absorbs or captures the impact of mortar during an armed conflict), and the cycling of time, as in the eventual returning to dust of bricks that are now beyond use but whose dust will eventually be formed into new bricks or other solids in some future time. While hiking along the vast Firth of Forth (Illustration 10.5), I noted that some beach areas were constructed from limestone pebbles intermingled with pieces of different colored bricks, some

Illustration 10.5. Bricks becoming pebbles and sand on the south shore of the Firth of Forth, Scotland, June 2018.
Photo by the author.

of which still had mortar attached and all of which had been smoothed by the continuing passage of the tides. There was no telling which buildings they had once been part of and who had constructed, lived in, or used those built spaces. They evoked thought of souls who had touched and lived in these spaces.

Uncovering Ghosts

Capitalist time has the effect of leapfrogging over points of chronological time. Large capitalist projects are heralded while the efforts of individual workers are forgotten. The disruption of personal histories and collective memories of communities of workers and their families adds to alienation in the capitalist world. This sense of alienation is the source of haunting. After outright decimation and gentrification, what is left of the brick structures? They may hold many ghosts. The collective memory thus becomes increasingly overwhelmed by the memories of capitalist employers and gentrified consumers. Over time, the stories of the brick workers and their families are diminished by means of both changing the "narrative" and altering and destroying physical evidence (Garrison, Chapter 8; Halbwachs 1992; Olick 2008; Surface-Evans, Chapter 9). As capitalist themes are infused into the time-space narrative, that narrative demolishes the times that matter to personal and collective memory. Applying our imagination, we can also envisage the collective memory as part of the intellectual "commons," building on my recent work on the notion of the commons. While scholarly work on the commons has focused mainly on natural resources such as air, water, and grazing lands, more recently it has been extended to include technology, culture, knowledge, intellectual space, and memory (Bechtold 2016; Sherman 2016). This nonorthodox approach to the commons includes a focus on resisting "privatization" of the collective memory and intellectual commons, to curtail the capitalist narrative and retain that of ordinary individuals. The memories of individual laborers emphasize family history, moral values, and the buildings built by labor.

Some types of social action can help reconnect people with the ghosts of the built environment. *Buildering*, for example, is the trend of exploring or taking over closed-off privatized spaces such as bricked-up passages between buildings. Buildering often uncovers traces of the physical evidence of destroyed, altered, or neglected brickwork. Some buildering involves feats by people who find a little niche in a tiny ally or a bricked-up window and turn it into a place to live. Other builderers will scale buildings to which they do not have authorized access, walk on tightropes between them, or explore and perhaps live in the vast underground tunnels that were constructed by bricklayers in a time long past. Whimsical trends of guerilla gardening, such as planting miniature gardens in potholes or in pavement cracks, yarn bombing, and seed bombing are other illustrations of individuals reclaiming their urban spaces from capitalist control.

In this way, everyday people reclaim what once was part of a physical commons and thus supplement, replace, or at least infuse human experiences into the dominant narrative. These activities contribute to resisting the overwhelming capitalist narrative. Buildering "hacks" the corporate capitalist narrative and reinfuses it with people's memories and experiences. While the memories that they create relate to traces of the past, however, these are "new" forms of collective memory created and maintained by everyday people. These subversive forms of social action may counteract or at least supplement the corporate narrative. They can reinforce a few strands in the fabric of the collective memory, connect with some ghosts that inhabit the layers of built spaces, and contribute to a cultural commons that belongs to ordinary folks.

When I revisit and walk in the spaces of my childhood, I no longer encounter bricklayers and the craft that so fascinated me. What was once the village's brick kiln is now parceled up into numerous private single-family houses with fenced-in gardens. Reflective of a crucial aspect of capitalism, everything in the physical built environment is now much more obviously private property rather than being part of an easily accessed commons. Yet, while the ghost of capitalism is very apparent in the residential subdivisions and the new industries, the haunting specters of the bricklayers and their culture linger. Personal memories like my own and those of others in generations past and present will continue to weave the memories and the "collective thoughts to which we remain closely related" (Halbwachs 1992: 139).

Dr. Brigitte Bechtold holds a PhD in Economics from the University of Pennsylvania. She is Professor of Sociology at Central Michigan University, where she teaches courses on racism and inequality, social justice and globalization, human trafficking, and research methods. Her recent publications include a focus on European society, the commons, community gardens, and infanticide. Her current research interests relate to *buildering* and social action in the urban setting. She is a member of the board of several professional journals, most notably the *Review of Radical Political Economics* and *Time and Society*.

Note

1. I thank Kettering resident Arnout Sellekaerts for giving me a guided tour of this neighborhood on 25 November 2018.

References

"Kasteel Isque." 2018. Agentschap Onroerend Erfgoed. Retrieved 21 January 2019 from https://id.erfgoed.net/erfgoedobjecten/40431.
Bechtold, Brigitte. 2016. "Introduction: Beyond Hardin and Ostrom: New Heterodox Research on the Commons." *Review of Radical Political Economics* 48(1): 5–8.
Bell, Michael Mayerfeld. 1997. "The Ghosts of Place." *Theory and Society* 26(6): 813–836.
Calow, Dennis. 2007. "Home Sweet Home: A Century of Leicester Housing, 1814–1914." Leicester, UK: University of Leicester, Special Collections Online. Retrieved 20 October 2018 from http://specialcollections.le.ac.uk/digital/collection/p15407coll5/id/1304/.
Clarke, Linda. (1992) 2011. *Building Capitalism: Historical Change and the Labour Process in the Production of Built Environment*. New York: Routledge Revivals.
Halbwachs, Maurice. 1992. *On Collective Memory*, trans. and ed. Lewis A. Coser. Chicago: University of Chicago Press.
Morrison, Kathryn A., and Ann Bond. 2004. *Built to Last? The Buildings of the Northamptonshire Boot and Shoe Industry*. Swindon, UK: Historic England.
Olick, Jeffrey K. 2008. "'Collective Memory': A Memoir and Prospect." *Memory Studies* 1(1): 23–29.
Sherman, Zoe. 2016. "Primitive Accumulation and the Cultural Commons." *Review of Radical Political Economics* 48(1): 176–188.
Stewart, Kathleen. 1988. "Nostalgia—A Polemic." *Cultural Anthropology* 3(3): 227–241.
Tanahashi, Kazuaki, ed. 1985. *Moon in a Dewdrop: Writings of Zen Master Dōgen*. New York: North Point Press.

Epilogue
Ghosts, Haunting, and Refusals to Erasure

KISHA SUPERNANT, APRIL M. BEISAW, A. E. GARRISON, AND SARAH SURFACE-EVANS

> I do not want to haunt you, but I will.
> —Eve Tuck

We have come to the end of our journey through time and space, wherein we have encountered the ghosts of Vassar College, the memories of loved ones at Teotihuacan, the intentional community of the City of David, the haunted landscapes of rural Michigan, the skeletons in the closet of biological anthropology, the Indigenous erasures of colonization, the echoes of loss of farmland in song, the quiet of a forgotten bridge, the trauma of a destroyed park, and the power of bricks to tell time. We hope these stories haunt you.

What happens when someone, some thing, some *time* refuses to be forgotten in the face of erasure? Ghosts are created through loss, sometimes traumatic, sometimes cyclical, but does a ghost exist if no one is haunted? The chapters in this volume speak to ghosts because those ghosts are not forgotten; they haunt places, objects, times, and people. Haunting is therefore *subversion to erasure*, a refusal against forgetting and an invitation to remember. From the farmlands of the Midwest, haunted by the echoes of family farms lost in the farm crisis of the 1980s (Brislen, Chapter 7) to the destruction of parks in Lansing, Michigan (Surface-Evans, Chapter 9), the chapters serve to bring forth narratives of time and place that are marked by loss and often by trauma (Van Wormer, Chapter 3). Many chapters engage with the systems that demand we forget, including those of late capitalism (Bechtold, Chapter 10; Brislen, Chapter 7; Garrison, Chapter 8; Surface-Evans, Chapter 9), Indigenous erasure (Lawton, Chapter 4; Supernant, Chapter 6), and disciplinary histories or practices (Burt, Chapter 5), but the very haunting evoked by these authors also resists that same ethic of forgetting, instead forcing us to remember and to bring the past into the present.

When ghosts are remembered, brought back into relations with the living, do they continue to haunt? Or do we, the rememberers, become their agents within the world? Throughout the volume, authors have *blurred timescapes*, bringing often forgotten pasts into the present, stepping across time to inhabit the past through affect and emotion (e.g., Begun, Chapter 2; Garrison, Chapter 8; Van Wormer, Chapter 3). Our trips through time, however, are always grounded in the present moment, our travel achieved through the materiality of memory and mnemonic that we encounter. Bricks evoke ghosts of the labor of craftsmen, their work made material but also subverted by capitalism (Bechtold, Chapter 10). The traces of an old bridge belie the destructive power of development and gentrification (Garrison, Chapter 8). Fragments of ancient objects encode memories of travels and homelands (Begun, Chapter 2), showing deep personal connections to peoples and places. Other ghosts are more ephemeral, remembered through song (Brislen, Chapter 7), through attempts to educate the public (Burt, Chapter 5), or sometimes through direct encounters with ancestors (Supernant, Chapter 6). The power of bringing these ghosts into these chapters is that they can continue to do their work, to have agency in the present, and perhaps to change the future.

What happens when ghosts are no longer a source of fear? Specters and hauntings are often portrayed in Western popular culture through horror movies, ghost-hunting shows, and literature, used to provoke fear or skepticism. The authors of this volume, however, are neither afraid of nor skeptical of ghosts. Ghostly encounters, rather than being something to avoid, are welcomed by these scholars, providing a chance to transform fear into empathy and emotional connection. We become allies of the ghosts, bringing their spectral nature into reality, making the invisible visible. Many of the hauntings in this volume encourage us to take action in the present (Supernant, Chapter 6; Surface-Evans, Chapter 9), reminding us that the ghosts of the past exist because their erasure is incomplete and that they have the power to impact our future. So, the next time you feel a prickle on your neck or a wave of unexpected emotion when in a place, we invite you to be haunted, to engage the ghosts, to blur the boundaries between past, present, and future. As a final step, we invite you to revisit the volume chapters *as* ghost stories, below.

Communicating across Timescapes

Each chapter in this volume presents the reader with a landscape and the people and events that can animate it. Pasts, presents, and futures blur together as what-once-was both enables and constrains what-is-now and what-may-soon-be. Here, April Beisaw presents the reader with a series of ghost stories inspired by her careful reading of each chapter. Consider this a "walking ghost tour" of *Blurring Timescapes*. We hope the retellings inspire you to consider the cycles of life and death that are contained in landscapes everywhere—and are part of you.

Inspired by "Material Memories: Interpreting Souvenirs and Heirlooms in the Archaeological Record" (Erica Begun)

My mother once had a Cuisinart food processor. Her relationship to it was unnatural. Around the holidays, Mom would find any reason to chop up ingredients. Sometimes I would catch her crying over the food processor. "Onions," she would say. Her holiday recipes always seemed to call for onions and I knew it wasn't the onions that she loved. Mom loved my grandfather, whose food processor she cherished until it too died.

Although we never talked about it, I understood how the Cuisinart spoke to Mom, because objects speak to me too. As an archaeologist, I spend a lot of time working with the possessions of those whom I will never meet in life. During normal working hours, I toil away in a noisy lab, listening to music and occupied with my own thoughts. But when I'm in the lab at night, the quiet takes over and I can hear the stories held by the artifacts.

One summer I was analyzing artifacts from Teotihuacan, a Mesoamerican city. These objects were over a thousand years old. They had many stories to tell. My favorite story came from the objects found in a small apartment within one of the Oaxacan neighborhoods. In that apartment were souvenirs from lives lived elsewhere: fragments of very shiny black and red pottery vessels, and some curious figurines or dolls. How sad the residents must have been when their cherished souvenirs broke into fragments! Did they too blame their despair on onions?

Inspired by "Journeys through Space and Time: Materiality, Social Memory, and Community at the City of David" (Heather M. Van Wormer)

In Benton, Michigan, a community was built on the premise that death is just another stage of life. The ghosts here are a proof of concept; immortality was possible for those who refrain from cutting their hair, consuming meat or alcohol, and engaging in sexual intercourse. Life could be made rich in other ways. To keep hands from being idle, daily work took the form of farming, blacksmithing, and all sorts of construction. There was ice cream and baked goods to satisfy one's appetite. The community zoo provided entertainment, and not just for residents. It brought in outsiders who might consider remaining for all time.

All was well for about twenty years, and then scandal ruptured the tranquility of this place. Allegations of sexual misconduct split the community into the House of David and the City of David, revealing the cracks in the faith of both groups. One remained focused on the goal of immortality while the other turned toward creating a profitable resort business. But this is not the common tale of money being the root of all evil. Instead, the City of David's prosperity may have made it the ideal place for both the living and the dead to linger.

In the City of David, the dead are remembered in a way that may make a visitor think they are still in mortal form. The literal fruits of one's planting labor continue to be ascribed to the person of origin. Mrs. Morrell may be long gone in the physical sense, but each year she provides us with peaches. Bob's tomatoes keep coming back, as long as he is happy with what we have done since his death. These are just two of the many spiritual advisors who linger in Benton. What are you willing to give up for this sort of immortality?

Inspired by "Recognizing Ghosts and Haunting in the Rural Midwest: Finding Community, Identity, and Wisdom in the Past" (P. M. W. Lawton)
Ghosts roam Michigan's Saginaw Valley and are especially active around the region's glacial erratics, the manitou stones. These massive boulders have sat on level fields for generations. They have witnessed changes to the land and the deaths of its residents. The valley was home to the Fox and Sauk peoples before the Chippewa. This transition was not a peaceful one. Then, settlers came and altered the landscape. Rivers were dammed. Wetlands were drained, woodlands clear-cut. The fields of farmers and their water-powered mills were all that the manitou stones could see. Then the new people began to destroy the manitous themselves. To some, large stones are obstructions; to others, they are raw materials waiting to be put to use. To the Anishinaabe, they are spirits. Big Rock Elementary School now sits beside one of the remaining manitou stones in Chesaning, Michigan. Chisin is the Anishinaabe word for "big rock." But another manitou stone is now missing from the park that once surrounded it. Its disappearance is a warning that change is coming to the valley once again. Who will witness these changes?

Inspired by "The Unwilling Student and the Ghost of Physical Anthropology: Public Perceptions of the Ethics of Physical Anthropology" (Nicole M. Burt)
I try not to work in the lab at night because museums are especially haunted places. You can encounter the ghosts of those whose bodies and objects fill storerooms and display cabinets, but also the ghosts of those who worked to develop the museum collections. There is much more to museums than what the average visitor can see. The people who started museums often did so with the admirable goal of providing access to the wonders of the world. But acquiring those wonders involved some shady dealings with those who claimed ownership and were willing to sell for a price. By today's standards, some of what came into museums should not have. Even when past acquisitions would have met current ethical standards, what was done with those collections may

not. Science has its own dark past, especially when it comes to eugenics and other assessments of human superiority. Museum collections were once used by scientists to justify colonialism and nationalism, at almost any cost. These heavy footsteps echo in museum hallways. We should not follow their lead.

Inspired by "From Haunted to Haunting: Métis Ghosts in the Past and Present" (Kisha Supernant)
Not so long ago, a woman on a journey found herself lost. The boat she was on was taking her someplace she was not meant to be. Then she heard a voice in the wind. "We are your ancestors. We have been forgotten but you can still remember us." The voice was unrecognizable and could have been a trick of the wind. But the woman was lost, so she began thinking more deeply about who she was and where she was meant to be.

When the voice returned, this time it came from a person whom she had just met. "We are related," the cousin said. "This will help you find your way." He handed her a photograph of her own great grandparents. Her ghosts now had names and faces, and she knew they wanted something in return. Again they spoke to her. "Remember that we still exist because you and your relations carry on. Learn our language. Preserve our culture. Look for us in our past places. We are more than what they say we are. We are you."

Bolstered by the faces and messages of her kin, the woman set out on a new journey. She went to the old overwintering places of the Métis. There she found crumbling architecture and lingering artifacts, but they meant more to her because she knew her culture. These Métis communities had rebelled against colonial Canada. With the blood of both First Nations and fur traders flowing through them, the Métis had become a distinct identity, and they were pushed to the margins of society. For some, this is where the story ends. But in these overwintering places where tight-knit communities lived through harsh winters, the woman could see how her ancestors had responded with resilience and ingenuity. The evidence was in the butchered bison, whose meat and hide provided resources to be shared, and in the tiny beads that adorned moccasins with affection. When the woman looked even closer she could see the paths that connected her peoples to their important places. The paths were not efficient routes; they were the connections from one family to the next. She had found her way back, through time.

Inspired by "Rain on the Scarecrow, Blood on the Plow: Haunting, Trauma, and the Cruelty of the Agrarian Dream" (Lilian Brislen)
Driving across the American Midwest can be boring. Architecture is dwarfed by seemingly endless farm fields until a small town appears and disappears almost as fast. If it wasn't for that one downtown traffic light you may have missed the town altogether. Slower forms of transportation, like a bicycle tour,

don't cover great distances but do give the spirits of past farmers a chance to communicate with you.

The haunted farmhouses are not that old, constructed in the late nineteenth or early twentieth centuries. You can recognize them because they are partially hidden by hay that refuses to stop growing. A "for sale" sign usually marks what is left of the driveway and seemingly invites the curious to witness this loss for themselves. As the house comes into full view, the porch may be seen to contain a worn rocking chair. From here, grandparents used to survey the land that provided for their multigenerational family. The porch is probably sturdy enough for visitors to step inside, and the front door is likely agape, beckoning for someone to witness the loss. The best evidence of what happened here may be found in the kitchen. There hangs a wall calendar that never advanced beyond August 1985, when the farm crisis was at its peak. Pushed to expand their farms from fence to fence, small-time farmers were given loans to grow up as the price of their products sunk to new lows. Many farms succumbed, and some took the neighboring towns down with them. There was no one left to go to church, to school, to the feed store.

If you find yourself in an abandoned farmhouse, do not go upstairs—it isn't safe. The broken windows and leaky roof have started the process of returning everything to the land it sprung up from. But before you go, there is something else you need to see. Directly across the road should be what is left of the farmer's barn. If you are lucky, it has already crumbled down around the tractor that refuses to let go of what once was. If the barn is still standing, listen carefully for a gentle whimper before entering. The barns are where some desperate farmers ended their lives, still wearing the jeans, T-shirts, and seed company hats that marked them as small-town farmers. Their spirits linger in the barn but they are too prideful be seen. Instead, take a look at what is left of their tools, many of which are not yet rusted but sit unused. These tools, including the tractor and its barn, are too small to be useful to the farmers who made the jump to the big time. Bigger is better for some.

Inspired by "Boneyard Quiet: A Ghost Story" (A. E. Garrison)

In Michigan's capital city, ghosts cry out for the living to pay attention to infrastructure that distances neighboring communities. The city's new rail trail is lovely for those walking their dogs or riding their bicycles in the daytime. At night, you can hear ghosts whispering in the wind. Why, they ask, does the trail follow the river yet rarely cross it? The ghosts themselves stay off the trail because the pavement seems to slither, like a pile of snakes. Along the trail's edge the ghosts gather at ruins. Small piles of stones stick out from seemingly empty fields, asking to be remembered for what they once were: places that mattered. One such pile contains the remnants of a bridge. A link has been severed, but you can still trip over it if you are brave. If not, venture down the trail to Moores Park. Here ghosts whisper about the community pool, a gathering place that brought some people together while intentionally keeping others apart. Enforcing pool rules was easier if the "undesired" did not have a direct path there. Ghosts remember the comfort that the living find in motion. If we keep moving, then we don't have to interact with strangers or confront injustices. The real danger comes when we linger in places we were not meant to be, in places where we are unwelcome.

Inspired by "Traumascapes: Progress and the Erasure of the Past" (Sarah Surface-Evans)
One of the most haunted places in Lansing, Michigan, is the city's new power substation. Those who follow the paranormal know that ghosts can feed off electricity. Here, there is plenty to go around, and the power station's ghosts have a right to all that energy.

This place was once the home of a Michigan Supreme Court justice, Edward Cahill. Justice Cahill is best remembered for leading Michigan's first African American infantry unit during the Civil War and for an 1890 court decision that prohibited racial discrimination in the state's public spaces. He was a man of fairness and equality, and those are characteristics that Lansing's residents cherish.

After Cahill's death, a neighbor and later president of the REO Motor Company (Richard Scott) transformed Cahill's former home into a sunken garden. In the 1960s, Scott Garden became city property to be enjoyed by all. This location provided the neighboring African American communities with much-needed green space, but its beauty attracted residents from all over the city. Many birthdays, graduations, and weddings were marked with a photo of loved ones at Scott Garden.

Changes to the garden came in 1978, when the city moved a historic house to the park. This house was once the home of Orien A. Jenison, eulogized as "one of Lansing's oldest and best known citizens." He spent forty-eight of his seventy-two years in Lansing, arriving at his new home on Christmas Day after walking most of the way from Jackson, Michigan. "Uncle Jen" was a collector of things, especially anything relevant to the history of Michigan. Some of his collections can still be found in the state library. Uncle Jen would have been pleased to have his home relocated to Justice Cahill's property. But he is surely not pleased with what happened next. Intended to serve as a community center, the house was not supported by all and it fell into disrepair. In retrospect, that decline should have been a warning of what was to come.

With the power station's construction, Uncle Jen's house and the Scott Garden were demolished. Chainsaws took down several trees that were likely just saplings when Cahill supported racial equality in Michigan's public spaces. Some say the wood from those trees was used to create a wall that encircles the power plant, adding insult to injury. The wall is often adorned by public art, but not all the works turn out as the artist planned. The energy that flows here reminds us that Lansing should be a city for all.

Inspired by "Brickwork, Capitalism, Collective Memory, and the Commons" (Brigitte H. Bechtold)

The modest brick home at 501 Cabot Way, South Pittsburgh, is an anachronism. In this densely populated neighborhood, fine workmanship is no longer as important as return on investment. Newer homes are built so close to the road that visitors have to turn sideways to climb the entryway stairs. Almost every square inch of the neighborhood is paved in asphalt. Children play inside their generic homes and neighbors come and go with such frequency that relationships between them are rare.

The corner inhabited by 501 Cabot Way includes a hand-laid brick building alongside a cobblestone road. To build this home, workers placed each brick and stone with care to ensure it was straight and true. Doors and windows were adorned by offsetting a row or turning a few bricks on their side. There is a defiance in this corner, a refusal to become something new just for the sake of newness. Yes, some want this place torn down and paved over. There is money to be made in a bigger and more modern home. Plus, cobbled streets are noisy. Every passing car is announced by the gentle rumble of its tires over the uneven surface.

But that rumble belongs here. It recalls the sounds that created this neighborhood: the slurping up of a trowel full of mortar, the scraping of that mortar onto a brick, and the pat-pat-patting of it all into place. Slurp, scrape, pat, and rumble. That soundtrack of the community has been replaced by the constant beep-beep-beeping of heavy machinery and car alarms, the hum of central heating and air-conditioning units, and the occasional police or ambulance siren. The spirit of South Pittsburgh is now inhuman.

Discussion

Academic writing is rarely as compelling as a ghost story. And academic discourse about ghost stories either discounts them outright as untrue or uses them as a metaphor for hidden political conflict and instances of social exclusion (Nagle 2018). But outside of academia, ghosts are something other than a metaphor (Lincoln and Lincoln 2015). They are a mechanism for talking about hidden dangers, the passage of time, and all varieties of loss. In ghost stories we can see truths that may be difficult to find through science alone.

This ghost tour of *Blurring Timescapes* shows us how landscapes and objects take on unexpected meanings and reveal deep connections. Nothing was made up. No one was lied to or even misled. The stories above simply highlight the main people and places where lives were experienced before loss occurred, without the academic discourse contained in the chapters that inspired them. Instead of focusing on the facts and their interpretations, my stories sought to bring the individuals and cultures alive for you in a way that is not easy to forget. If any of these people and their places linger in your mind after you have closed the book, then you have experienced a haunting.

These ghosts have messages for you. When Nicole Burt challenges us to think about the human actions that went into the creation of museum collections, the ghosts are there to be confronted. Maybe their spirits will rest when we, the living, do a better job of educating ourselves and our audiences about past wrongs. Like Jacob Marley in Dickens' holiday classic, these ghosts can prevent us from meeting the same fate. Learning from ancestors was the key to Kisha Supernant's professional and personal journey. She found her new path in the well-worn paths of those who came before her—paths that others had not seen. Looking closely at things, Erica Begun found thousand-year-old souvenirs from Teotihuacan in an Oaxacan neighborhood. That act of cherishing a trinket from another place shows the shared humanity between then and now. Some objects are not about functionality. I keep a handkerchief in a small lockbox. My Sicilian grandmother left it behind when she stayed in my room one summer. It is all that I have left of her.

Ghosts are simply reminders of lives lived and lessons learned, and sometimes their messages are for society at large. When Lilian Brislen brings us to the not-so-distant past of the 1980s, she reminds us of the farm crisis that has yet to make it into history books. Pressured to maximize output, some farmers literally worked themselves to death to provide the United States with cheap food. A. E. Garrison's lost bridges in Lansing, Michigan, and Sarah Surface-Evans's lost park from the same city reveal how urban improvement projects can sever links between the living and the dead. The demolition of a bridge and the rules of city managers dictate who is welcome in a park. Replacing a park that had brought people together with a power station surrounded by a wall is a message about what is considered most important by those in power (pun intended). Communities' losses are not easily spoken about.

P. M. W. Lawton's account of the changes that settlers brought to the Saginaw Valley and Brigitte Bechtold's collective memory of brickwork both ask us to consider how nonhumans bear witness to human action. Things seemingly under human control (stones, trees, bricks, etc.) can persist on a landscape far longer than a single human life, if we let them. But the human obsession with the afterlife does make claims on our planet that go on for eternity. For example, Heather M. Van Wormer had trouble determining just how many people lived in the City of David. Residents consider those who have gone into an afterlife to still be part of the day-to-day functioning of this place. So, here she may need to be explicit that she is seeking to tally the number of mortal residents, or mortal and immortal. It seems like such a basic question to ask—How many people live here?—but such a question assumes that lives end. Academic discourse can easily assert truth and fact where there is more uncertainty than we would like to admit. When we step away from the trappings of science, we can see more humanity than we can ever quantify.

Blurry Timescapes and Ghostly Presences

Academics can dissect these stories to test their truth value or highlight the metaphorical struggles that the stories reveal, but that does not make the stories any less powerful. Ghost stories and hauntings are ways of experiencing the past in the present and of considering how comfortable we are in our own space and time. No paranormal powers are necessary. All that is needed is a place about which a vivid story of loss can be told. Knowledge of, and empathy for, those who came before turns any landscape into a timescape and manifests its ghosts. Ghosts connect seemingly disparate peoples, places, and times into a larger human story.

In *Blurring Timescapes*, academics have allowed ghosts and hauntings to enter their usual academic discourse. The resulting chapters contain some of the best of both worlds, revealing the human emotions behind the landscapes they explored. What you get from a ghost story are memories, not facts. Let these tales linger in your mind and see what meaning you can find in them.

Dr. Kisha Supernant is Métis and Associate Professor in the Department of Anthropology and Director of the Institute of Prairie and Indigenous Archaeology at the University of Alberta. She is the Director of the Exploring Métis Identity Through Archaeology (EMITA) Project and has published widely in national and international journals, including *PNAS*, *Journal of Archaeological Science*, *Journal of Anthropological Archaeology*, and the *Canadian Journal of Archaeology* and is co-editing a forthcoming book entitled *Archaeologies of the Heart*. An award-winning researcher, teacher, and writer, she is actively involved in research on cultural identities, landscapes, collaborative Indigenous archaeology, Métis archaeology, and heart-centered archaeological practice.

Dr. April M. Beisaw is an Associate Professor of Anthropology at Vassar College, Poughkeepsie, NY. There she teaches courses on Native North America, repatriation, forensic anthropology, and historical archaeology. Her most recent book is *Identifying and Interpreting Animal Bones: A Manual*, published by Texas A&M University Press. Her next book will be on the New York City water system and the towns that have been sacrificed to create and maintain city reservoirs. She is also an associate editor for the journal *Historical Archaeology*.

Dr. A. E. Garrison is Assistant Professor of Sociology at Central Michigan University. She earned her doctorate in Rural Sociology from the University of Missouri in 2011. Her work focuses on the development of graphic sociological methodology for scholarship and pedagogy. Her graphic work includes "Ghosts of Infertility: Haunted by Realities of Reproductive Death" (2016). Garrison's research interests also include social consequences resulting from urban planning policies, impacting urban infrastructure in Rust Belt cities. Her work in this subject area includes "Boneyards of the *Sortatropolis*: Exploring a City of Industrial Secrets – Lansing, Michigan (Part 1)" (2017).

Dr. Sarah Surface-Evans is Associate Professor of Anthropology at Central Michigan University. Her community-based archaeological research investigates cultural landscapes in the Great Lakes region of the United States. Her recent publication "A Landscape of Assimilation and Resistance: The Mount Pleasant Indian Industrial Boarding School" in the *International Journal of Historical Archaeology* examines the gendered and powered components of institutional design at Federal Indian Boarding Schools. This ongoing research was recognized for a Michigan Governor's Award for Historic Preservation in 2016. She has a forthcoming publication that utilizes "haunting" as a way conceptualize the trauma of colonial landscapes.

References

Lincoln, Martha, and Bruce Lincoln. 2015. "Toward a Critical Hauntology: Bare Afterlife and the Ghosts of Ba Chúc." *Comparative Studies in Society and History* 57(1): 191–220.
Nagle, John. 2018. "Ghostly Specters, Haunted Ruins and Resistance to the Amnesiac and Exclusivist Divided City." In "Urban Public Art: Geographies of Co-production," special issue, *City & Society* 30(1): https://doi.org/10.1111/ciso.12149.

Index

A
adult learning, 76–79
affect, 2
agrarian communities, haunting and trauma, 105–117
 dealing with failures, 108–110
 early success, 106–108
 emotional struggle and failure, 112–115
 haunting memories, 115–117
 sufferings, 110–112
alienation, strategies for, 143
American Association of Physical Anthropology (AAPA), 74
ancient and colonial-era sites, destruction of, 66–68
ancient Mexico, memory and material culture in. *See* material memories
Andersen, Chris, 90
archaeological materials and haunting, 62. *See also* haunting
archaeology and haunting, 2–3. *See also* haunting
archaeology and traumascapes, 61–68. *See also* trauma
authenticity, 124

B
Barkun, Michael, 39
Bartlett, Peggy, 111
Beaver Wars, 63
Bechtold, Brigitte, 147
Bekerman, Zvi, 154
Bell, Michael Mayerfeld, 14, 173
Berlant, Lauren Gail, 112
Bernstein, Basil, 82
Berry, Brian J. L., 39

biological anthropology, history and ethics in, 73–75
Blakey, Michael, 73
Bond, Ann, 176
brickworkers, disruption of history and collective memory, 171–184
 brickwork and chronology, 181–182
 capitalism, 174–177
 capitalist time, 178–181
 collective memory, 182–184
 history, 171–173
 rapid changes, 173–174
Brown, Susan Love, 38
Bryan, Luke, 112–114
Bryant, Lia, 115
Building Capitalism (Linda Clarke), 173
burials and cultural identification, 26–27
Burley, David, 93
Buttel, Frederick H., 111–112

C
capitalism, 12
 and brickworkers (*see* brickworkers, disruption of history and collective memory)
 and cities of American Midwest, 149–150, 154–157
 global, 106–107, 110–116
 and late modernity, 6–8, 87
 and loss of agrarian culture (*see* farm crisis, impact on agrarian subjectivities)
Chesaning, haunting of urban landscapes, 61–69
 disposing indigenous people of their land, 66–68
 false mementos of identity, 65–66

memories and politics of power, 62
Saukenauk, 63–65
Christian Israelites, 40–42, 54–55
City of David, history, 40–49, 52
  Christian Israelites, 40–41
  colony, expansion, 43–45
  colony and its ideology, 41–42
  colony, split, 45–46
  Mary's City of David, 47–49, 52
  memory at, 53–55
  new colony's architecture, 47
City Pulse (newspaper), 132
Clarke, Linda, 173
collective loss, expressing, 109
collective memory, 53. *See also* memories; social memories and colony identity
  of communities of brickworkers (*see* brickworkers, disruption of history and collective memory)
  of community at the City of David (*see* City of David)
colony identity. *See* social memories and colony identity
commodity agriculture, 114, 116
community-based archaeology, 152–153. *See also* Lansing, Michigan; Métis archaeology
community identity and cohesion, 156
community memory, deliberate erasure of, 151–152
Cothran, Boyd, 62

D
Dōgen, Ehei, 181
dairy crisis, 114–115
dangerous memories, 154. *See also* haunting; memories
Darwin, Charles, 73–74
Dawdy, Shannon Lee, 14
De Blasio, Bill, 150
Dean Foods, 115
Descent of Man (Charles Darwin), 73
Dewhirst, Thomas, Judge, 45
Di Domenico, MariaLaura, 75
Dudley, Kathryn Marie, 108, 109–110, 115

E
eminent domain, 67–68
empathy, 2, 3–4
Epstein, Griffin, 164

ethical conversation
  anatomy of, 79–81
  pedagogy of, 81–82
ethics. *See* physical anthropology, public perceptions of the ethics of
ethnic identity and burial goods, 30
Exploring Métis Identity Through Archaeology (EMITA) project, 93

F
Faimon, Mary Beth, 154
false mementos of identity, 65–66
farm crisis, impact on agrarian subjectivities, 105–117
farmer identity, loss of, 109–110
Fine, Lisa, 124
Forster, Peter, 39
Frers, Lars, 110

G
Garnham, Bridget, 115
Gazi, Andromache, 75
gentrification. *See* historical trauma and gentrification
ghost stories, narration, 13–14
ghosts and haunting, 20–21. *See also* haunting
Giddens, Anthony, 36
Gómez, Sergio, 25–26
González-Tennant, Edward, 165
Gordon, Avery, 105, 109, 116, 124, 154
Grabur, Michael, 23

H
Halbwachs, Maurice, 53–54, 172
Hanks, Michele, 14
Haraway, Donna, 116
haunting
  and agrarian communities (*see* agrarian communities, haunting and trauma)
  and archaeology, 2–3, 86–88
  and brickworkers (*see* brickworkers, disruption of history and collective memory)
  and community in Lansing (*see* Lansing, Michigan)
  concept of, 1–2
  Gordon on, 124
  in the rural midwest (*see* Chesaning)
Heffernan, 108

heirlooming, 24–25
Hirsch, Marianne, 152
historical trauma and gentrification, 149–150, 152–154, 156–158, 160–162, 164–165
Houghton, Douglas, 64
Hrdlička, Aleš, 73
Hume, 23
Hutchison, Anthony, 106

I
Indigenous archaeology, 87–88
individual loss, expressing, 109
informal learning, 76
informal teaching, case study, 77–79
Instrumental Neutron Activation Analysis (INAA), 29
intellectual commons, 183
intentional communities, 37–40
invisibility, 85, 121, 134, 183, 196
Ireland, Irma, 62
Ireland, Mark, 62

L
Lake Cuitzeo, 29
Lansing, Michigan
  change in city's landscape, 125–143
  defining traumascapes, 152–154, 156–157
  history, 149, 152
  protecting the past for communities, 164–165
  trauma, haunting, and gentrification, 157–158, 160–162, 164
Little, Barbara, 165

M
MacFadden, Bruce, 74
Mallach, Alan, 150
Marandino, Martha, 82
Marshall, John, Supreme Court Justice, 67
Mary, Benjamin, 42, 45
Matarese, Susan, 39
material memories, 20–30
  evidence for a Michoacán presence at N1W5:19, 26–27, 29
  heirlooming, 24–25
  objects of memory at N1W5:19, 29–30
  overview, 20–23

souvenirs as memory of time and place, 23–24
  teotihuacan background, 25
materialism, 36, 45–46
Mellencamp, John (Cougar), 108–109, 113
memories, 4–5. *See also* collective memory; haunting; material memories
  and politics of power, 62
Metcalf, William, 39
Métis archaeology
  families and kinship, 95–97
  haunting, 86–88
  haunting, case study, 88, 90–91
  introduction, 85–86
  Métis Daily Life, 93–94
  remembering through physical remains of past, 97
  reviving history, 91–93
  tracks and trails, 94–95
Michoacán-style grave goods, 26–27, 29–30
Miller, Timothy, 37–38
Miller, William, 39
Morrison, Kathryn, 176
museum teaching, 75–76

N
N1W5:19, 25–27, 29–30
  evidence for a Michoacán presence at, 25–27, 29
  objects of memory at, 29–30
native Americans, 62–69, 152–153, 165
nostalgia, 4–5
Nouvel, Henry, 63

O
Oaxacan barrio, 26–27

P
Patzcuaro style figurines, 27
pedagogy of ethical conversation, 81–82
physical anthropology, public perceptions of the ethics of, 72–83
  building a pedagogy, 81–82
  case study, 77–79
  haunting, 72–73
  history and ethics in biological anthropology, 73–75
  museum teaching, 75–76
  verbal interaction, 79–81

Pitzer, Donald, 38
Popkin, Mary, 23
public informal learning pedagogy, 81–82
Purnell, Benjamin, 41, 42, 45

R
Ramírez-Ferrero, Eric, 108, 111
Ree, C., 86
relational ontologies, 87
Remembering the Modoc War: Redemptive Violence and the Making of American Innocence (Boyd Cothran), 62
research ethics, 74–75
restrictive power, 143
ritual worship, 29

S
Saginaw Valley, 63–65
Salmon, Paul, 39
self-identity formation, 24
sense of identity, 115
Shackel, Paul, 165
Shiloh Messenger of Wisdom, 42
social justice through archaeology, 165
social memories and colony identity, 33–55
  City of David, history, 40–50, 52
  communitarian movements and intentional communities, 37–40
  memory at the City of David, 53–55
  social and collective memory, 53
social time, 178
Southcott, Joanna, 40
souvenirs as memory of time and place, 23–24. *See also* material memories
spaces for sharing, 143
Stewart, Kathleen, 181
Stottman, M. Jay, 165
subverting erasure, 3. *See also* haunting; memories
  subversion, 13, 72, 96, 195

T
temporal curation, 24
Thomas, Eli, 62
tomb construction, 26
Totush, 62
trauma
  and agrarian communities (*see* agrarian communities, haunting and trauma)
  and capitalism, 7
  of colonialism, 65–66
  and hauntings, 20–21
  historical, and gentrification, 149–150, 152–154, 156–158, 160–162, 164–165
traumascapes
  and archaeology, 61–68
Tuck, 86
Tucker, Elizabeth, 17–18
Tumarkin, Maria, 139, 153
Twain, Mark, 17

V
van Dernoot Lipsky, Laura, 152
Van Wormer, 24
Vassar College, 15–19
  architecture, 15–16
  ghost tours, 18–19
  storytelling event, 17
  suicide-related ghost stories, 17–18
  visit by Mark Twain, 17
Vassar, Matthew, 16
vulnerability, 3

W
Walmart, 114–115
White, Christine, 26

Z
Zembylas, Michalinos, 154

www.ingramcontent.com/pod-product-compliance
Lightning Source LLC
Chambersburg PA
CBHW071343080526
44587CB00017B/2940